W9-AHF-491

Berlin

Berlin

Norbert Schürer

Interlink Books

An imprint of Interlink Publishing Group, Inc.
Northampton, Massachusetts

First published in 2015 by
INTERLINK BOOKS
An imprint of Interlink Publishing Group, Inc.
46 Crosby Street, Northampton, Massachusetts 01060
www.interlinkbooks.com

Library of Congress Cataloging-in-Publication Data available
ISBN 978-1-56656-938-5

Front cover image: Sony Center © Locha79 | Dreamstime.com;
Back cover image: MLenny | iStockphoto

Printed and bound in the United States of America

To request our 48-page, full-color catalog, please call us toll free at 1-800-
238-LINK, visit our website: www.interlinkbooks.com, or send us an email:
info@interlinkbooks.com

Contents

Introduction

Any attempt to capture the essence of a city like Berlin in one book is likely to end in failure. What could a hippie in Kreuzberg, a socialite in Wannsee, an industrial worker in Marzahn, a banker at Potsdamer Platz, and an unemployed university graduate in Friedrichshain possibly have in common? How could a medieval fortress, an Enlightenment ruler's capital, the Nazis' metropolis, the bastion of the Cold War, and the center of a new Europe be considered the same place? Why should Berliners established here for many generations, the ethnically Turkish population, French Huguenots from centuries ago, and more recent immigrants from Poland, Russia, and Swabia think of their city in similar ways? In a city with no real center, or two, or twenty, what counts as characteristic? There are no easy answers to these questions.

Instead, it might be more helpful to think of Berlin as the site of converging or intersecting stories. Over the centuries, the various parts and constituents of the city have interacted, picking up political, cultural, linguistic, and culinary habits from each other. This interaction has fortunately not resulted in uniformity, but Berliners might recognize certain aspects of each others' lives, experiences, and histories as common. This book, then, is an attempt to describe some of those stories.

Of course, it is also impossible to cover Berlin's experiences and histories in any kind of comprehensive fashion, so many details that might immediately strike a visitor are only mentioned in passing or not at all in this book. For instance, I have not been able to write sufficiently, if at all, about Berlin's cuisine (especially the *Currywurst*, which even a vegetarian such as myself can appreciate, and the delicious *Brötchen*—bread rolls—and pastries); bicycle paths (beware!); the district of Pankow (home of the East German leadership and destination of Udo Lindenberg's song "Sonderzug nach Pankow"); paternosters; the beautiful libraries at the Free University, Technical University, and Humboldt University; Buddy Bears; the statue of Marx and Engels near Alexanderplatz; the disaster of the new Berlin airport (which may or may not finally open in 2014); or the ubiquitous graffiti—all of those remain for you to discover on your own.

I first came to Berlin at the age of two, but obviously I have no memory of that time. I returned in 1972–73, when I attended first and then second grade at the Erich-Kästner-Grundschule (elementary school) in Dahlem. In 1976 I came back, and this time I stayed until 1994. During these eighteen years I lived in Charlottenburg, Spandau, Wilmersdorf, and Neukölln, and I studied at the (then) Hochschule der Künste (conservatory in West Berlin), the Free University, and the Hochschule für Musik Hanns Eisler (conservatory in East Berlin—right after the fall of the Wall). Like most Berliners, I was anchored in the districts where I lived, studied, and worked, but I also tried to explore the city as much as possible. Since 1994 I have lived in the US, but visiting Berlin every year to see family and friends I have made a point of keeping up with changes in the city and literature about it. I hope that my love of this vibrant and diverse city comes through in these pages, and I hope this book will encourage you to learn even more about Berlin—and hopefully visit.

Glossary

Most of the names of people, streets, and sites are given in the original German throughout this book (including the *Umlaute* ä, ö, and ü), since that is what you would encounter in Berlin. However, the German letter ß (which sounds like an s) has been consistently changed to ss. Only when the individuals or places are commonly known in English, for instance the Brandenburg Gate and Frederick the Great, have I given their names in English. The two main names that might sound slightly unfamiliar to English speakers are Friedrich and Wilhelm (for Frederick and William). German terms are printed in italics and followed by an approximate translation. For words that occur frequently in the names of streets and sites, a glossary might be helpful:

alt	old
Bahnhof	train station
Berg	mountain/hill
Bibliothek	library
Brücke	bridge
Chaussee	avenue
Fluss	river
Garten	garden
gross	large
Hafen	port/harbor
Haupt-	main
Insel	island
Kanal	canal
Kirche	church
klein	small
Markt	market
neu	new
Norden	north
Osten	east
Platz	square/plaza
Schloss	castle/palace

See	lake
Staat	state
Stadt	city
Strasse	street
Süden	south
Tor	gate
Turm	tower
Viertel	quarter
Vorstadt	suburb
Wald	forest/woods
Westen	west

Acknowledgements

First of all, I would like to acknowledge my literary sources, especially the books published by Berlin Story Verlag, Jaron Verlag, Vergangenheitsverlag, and Stadtwandel Verlag. It would be worth learning German simply to be able to read their excellent books. Unfortunately, I was not able to give the exact source for every single piece of information in this volume.

In addition, this book would have been impossible without my past and present friends and family in and around Berlin. Over the course of several years, Connie, Hannes, Inken, and Tomke Behrmann as well as Frank Schürer-Behrmann, Fritz and Uschi Brückmann, Gerd Harders, Thoralf and Sabine Kerner, Oliver and Naomi Lubrich, Cary Nathenson and Katrin Völkner Nathenson, Jörg Schendel, Dirc Simpson, Gerd and Hanne Völkner, and Almute Zwiener have indulged my obscure interests with good humor and patiently tried to answer any questions I posed. Friends from the US including Clorinda Donato, Tim and Kathleen Keirn, Claire Martin, and Kim Trimble have gone on exploratory adventures across the city with me and provided a visitor's perspective on Berlin. Gerlinde Hollweg and Wolfgang Krüger have been amazingly hospitable over and over again for more than two decades, and extremely knowledgeable about everything from literature and breads to beers and industrial history. Over the last 35 years (or so), Judith Brückmann (more recently with Finn and Eske) has been a wonderful friend and co-explorer of Berlin, introducing me to culture and history I would otherwise have missed. My wife Susan Carlile (from the US) has accompanied me on many trips to Berlin and helped me see the city in an entirely new light. She is my perfect audience, so this book is largely written with her in mind. Finally, this book is dedicated to my mother, Gretel Schürer, who holds down the fort in, provides a constant stream of information on, and originally brought me to, Berlin.

1 | **Contours**
| Geography and Topography

Berlin is located in a valley left by retreating glaciers some ten thousand years ago, geologically between the Barnim plateau to the north and east, and the Teltow plateau south and west. The moderate climate and glacial soil mean that the land is generally fertile, allowing oak forests to grow and offering a welcoming habitat to wildlife such as deer and wild boar. (An etymological explanation attributing the name "Berlin" to a bear crossing a ford was unfortunately exposed as a myth.) Berlin's natural contours include two major rivers (Spree and Havel), significant bodies of water (Wannsee and Müggelsee), various elevations (Müggelberge and Teufelsberg), and expansive forests (Müggelsee area and Grunewald) within the city limits. Since there are so many natural features that act as obstacles to urban growth, Berlin never really merged into one large city; to this day, it remains (to some extent) a conglomeration of villages connected by water and green spaces. There are, according to Spiegel TV, 4,160,000 trees in Berlin, and in many parts of the conurbation it is easy for visitors to forget entirely that they are in one of Europe's largest cities.

Water: Rivers

The Havel and Spree rivers (in the former glacial valleys) form the skeleton of Berlin's natural contours, and without them there would probably be no city here. The Havel is the longer river, and the Spree is actually its tributary, but since the historic center of Berlin grew on an island in the Spree, this river is etched into the Berlin psyche much more than its larger counterpart—in fact, one of Berlin's nicknames is "Spree-Athen," Athens on the Spree. The Spree runs through the middle of the city for 28 miles from the Müggelsee (in former East Berlin) to its confluence with the Havel in Spandau (in

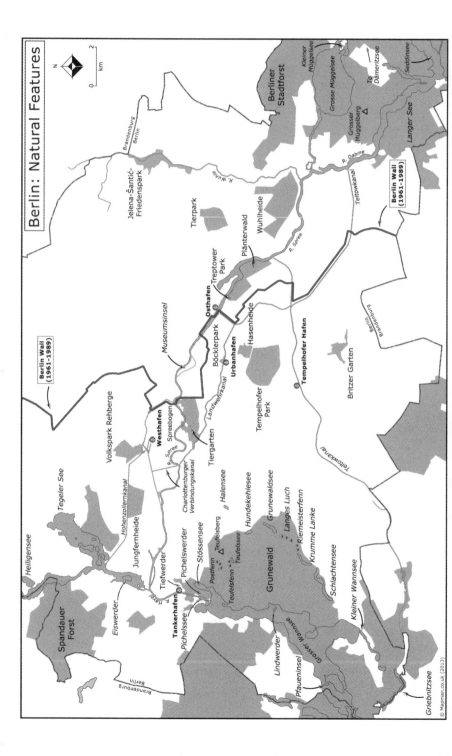

Berlin: Natural Features

former West Berlin) through the historical center of Köpenick, Berlin's main old harbor, the city's oldest parts around the Schlossinsel, the new government quarter, and the old town of Charlottenburg. As it winds its way through Berlin, the Spree travels past facets of the city's government, transportation history, culture and entertainment, military protection, and trade and economy.

In central Berlin the Spree flows tranquilly in the vicinity of several old and new landmarks: the government quarter, the Hauptbahnhof (main train station), the Museumsinsel, and the Schlossinsel. When the German government moved to Berlin after reunification, the Spreebogen (Spree curve) at the edge of Tiergarten in the city center was one of the few spaces available to construct new buildings for parliament and parliamentarians. The Bundeskanzleramt (chancellor's office), built between 1997 and 2001, is a colossal ensemble by Axel Schultes and Charlotte Frank known colloquially as the Kohllosseum (after the chancellor who initiated it) or as the "Washing Machine" (after the distinctive central building). On the other side of the Spreebogen are two complementary buildings on either side of the river (formerly West and East Berlin), the Paul-Löbe-House and the Marie-Elisabeth-Lüders-House. Architect Stephan Braunfels conceived these buildings as symbolizing the reunification of the city and as countering the north-south design of the Nazi reimagining of Berlin as Germania (see p.59) with its east-west orientation. There are two bridges connecting the buildings, the lower open to the public and the upper only to people working there. The latter is wittily called *Gehobene Beamtenlaufbahn*, which translates either as "upper civil service career" or "raised civil servant's catwalk"—take your pick.

To the north of the Spreebogen is the new Hauptbahnhof, a reminder of Berlin's transport history, built on the site of the former Lehrter Stadtbahnhof, a smaller station mainly for journeys north. The glass and steel main station, designed by Meinhard von Gerkan and opened in 2006, is a wonder to behold and impressive by most standards, but not exactly beloved by most Berliners. For one thing, the construction did not take into account the actual length of trains, so travelers on both ends of some platforms were left exposed to the elements. For another, the station is difficult to reach by public transport, which is how most Berliners get around. A shiny new U-Bahn connecting the station to the S-Bahn was opened in 2009, but still requires changing lines.

Moving upstream, the Spree passes the Reichstag and the Friedrichstrasse train station and splits around the Spreeinsel, an island which is important enough for its three parts to have their own names. At the northern end, the Museumsinsel is home to Berlin's most famous museums and thus forms a center for culture and entertainment; the middle was the site of the castle of the Hohenzollern rulers and is still known as Schlossinsel even though the castle no longer exists; and the southern end is named Fischerinsel after the fishermen who mainly settled there back in the thirteenth century. Further upstream on the north shore is O2 World, Berlin's largest indoor event and concert venue with seating for 17,000 spectators. Opened in 2008 and designed by the architects of HOK Sports, O2 World has a base made of Chinese black granite, walls of Portuguese limestone, and a distinctive roof of blue plastic. The front towards the Spree has a wall of glass that leans slightly outwards and contains 300,000 LED diodes to illuminate the building or announce forthcoming events.

A structure like O2 World might be found in any modern city, but its immediate juxtaposition with an old structure such as the neo-Gothic Oberbaumbrücke (and some remnants of the Berlin Wall) is perhaps unique to Berlin. A bridge existed in this location, then the city border, from the early eighteenth century and was named after the tree (*Baum*) that was lowered at night to stop traffic on the water and offer the city protection. The current bridge was built in the style of a Brandenburg castle with two crenelated towers in 1895, destroyed in World War II and restored provisionally to function as a pedestrian border crossing between the two quarters on either side of the river that are now one district, Friedrichshain-Kreuzberg. After the Cold War, the bridge was rebuilt with a new middle section by the Spanish architect Santiago Calatrava. With its two levels—one for cars and pedestrians, and one for the U-Bahn, which runs overground here between Schlesisches Tor and

Warschauer Strasse—the Oberbaumbrücke is one of Berlin's most iconic structures.

Outside the old city border, between the Oberbaumbrücke and the Elsenbrücke, the north side of the Spree is occupied by the Osthafen (east harbor) for just under a mile. This used to be one more industrial stretch of the river, but recently it has been transformed into a thriving hub of architecture and entertainment. A new harbor had been built here in the early twentieth century (with a counterpart, the Westhafen, in the Moabit quarter) because Berlin's dock capacity for water-based trade no longer sufficed. When the Osthafen was opened in 1913, it had a symmetrical layout with an eight-story neoclassical granary (featuring reliefs of dock workers on the façade) flanked by two-story halls. Over 15,000 tons of grain and over 10,000 tons of other goods could be stored in the buildings, and forty ships could dock at the straightened Spree quay, so it contributed significantly to Berlin's trade and economy. During the Cold War the Osthafen fell on hard times because it was in the Eastern sector while the other side of the Spree was in West Berlin, and because trade was generally moving away from the water.

Since the reunification of Berlin, though, the Osthafen has experienced an extraordinary renaissance as a center for the media industry. The cable television company MTV occupies one of the large halls (barely changed on the outside, but completely remodeled inside), and Universal Music has its headquarters in a building known as the Eierkühlhaus. This "egg refrigerator" is a nine-story structure added to the harbor in 1928 with the capacity to store seventy million eggs. In Universal's remodel, the diamond-shaped façade was highlighted by a gigantic glass opening in the middle of the building towards the river. The structures in the entire area have been renamed "Labels." For instance, Label I is now home to Hugo Boss, Escada, and others. Label II is an astounding new building by the Swiss architects HHF, with each of the five floors defined by concrete painted olive-green and shaped in the form of undulating parabolas. From the Spree, the building looks like an extension of the waves on the river, fitting its location even though it is very different from the neoclassical Osthafen. Standing in the Spree across from Label II and next to the Elsenbrücke is Molecule Man, a hundred-foot sculpture by US artist Jonathan Borofsky. The flat aluminium sculpture shows the silhouette of three men leaning towards each other, each riddled with holes to symbolize their molecules. Molecule Man is in the water where East and West meet—the sculpture suggests that the coming together of human beings here is a meeting of all humanity. The symbolism may elude Berliners and visitors, but it is still thought-provoking to see a sculpture rising out of the river.

Across from the Osthafen in Kreuzberg, where the Landwehrkanal (see below) enters the Spree, is another of Berlin's newer and more exciting destinations: the Badeschiff (bathing ship). In the past, Berliners actually swam in the Spree, but today the river water is no longer clean enough. Instead, Gil Wilk and his AMP *arquitectos* submerged the hull of a 105 x 26-foot rebuilt vessel almost to the level of the Spree and filled it with clean water. Thus, since 2004 visitors have been able to imagine they are swimming in the river, without the associated risk of infection. The Badeschiff is attached to the shore through a series of piers that are widened in some spots to offer bathers a place to spread their towels and soak in the sun—a kind of artificial lido.

Still moving against the current, past the Elsenbrücke, is the Treptow quarter of the Treptow-Köpenick district with two parks to the south. Treptower Park is home to the Soviet War Memorial, built in 1949 to honor the soldiers of the Red Army. On top of a round mausoleum is a 45-foot bronze statue of a soldier holding a sword in one hand, carrying a child in the other arm, and stamping on a swastika. This is hardly a subtle memorial—not to mention one that whitewashes any issues Berliners may have had with the behavior of the Red Army (see p.80)—but it is certainly impressive. The second park, Plänterwald, was planted in the eighteenth century for forestry but turned into a public green space in the nineteenth. Right on the river is the Spreepark amusement park, which was built by the GDR, briefly resurrected after the Cold War, but now remains closed without prospects for reopening (though it is occasionally used as scenery in films). Between Plänterwald and Treptower Park is a small island in the Spree that has had many names: Rohr-Insel, Neu-Spreeland, and Abteiinsel among others. Since 1915 the island has been accessible from the riverbank on Germany's first composite steel bridge. In 1949 the island was renamed Insel der Jugend (Island of Youth) and became a destination for concerts and other events. In 2010 it was once again renamed as Insel Berlin and serves as an example of the city government's desperate (and usually unsuccessful) attempts to be fashionable. Further south on both sides of the Spree past Plänterwald is the district of Schöneweide (pretty meadow), which because of the heavy industry located there has received the less flattering nickname "Schweineöde"—pig's wasteland.

Further upstream, the Spree splits again and surrounds the center of Köpenick, formerly a city in its own right and now part of the Treptow-Köpenick district. Köpenick was settled by Slavs before the Middle Ages and is documented as far back as 1210. The Sprewans people controlled the area early on, but by 1245 the town was ruled from Brandenburg. From the river, one of Köpenick's landmarks is visible on a little island: the castle, built from 1677 by the architect Rutger van Langerfeld in the Dutch style, with a neoclassical chapel added in 1684–85 by Johann Arnold Nering. After the Brandenburg rulers moved to Berlin, Köpenick Castle was neglected, but recently it has been renovated and is a satellite of the Museum of Decorative Arts in the city center. To most Germans, this district is best known for Carl Zuckmayer's play *Der Hauptmann von Köpenick* (*The Captain of Köpenick*—see pp.213–14). Around Köpenick, two smaller rivers enter the Spree—the Dahme from the south and the Wuhle from the north—and the castle island is technically on the Dahme. The Wuhle gives its name to the Wuhlheide park, which is remarkable for its miniature railway, where children (and grownups) can learn about how to become train conductors. Beyond Köpenick, the Spree is called Müggelspree because it connects to the Grosser Müggelsee (see below).

But to return to the center of Berlin: around the north side of Tiergarten, near the Spreebogen, the river enters the Moabit quarter (part of the Mitte district), where at least a dozen bridges cross the Spree. In the early twentieth century this was a hotbed of the workers' movement, and during the Cold War it was a slightly dingy quarter because of its vicinity to the Wall. Unfortunately, it is still known mostly because of the justice system, as in Berlin it is synonymous with its jail. Around Moabit, canals branch off the Spree: the Charlottenburger Verbindungskanal connects the Spree to the Westhafen to the north, while the Landwehrkanal heads south. Past Moabit, and now going downstream with the current, the Spree skirts the park of the Schloss Charlottenburg. After that, the shores of the river are not exactly a pretty sight due to industrial buildings and sewage treatment plants. The Siemensstadt quarter to the north is interesting because of its turn-of-the-century and early modernist architecture, a place where industrialists tried to settle their workers close to their factories. Finally, near the Spandau Citadel in the north of Berlin the Spree flows into the Havel.

The Havel runs north to south through Berlin (before it turns west to join the Elbe). Before it meets the Spree, the Havel has formed several lakes—Niederneuendorfer See, Heiligensee, and Tegeler See—and it has passed two historically and culturally important sites. First, near Heiligensee are the Papenberger Wiesen (meadows), a reminder of Berlin's recent past. During the Cold War, this area on the eastern shore of the Havel was an exclave of West Berlin (or an enclave within the GDR, depending on your perspective). This meant that the area belonged to West Berlin, but was not accessible by a direct road. In other words, West Berliners had to pass through East Berlin in order to get to their homes or community gardens. This was not unusual around Berlin: the Steinstücken exclave to the south was quite famous, and a little bit south of Heiligensee are the Fichtewiese and Erlengrund colonies, which could only be visited (from the Spandau district) by West Berliners with special passports and permits documenting that they owned property there. The Papenberger Wiesen are unusual because this exclave could only be reached by boat across the Havel.

Secondly, on the shores of the Tegeler See is the Dicke Marie (Fat Marie), an oak tree that at the age of eight hundred years is supposedly Berlin's oldest tree—though botanists suspect that it is "only" four or five centuries old. Nearby is the small Humboldt-Schloss (palace), originally built in the sixteenth century and then reconstructed various times, finally by Karl Friedrich Schinkel in the 1820s in the neoclassical style. Two famous brothers—the traveler, botanist, and writer Alexander von Humboldt and the politician and founder of the Berlin university (now Humboldt-University) Wilhelm von Humboldt—lived here in the late eighteenth and early nineteenth centuries.

The confluence of the Havel and Spree was the site of a ford across the Spree. A Slavic village grew here with a medieval castle that later developed into the Spandau Citadel. The Juliusturm (tower), now part of the citadel and the emblem of Spandau, was built some time in the thirteenth century. The citadel itself was built during the Renaissance (by the Italian architect Francesco Chiaramella de Gandino) and did not change much over the following centuries. The plan is fairly square, with arrow-shaped bastions pointing out on all four corners so that every inch outside the fortress could be covered by cannon fire. In fact, the only time the Spandau Citadel saw any action was during the Napoleonic Wars, and then the soldiers in the fortress did not put up much of a fight. It is preserved close enough to its original state to convey a sense of what life in the late sixteenth century here might have been like. The Juliusturm is particularly interesting because of its underground dungeon, the alarming spiral staircase along the inside of the round walls (with nothing to protect those scaling the heights from falling down the middle), and the view from the top over the battlements, which were added by Schinkel after the French burnt the old ones down in the early nineteenth century. It would probably not have been much fun to be a soldier here during the Renaissance—and even less so to be a prisoner in the dungeon.

The moat around the citadel seems stagnant, but is actually part of the Havel. The river narrows once again and continues south along the Wilhelmstadt quarter of the Spandau district. After another harbor (Tankerhafen), the Havel splits into two branches, though the eastern one is barely recognizable as such. To the west, the river passes under the Freybrücke into the Pichelssee; to the east into a series of tiny canals under the Stössenseebrücke into the Stössensee. Officially called Tiefwerder, this area to the east is known as Little Venice because of its canals. There are no major streets here, and most of the development consists of weekend houses or community gardens. Between the two branches of the Havel is Pichelswerder, a small wooded area close to which I grew up. Once the Havel reunites, the Grunewald is on the east and the Gatow quarter on the west for many miles before Wannsee and the Pfaueninsel (see below). Thus the Havel traverses a wide spectrum of Berlin's nature and history.

Water: Canals

As already mentioned, there are numerous man-made waterways that contribute to Berlin's contours and environment. One of the most famous is the Landwehrkanal, which connects two points along the Spree by running for about seven miles between Kreuzberg and Moabit via Neukölln, Charlottenburg, and Tiergarten. *Landwehr* literally means "defense of the country," and indeed at one point the canal served as a kind of moat outside Berlin's city walls. But more importantly, it took some of the pressure off the Spree as the main waterway through Berlin, connected Osthafen and Westhafen, and allowed ships to circumvent the city center. Built between 1845 and 1860, the canal is 72 feet wide and six feet deep.

Since canals are no longer used much for trade, the Landwehrkanal has been repurposed for a variety of other functions. Gastronomy is certainly one of them, with canalside establishments taking appropriate names: the Freischwimmer—the designation of the test German children have to take before being allowed to swim on their own—is right on the canal at the confluence of the Spree and the Landwehrkanal in Kreuzberg; the Ankerklause (anchor or anchorite's cell) hangs over the canal near Kottbusser Tor in the most Turkish part of Berlin; and the Schleusenkrug (lock bar) is a beautiful beer garden next to a lock in the Tiergarten, with a view of some of the enclosures of the Berlin Zoo. On the south side of the canal, a popular Turkish market is held on Tuesdays and Fridays on Maybachufer (shore). The Admiralbrücke near Kottbusser Tor in a quarter called Graefekiez has recently become an object of significant contention. For reasons not entirely understood (probably involving inadvertent advertisement through travel guides), the short bridge has become the preferred meeting point for sometimes hundreds of young travelers, who congregate, play music, drink, smoke, and party—enjoying themselves or becoming a nuisance, depending on perspective. So far, the only solution to the situation seems to be cold or bad weather, which drives the revelers away.

In contrast, what used to be the Urbanhafen on the Landwehrkanal in Kreuzberg has been turned into the beautiful Böcklerpark, where Berliners can sit quietly, observe the swans, and enjoy the water moving by slowly. A synagogue near Böcklerpark is the only part of a larger complex that survived the 1938 Reichskristallnacht (Night of Broken Glass). Through other parts of Kreuzberg, the raised subway runs over the Landwehrkanal. In Tiergarten, houseboats are moored in the canal. At the edge of Tiergarten, the Landwehrkanal gained notoriety when the communist Rosa Luxemburg was assassinated in 1919 and her body thrown into the water. The site was commemorated with a sculpture in 1987: simply her name raised in concrete profile. Between sidewalks and park paths, it is not difficult to walk or run the entire length of the Landwehrkanal.

The other famous canal that shapes Berlin's layout is the Teltowkanal, which stretches about 25 miles from Griebnitzsee, one of the lakes in the Havel around Wannsee, to the Dahme river at Köpenick. Built between 1900 and 1906 by some 2,500 workers and using the course of the Bäke river, the Teltowkanal runs through southern Berlin—and partly through the adjacent state of Brandenburg—relieving the burden on Berlin's waterways and shortening the trip between the Elbe and Oder rivers. There is only one set of locks on the entire canal. Unusually, boats were towed by locomotives, so the towpath was actually a railway. The tracks were destroyed during World War II and never restored, though one locomotive serves as a memorial at the Emil-Schulz-Brücke, about halfway along the canal in the Lichterfelde quarter.

At the western beginning of the Teltowkanal, the Glienicke Hunting Lodge is on the north shore, and a pump station supplying the great fountain in the Sanssouci grounds and designed by the architect Ludwig Persius 1841–43 in the Moorish style is to the south. These waterworks were built at a time when even industrial architecture was supposed to look appealing. Coming out of Griebnitzsee, the canal forms the border between the German states of Berlin and Brandenburg—and used to be the border between West Berlin and the GDR. At the Knesebeckbrücke over the canal between the Berlin district of Steglitz-Zehlendorf and the Brandenburg city of Teltow, there is a memorial to the unnamed individual (actually Roland Hoff) who was shot on 29 August 1961 when he tried to swim across the canal here. More strangely, one of the former East German guard towers has been integrated into a camping site in the Kleinmachnow district of Teltow.

Back in (former) West Berlin, the Teltowkanal runs past the University Clinic Benjamin Franklin, one of Europe's largest hospitals. This hospital used to be part of the Free University, but since reunification has become administratively part of the Charité, the teaching hospital in (former) East Berlin. Almost across from the clinic is the former Steglitz Power Station, a beautiful example of early twentieth-century industrial architecture. The power station was finally closed in 1996 and is now home to the semi-public Energy Museum. A few miles further to the east is the Tempelhofer Hafen, once a major shipping center. The most remarkable building at the harbor is the Ullsteinhaus, named after the publishing family who printed Erich Maria Remarque's *All Quiet on the Western Front* (1928) and Carl Zuckmayer's *The Captain of Köpenick* (1931). This was Berlin's first skyscraper made from concrete, but that fact is obscured by walls decorated with red brick. The northwest corner towards the Teltowkanal is watched over by an owl, the symbol of the Ullstein family (since the "Ull" in their name is etymologically related to the German word for owl). Since the Ullsteins were Jews, they were forced to sell the site in 1934, though they regained their property in 1952. More recently, the Ullsteinhaus has become a fashion center and unfortunately has been "complemented" with an ugly modern extension.

Near the harbor, a vintner made a valiant attempt to grow grapes in the early 2000s on the Antennenberg on the sunny south side of the canal, but ultimately failed. The Sarotti factory was more successful in making chocolate next to the Teltowkanal from 1911 to 2004, but had a different kind of public relations fiasco: its mascot was the Sarotti-Mohr (Sarotti-Moor), a black-skinned child carrying a serving tray with chocolate, familiar to any German who grew up prior to 2004. That year, however, the mascot was deemed racist and was redesigned white, without the serving tray, and renamed Sarotti Magician of the Senses. Unlike the Sarotti-Mohr, the Teltowkanal was not redesigned and still flows along the Britz, Johannisthal, Rudow, Alt-Glienicke, and Grünau quarters into the Dahme river.

Water: Lakes

Wannsee is technically not one lake, but two (Grosser Wannsee and Kleiner Wannsee), and strictly speaking it is not a lake at all but a bay in the Havel river. Even more specifically, Wannsee is really an island surrounded by the Havel to the east and north, the two Wannsees (and others) to the west, and the Griebnitzsee and Teltowkanal to the south. Wannsee was developed into a high-end residential area with expensive villas in the late nineteenth century, and it was long known as an extremely wealthy suburb. In fact, the residents resisted bringing large roads and public transport to Wannsee, since that would have made it easy for anyone to visit. Almost all of these villas have beautiful gardens right on the lake. (Today, resistance to visitors is mostly expressed in gates and tall fences obscuring views of buildings and the lake.) Some of the villas survive and are open to the public: the painter Max Liebermann's summer home is now a gallery, as is the Villa Thiede next door. Both were built (in 1909 and 1906, respectively) by Paul Baumgarten, who, through no fault of his own, was one of Adolf Hitler's favorite architects.

Many famous Berliners are buried in the Wannsee cemetery, including the surgeon and medical researcher Ferdinand Sauerbruch, Nobel Prize winner (for chemistry) Emil Fischer, and Gustav Hartmann, the hackney coach driver who drove his coach all the way to Paris (to protest, presciently, against the rise of automobiles) and was immortalized in Hans Fallada's novel as *Iron Gustav*. On the east side of the Kleiner Wannsee is a memorial to the Romantic poet Heinrich von Kleist near where he committed murder-suicide with his partner, Henriette Vogel (see pp.91–92). Most notoriously, the Villa Marlier (also by Baumgarten) was home to the Wannsee Conference in 1942, where the Nazis developed strategies for their "final solution" to the "Jewish question." Surprisingly, the villa was long used as a youth hostel, but more recently it has become a museum dedicated to explaining the conference.

Many Berliners have happier associations with Wannsee because of its open-air bathing area, Europe's largest lido (Strandbad Wannsee) with an artificial beach 4,100 feet long and 260 feet wide. The "pool" was first opened in 1907 and expanded in 1929 according to plans by the architects Martin Wagner and Richard Ermisch. The 1,650-foot promenade in yellow brick in the New Objectivity style has changing cabins (unnecessary for the nudist portion of the beach, of course), snack bars and restaurants, and fine views of the beach and lake. Visitors can rent *Strandkörbe* (beach baskets), a uniquely German seating option with comfortable cushions, leg rests, and a reed roof creating shade. In its first season in 1930, 1.3 million Berliners visited the improved Strandbad Wannsee, and today some 30,000 crowd in on a sunny day. Bathing here is not necessarily relaxing, but the trek from the S-Bahn or car park, the search for an empty spot to occupy with a towel, and the attempt to enjoy the chaos are certainly typical Berlin summer experiences not to be missed.

Off the west coast of Wannsee is one of Berlin's strangest and most interesting curiosities, the Pfaueninsel (Peacock Island) in the Havel river. As described by the publicist Wolf Jobst Siedler in *Auf der Pfaueninsel*, this 210-acre island was settled as far back as the Iron Age, and the Wend tribe had a village here. In more modern times (the seventeenth century), the Prussian rulers raised rabbits on the island, which was therefore known as Kaninchenwerder. From 1685 to 1692, the island was gifted by the Great Elector Friedrich Wilhelm to the alchemist (scientist) Johannes Kunckel, who was supposed to improve Prussian glass production. Kunckel managed to scare villagers on either side of the island with his smoky and smelly (and unsuccessful) experiments, and in 1689 he burnt down his entire operation.

A century later, the Pfaueninsel was developed by two rulers into a quaint folly with structures mimicking buildings from various countries and time periods. The Prussian King Friedrich Wilhelm II had an attachment to the island because he spent happy hours there with Wilhelmine Encke, his mistress for some thirty years (parallel to two marriages) and mother of five of his children. In the 1790s he built a small castle at the southwest end of the island in the style of a romantic ruin with only one completed tower (and a distinctive bridge between them, the first cast-iron bridge in Berlin) and a third half-story of "broken" windows. At the opposite end of the island, Friedrich Wilhelm II had a dairy constructed in the style of a Gothic monastery. He also brought the now ubiquitous peacocks to the island, though it remains unclear whether the name or the peacocks came first. Under his direction, nature was tamed to look wild while revealing the structures in intricate lines and perspectives both on the island and from the shore.

Under his successor, a unique structure was added in the middle of the island. A Kavaliershaus (guest house) had been built here around 1804, but was no longer large enough for visitors. In 1824 Friedrich Wilhelm III found a late Gothic patrician house he liked in Gdansk (now Poland), where it had supposedly been brought in 1480 after having been built a century earlier in Nuremberg. The house was dismantled in Gdansk and reassembled on the Pfaueninsel and attached to the guest house by the architect Karl Friedrich Schinkel. Schinkel also designed the Schweizerhaus, which was not very Swiss at all but rather neoclassical, and was perhaps responsible for the Luisentempel, a neoclassical memorial to Friedrich Wilhelm III's popular wife. Aviaries for the peacocks and other birds were added, as was a large greenhouse that burnt down in 1880. Today, the island is a popular destination, partly because it is only accessible by a quick ferry that runs every fifteen minutes and thus has no cars. In supposedly typical German fashion, visitors are greeted with a long list of prohibitions in force during their stay on the island, but once past the notice the Pfaueninsel represents a little island paradise. There may be crowds, but the island is large enough to find a quiet and shady spot—though perhaps illegally off the path.

The Wannsee also feeds Schlachtensee, the southernmost of the Grunewaldseen. Around these five lakes created by a glacial depression in the last Ice Age—Schlachtensee, Krumme Lanke, Riemeisterfenn, Grunewaldsee, and Hundekehlesee (from south to north)—Berlin's natural contours are still easy to recognize. (The chain of lakes is started by Nikolassee in the south and continued by the smaller Dianasee, Koenigssee, Herthasee, Hubertussee, and Halensee in the north, but those are not in the Grunewald, and they are fed by underground pipes rather than waterways above ground.) The Grunewaldseen are supposedly home to almost twenty species of fish including pike, carp, tench, and eel, and some fishing is allowed. Starting on the northern sides of the Schlachtensee and Krumme Lanke, the entire chain of lakes forms one of Europe's largest dog parks. Fortunately, dogs have to be kept on leashes around bathing areas (some of which allow nude bathing).

Since the water entering the Schlachtensee is cleaned, the water quality is good. The 3.5-mile path around the circumference is a popular jogging route, but there can be heavy traffic here with walkers, baby strollers, runners, dogs, and cyclists competing for space. The next lake is appropriately called Krumme Lanke, *Lanke* being an old Slavic word for "lake" and *krumm* meaning "crooked." Northeast of Krumme Lanke there used to be another lake as late as the early twentieth century, but now this has become a swampy area called Riemeisterfenn, something of a tautology since Riemeister is a bowdlerization of *Riedmeister*, which means "swamp warden," and *Fenn* is a cognate of the English word "fen." Right next to the swamp is an old restaurant (now also a horse-riding school on the edge of the Grunewald) founded in 1885 that was soon nicknamed "Onkel Toms Hütte" (Uncle Tom's Cabin), alluding to Harriet Beecher Stowe's famous novel, perhaps because of the restaurant's straw roof. In the 1920s one of Berlin's modernist housing developments nearby (and the U-Bahn station there) was also called Onkel Toms Hütte. After Riemiesterfenn, the glacial depression moves through another swamp, the Langes Luch. This nature reserve used be to home to distinctive flora and fauna (apparently, there were unique spider species), but the encroachment of the city has led to there being mostly birch and alder trees today. The final and largest lake in the series is the Grunewaldsee with its hunting lodge (see below) and dog bathing area, which has been a bone of contention among Berliners for many years.

Green Spaces: Forests and Hills

Berlin's largest lake at almost three square miles is actually the Grosser Müggelsee (Great Müggel Lake) on the southeastern edge of the city. Above the Grosser Müggelsee rises the somewhat euphemistically named Grosser Müggelberg (Great Müggel Mountain), the highest natural elevation in Berlin at 377 feet. With their "small" counterparts, the Kleiner Müggelberg and Kleiner Müggelsee, as well as the Dämeritzsee, the Seddinsee, and the Langer See (Long Lake—technically just an expansion of the Dahme river), this entire area covers almost six square miles and constitutes Berlin's largest green space. To the northwest, where the Spree leaves the Grosser Müggelsee (see above), the Friedrichshagener Spreetunnel was built under the river in 1926 so that boat traffic was not interrupted. This pedestrian tunnel is approximately four hundred feet long and about 26 feet under the surface of the river. Because of the tunnel, the energetic can hike all the way around the Grosser Müggelsee and in the Müggel mountains—but that would certainly be an all-day excursion.

In this area it is easy to imagine the wilderness that existed before the advent of civilization and the founding of Berlin, but there are also random reminders of the presence of humans. For instance, there was competition between the Müggelberge and Alexanderplatz for the TV Tower (see p.131), and a hundred-foot-high stump survives where the GDR first intended to build it on the site of a memorial for Bismarck, blown up in World War II. The project was abandoned, however, when it was realized that it would interfere with flights in and out of East Berlin's Schönefeld airport. The 46-foot-high Wendenturm, a nearby tower built in 1900 and named after the

17

West Slavic Wend tribe, is now part of the Hotel Müggelsee. There are no views, but the tower can be rented for faux-medieval banquets. More appealing (in a nostalgic kind of way) is the 165-foot modernist Müggelturm (1959–61) south of the lake on the site of a nineteenth-century tower that burned down in 1958. Built in the International Style, the Müggelturm offers vistas from nine levels of viewing platforms of some thirty miles in each direction. There used to be a restaurant attached to the tower, but it has remained unoccupied for several years now and is currently more interesting as a relic of GDR architecture and culture.

Two other sites of past glory in the Müggelsee area are in a similarly derelict state. The Kanonenberge (Cannon Mountains) are an 820 x 260-foot pit where a nineteenth-century contractor had excavated sand for construction in Berlin. When the residents in the area objected, the operation was shut down, but instead the Prussian military and, later, the Wehrmacht used the pit for artillery practice before the two World Wars—which probably displeased the residents even more. An old viewing platform over the pit is accessible again. Secondly, there is a toboggan run between the two Müggelberge affectionately known as "Death Run." The future of the derelict course is uncertain, though it is often used (unofficially) by mountain bikers.

The counterpart to the Müggelseen and Müggelberge area in the southeast of Berlin is the Grunewald in the southwest. The Grunewald forest covers over 7,400 acres, has Berlin's second-highest elevation at the Teufelsberg with 376 feet, and includes in its area (or borders on) water in various forms: the Havel river, the Wannsee, and the Grunewald series of lakes. The northern part of the forest is in the district of Charlottenburg-Wilmersdorf; the other end, many miles to the south, is in Steglitz-Zehlendorf. There are swamplands such as the Postfenn, the Teufelsfenn, and the Riemeisterfenn, and the retreating Ice Age created various smaller ponds and lakes. With the Müggelsee area in the east, the Grunewald functions as Berlin's lungs.

Over half of the forest is comprised of pine trees, about a quarter is oak, and the rest includes birch and beech. Trees have been harvested here at least since the Middle Ages, so the Grunewald is by no means in its natural state. At the same time, the size and condition (partly due to diminishing city resources for maintenance) make it feel like an ancient forest. With a good map, it is not difficult to wander here for four or five hours without leaving the forest. Some hikes go up and down the various peaks in Grunewald; others follow the Havel ridge with views of the river; still others hop from lake to lake. The forest is large enough to sustain significant wildlife populations, and encounters with deer and wild boar are quite common. Some of the man-made environment actually enhances the natural parts. The 180-foot Grunewaldturm is a red brick neo-Gothic tower built in the late 1890s to honor the Prussian King and German Emperor Wilhelm I, but today it is more popular because of its viewing platform and is safe to visit again after several years of renovation. Throughout the forest, there are small foresters' lodges that confirm stereotypes about Germans' enjoyment of the outdoors and hunting—though nobody should mistake a Berlin forest for Bavarian woods, since the rivalry between southern and northern Germany continues to thrive.

But perhaps most interestingly, the highest elevation in the Grunewald is also man-made. After World War II Berlin was presented with the problem of how to dispose of the rubble resulting from a city bombed into ruins. Some sites within the city were used for the detritus, but those were full by the end of the 1940s. Then, from 1950 to 1972, rubble amounting to the equivalent of 15,000 buildings was taken to a site in the Grunewald which was subsequently covered with earth, planted with trees, and named Teufelsberg (Devil's Mountain—after the adjacent Teufelssee lake, not because of satanic associations). The Allied Forces in Berlin decided this would be a good place to listen in on East German and Russian radio traffic, so they built a large bulbous station on top of the mountain. At the same time, Berliners used the hillside for sledding and skiing in the winter, and cultivated grapes for Berlin wine in the summer for several years. After the end of the Cold War the listening station was used for various other purposes and was supposed to be developed into a hotel, a conference center, or a "peace university"—all of which failed or were stopped by environmentalists, so now the site is a slowly decaying futuristic ruin. The sledding run is closed as well, but mountain bikers, snowboarders, and even hang-gliders use the hill. On New Year's Eve, it is one of the best places in Berlin to observe official and unofficial fireworks all over the city.

Three major streets traverse the Grunewald today. The Havelchaussee (Havel Avenue) mostly skirts the western edge of the forest along the Havel river and passes sights such as the Schildhorn monument (see pp.68–69), the Grunewaldturm, and Lindwerder island. The Avus Highway cuts straight through the middle of the forest and for a long time was the last road in Berlin without a speed limit—another German cliché. Towards the eastern side of the forest, the Koenigsallee and Onkel-Tom-Strasse are home to some of the most exclusive addresses in Berlin in the quarter also known as Grunewald. This has been a high-class area for a long time (even though wild boars will occasionally cross the roads at a leisurely pace): Berlin's oldest surviving castle, the Hohenzollern ruler Joachim II's hunting lodge, was built here around 1542 in the Renaissance style. This Jagdschloss Grunewald feels forgotten by time since it is on a lake on one side and surrounded by the forest on the other three (and hence only accessible on foot); the cobblestone yard and half-timbered houses also contribute to that impression. Of course, there is a lovely museum gallery and a nice café.

Green Spaces: Parks

With their rivers, lakes, mountains, and forests—as well as towers, lodges, and infrastructure—the Müggelsee area and the Grunewald served for many years as recreation areas for East and West Berlin, respectively. Both were large enough to let East Berliners feel that they could escape their repressive regime, and to allow West Berliners to forget they lived in a walled-in city. Together, the two areas form an important part of Berlin's environment. Yet they are far from the center, so Berlin created two alternative green spots—which more recently have been supplemented by a third—in the middle of the city.

The Britzer Garten, Berlin's largest park created after 1945, was originally constructed for the Bundesgartenschau (Federal Garden

Exhibition) in 1985 and located in Britz to offer the citizens of the southeastern parts of West Berlin—Britz, Buckow, Rudow, and Tempelhof—a park. This was necessary because they were cut off from their natural green resource, the Müggelsee area, by the Wall. In contrast to other Berlin parks, the Britzer Garten has an entrance fee, but it is well worth the price (no dogs or cyclists are admitted). Even today, the garden receives around one million visitors per year. Those who have trouble walking can take a small railway around the grounds. On 225 acres of cultivated land and community gardens, landscape architects dug a 25-acre lake and used the soil to create three hills around it, the highest with an excellent view of the park and surrounding areas. The shores of the lake were given a variety of surfaces: meadows, gravel, sand, reeds, and a promenade. There are various man-made brooks that wind their melodious way through the park. Supernaturally inclined visitors can check out the Witches' Garden with plants and herbs that were popular in the Middle Ages. The designers even made an effort to accommodate the needs of non-human visitors by creating habitats for insects, amphibians, and birds.

Similarly, the architecture of the garden is related to its nature. The most distinctive structure is the Rhizomatic Bridge, which has walkways mounted on tall tripod-like structures topped with what look like copper needles. "Rhizomatic" has two meanings: it refers to root-like structures, which would be appropriate in a park but does not really fit the bridge; and it means interconnected, which is probably the significance it takes here. The café on the lake is a design by Engelbert Kremser in his unique style of Earthwork Architecture and looks like a charming pile of mud dropped next to the lake. The Liebesinsel (Love Island) in the lake has a stone house that remains mysterious because it cannot be visited. Most of all, though, Berliners love the Britzer Garten because of its beautiful trees and flowers such as rhododendrons and roses; its main path with millions of crocuses, daffodils, and hyacinths; and especially its annual spring exhibition of hundreds of thousands of tulips.

Berlin has many other large parks, but after the Britzer Garten the most famous is the Tiergarten in the center of the city, between the Spree to the north, the Brandenburg Gate to the east, the embassy quarter in the south, and the Technical University in the west. In the sixteenth and seventeenth centuries this 520-acre expanse was the elector's personal property and was used mainly for hunting. Animals were set free here, and fences kept them from destroying the surrounding farmland (and escaping the elector's hunting parties). Towards the end of the seventeenth century the first roads were constructed through the area, especially the Grosser Stern (Great Star) where four streets form an intersection that is now the site of the Siegessäule (Victory Column). In the eighteenth century Frederick the Great was not much interested in hunting and directed landscape architect Georg Wenzeslaus von Knobelsdorff to transform the hunting reserve into a public park. One of Knobelsdorff's innovations was a pheasant aviary, which formed the nucleus of the Berlin Zoo. The Tiergarten (Animal Garden) may have received its name from the original animals that were hunted there, or for the zoo. In the nineteenth century the Tiergarten was redesigned by Peter Joseph Lenné as an English-style garden with straight paths and long views, as well as whimsical details such as the Luiseninsel, a rose garden, and various bridges over natural or man-made rivulets. Statues of German grandees in politics and the arts were spread all over the park to promote German national pride. Many foreign embassies settled at the southern edge.

In contrast, the twentieth century held many challenges for the Tiergarten. The Nazis widened some of the streets, reducing the green areas. After World War II, so many trees were used as firewood that only about seven hundred were left. In the post-war period, various buildings and monuments were constructed within the borders: the Soviet War Memorial (which was guarded by Soviet soldiers throughout the Cold War) in 1945, the Kongresshalle (a convention hall known variously as the Pregnant Oyster or Jimmy Carter's Smile—which makes perfect sense when you see it—and now home to the Haus der Kulturen der Welt, see p.145) in 1956–57, and the Carillon (the fourth-highest in the world) in 1987. The embassies fell into disrepair as most countries moved their representation to Bonn.

Fortunately, things have been looking up for the Tiergarten in the twenty-first century. There were two brief scares: one when a tunnel was laid under the park to connect the new government district to the surrounding streets, and another when the Love Parade (an open-air rave) with over one million participants posed an ecological threat. However, it seems the tunnel has not harmed the trees' roots after all, and the Love Parade has moved to other cities. At the same time, the embassies have been renovated or replaced, and barbequing in the park has been banned—to the chagrin of many locals. But more importantly, the Tiergarten is once again a beautiful park, an oasis of green in a hectic city, a man-made design that offers a seemingly natural environment.

Most recently, a third large park has been created in the middle of Berlin: the Tempelhofer Park, aka the former Tempelhof airport. The old airport goes back to the turn of the twentieth century when none less than Orville Wright flew an airplane on a parade ground here in 1909. The parade ground was officially turned into an airport in the 1920s, and the Nazis rebuilt it on a monumental scale in the 1930s. Tempelhof Airport was crucial in the efforts of the Berlin Airlift of 1948–49 (see pp.81–82), but it was used less and less as Tegel Airport gained prominence, and finally closed in 2008 when construction for Berlin's new (and still unfinished) mega-airport was under way. After renting out the terminal buildings at Tempelhof, the city decided to turn the runways and surrounding areas into a park, which opened in 2010.

This Tempelhofer Park, part of a larger urban development project called Tempelhofer Freiheit (freedom), covers almost 750 acres and thus constitutes the largest park in Berlin. Like the Britzer Garten, the Tempelhofer Park is closed at night (it is fenced in), but like the Tiergarten it is free to visit (through various entrances open during the day). The runways have not been removed (or even their markings erased), so visitors have the eerie feeling that an airplane might land at any second. Apart from sanitary facilities and a small look-out tower, not much has changed, but nature is slowly reasserting itself across the park, with grass growing high and birds and other animals returning (except in the dog exercise area). In one corner squatters have started to grow vegetables. However, this idyllic park is already under threat: the city is encroaching with apartment buildings on the southern edge and plans to construct a new S-Bahn station. Even more alarmingly, Mayor Klaus Wowereit wants to develop the entire area into an "Education Quarter," which is supposed to include a new State Library as well as various educational institutions. This scheme is likely to fall victim to Berlin's poor financial situation—and leave the city with its newest and most exciting park.

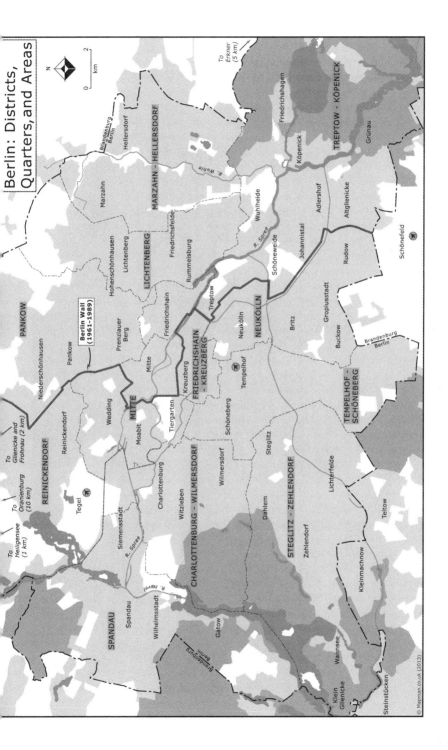

Berlin: Districts, Quarters, and Areas

© Mapman.co.uk (2013)

Bird's eye view of central Berlin around 1850, with the Forum Fredericianum, the Humboldt University across the street, the opera, and the Hohenzollern castle across from the Lustgarten (right to left), all along Unter den Linden (and the Spree in the

2 | The Urban Map
Growth and Development

Berlin grew where it did mostly for two (related) reasons: because of a glacial valley and because of trade routes. Between the Barnim and Teltow plateaus, the Warsaw-Berlin glacial valley narrows to a width of between three and four miles, and the east-west trade routes between the Rhine and Oder rivers cross the north-south routes between the Baltic Sea and southern Germany. For the same geographical reasons, there was originally limited space in which the city could expand, so it remained rather small for a considerable time. Meanwhile, similar towns were developing further up and down the rivers and trade routes. These towns, such as Köpenick in the southeast and Spandau in the northwest, maintained their independence for centuries, but eventually they were swallowed up and demoted to mere districts as Berlin acquired more and more political power. These developments can be traced in the four Berlin walls, all of which have left traces in the urban map almost in concentric circles: the medieval city wall, the seventeenth-century so-called Fortification, the eighteenth-century Akzisemauer or Excise Wall (with its immediate predecessor, the palisade fence), and, of course, the notorious Berlin Wall.

The Medieval City Wall

The medieval wall was probably built in the thirteenth century soon after the city was founded, and it surrounded the twin cities of Berlin and Cölln. (Any statement about "Berlin" until the early eighteenth century should always be understood as referring to these twin cities.) Its main purposes were military security and control of imports and exports. The wall was up to fifteen feet high and about six feet wide, with a parapet and crenellation. At irregular intervals there were towers or half towers open on the inside. Following the outline of Berlin-Cölln, this wall crossed the Spree river at both ends of the twin cities, surrounding the Schlossinsel (see p.4) and most of what now constitutes the district of Mitte. The Berlin section started around today's Jannowitzbrücke and followed what is now Littenstrasse north. Here (between Littenstrasse and Waisenstrasse) stands the only remaining part of the wall, which was discovered during construction in 1948 and restored in the 1980s. Other sections are periodically found under similar circumstances, but they are usually not preserved. From Littenstrasse the medieval city wall went through the area now occupied by the TV Tower and turned west on Rochstrasse to rejoin the Spree at today's Friedrichsbrücke, following the river back southeast. On the outside of this Berlin section was a small moat, and there were also three gates named after the places closest to them: the Stralauer, Oderberger, and Spandauer Tor.

On the Cölln section over the Rathausbrücke—which was long under (re-)construction and (re-)opened in late 2012—the wall approximately followed the southern edge of the Schlossplatz to the other arm of the Spree. (When the castle was built in the fifteenth century, the wall may have been adjusted; sources disagree.) From the Gertraudenbrücke (with the Teltower Tor), it went northeast again to the Inselbrücke (which is actually no longer a bridge but simply a street name), where it passed the Köpenicker Tor and met the Spree. Thus, the medieval city wall was about one and a half miles long and surrounded an area of 175 acres. As few as 2,000 people (around 1250) and as many as 12,000 (around 1620) lived here, and by the seventeenth century the twin cities were becoming crowded.

Fortification

The medieval wall served Berlin well for about 350–400 years, until the city was devastated in the Thirty Years' War (1618–48)—the population dropped from 12,000 to 6,000, and over a third of the 1,200 houses stood empty. After the war, the Great Elector Friedrich Wilhelm decided to construct a new bulwark for military protection, and between 1658 and 1683 the Fortification was built. Rather than a simple wall, this was supposed to be a rampart designed to the latest specifications (though the plans were soon out of date as technology developed). The Fortification turned Berlin into a water fortress, i.e., the entire city was surrounded by a moat. In total, the bulwark was about 250 feet wide: the new wall was some twenty feet wide (and over 25 feet high) with a walkway at its summit; in front of it was a smaller subsidiary wall; both of those were constructed with earth excavated from a new 150-foot-wide moat. The water level in the moat was regulated with a system of locks and inlets, which in turn were controlled by little round structures called *Bären*. One of these, the Wusterhausener Bär, survives in the park next to the Märkisches Museum, though it is actually a newer version built in 1718 rather than the seventeenth-century original. At intervals, thirteen five-point bastions stood out from the Fortification so that cannons could cover the entire area in front of the walls and on the water. The shape of the bastions can still be imagined at Hausvogteiplatz, which was designed on the site of bastion no. 3 and retains its pentagon shape. In total, this wall enclosed an area of a little over five acres in which some 15,000 people lived.

The construction of the Fortification was a huge project for which no significant funds were available, so Friedrich Wilhelm decided simply to force Berliners to participate in its building. Every single day, a quarter of the working population was required to report for duty, and farmers in the areas around Berlin were drafted as well. Thus, around 1,000 individuals worked every day for 25 years, contributing an estimated seventy or eighty million hours of labor. This was, of course, a huge drain on the Berlin economy, and it is not entirely clear whether the intended military improvement warranted the project—the Fortification was never really tested in war. Work started in 1658 on the Berlin (eastern and northern) side, and that part was completed in four years under the direction of the Dutch-trained architect Johann Gregor Memhardt. (Earlier, in 1652, Memhardt had engraved Berlin's earliest map.) Here, the Barnim plateau in the form of the Prenzlauer Berge did not allow for much development, so the Fortification simply followed the course of the medieval city wall, except for the addition of the moat. In subsequent centuries the moat was filled up, and in the late nineteenth century the new elevated S-Bahn followed its course. Today, the street along the S-Bahn is named after its architect Ernst Dircksen.

On the Cölln (western and southern) side, the Fortification extended beyond the medieval wall and incorporated two new areas that had grown outside the old twin cities. To the south, Neu-Cölln am Wasser was a narrow strip along two streets: Neu-Cölln am Wasser (now Märkisches Ufer) and Neu-Cölln am Wall. The latter is called Wallstrasse today and follows the contours of the Fortification in this area. At 47 acres, Neu-Cölln am Wasser was populated by the Dutch specialists who were involved in the construction of the bulwark. To the west, the Fortification enclosed Friedrichswerder. The first houses on this river island ("Werder") were built in 1631, and it was recognized as a city in 1662; Memhardt himself lived here after 1669 and a city hall was built in 1678. Today, the designation lives on in Schinkel's Friedrichswerdersche Kirche.

Suburbs

Though it contributed significantly to the urban map, the Fortification turned out to be useless as protection against military threats and a failure with regard to planning. In the fifty years after its completion in 1683, a belt of various *Vorstädte*—suburbs, literally "in front of the city"—developed all around the city walls anticlockwise around the center of the Fortification: Dorotheenstadt, Friedrichstadt, Luisenstadt, Stralauer Vorstadt, Königstadt, and Spandauer Vorstadt.

The first suburb, which existed even before the Fortification was finished, was Dorotheenstadt. As a matter of fact, there were plans to extend the city wall around this district, and at least one popular map mistakenly portrayed the extension as accomplished, even though it never was. Friedrich Wilhelm, the Great Elector, had presented this area to the west of the city between the Fortification and the Tiergarten, originally called *Neustadt* (new city), to his second wife Dorothea in 1670. After a street grid was developed, the area was recognized as a city in 1674, and in 1681 it was renamed Dorotheenstadt in honor of its owner. To the east, Dorotheenstadt abutted the Fortification and was connected through the

Dorotheenstädtisches Tor, which no longer exists; to the west, its border was later marked by the Brandenburg Gate.

The suburb's name is remembered in today's Dorotheenstrasse, but its most famous street is Unter den Linden. Developed in the seventeenth century and lined with a thousand lime trees from the beginning, Unter den Linden became Berlin's most celebrated thoroughfare in the 1700s and 1800s. With the Hohenzollern castle, the opera, the Berliner Dom (cathedral—see pp.155–56), the Forum Frediricianum, the university, the academy of arts and sciences, and the Brandenburg Gate—to name just a few landmarks—there was no street more significant. The Nazis cut down the trees to make room for military parades, and most of the buildings on either side were destroyed during World War II, but the street was resurrected almost immediately under the GDR regime. Local writers such as Günter de Bruyn and Christa Wolf (see pp.102–3 and 106) have written entire books about the boulevard.

Friedrichstadt to the south of Dorotheenstadt and west of Friedrichswerder (so southwest of the original twin cities of Berlin and Cölln) was developed only slightly later. The son of Friedrich Wilhelm, Elector Friedrich III (later Friedrich I as King in Prussia—see below), decided to build a new district here in 1691, and one year later there were already three hundred buildings. Many Huguenot refugees settled here to escape religious persecution in France, and in the early 1700s they built their own church. This French Church was symmetrically complemented by the German Church to frame the Gendarmenmarkt, one of the most beautiful squares in all of Berlin. In 1706 the development was named Friedrichstadt. Its eastern end was the Leipziger Tor in the Fortification; its western end was a newly constructed octagonal plaza (originally intended for military exercises) that was later called Leipziger Platz.

When Friedrichstadt was extended further south in 1732–34, the street plan was changed so that the three main thoroughfares—Lindenstrasse, Friedrichstrasse, and Wilhelmstrasse (from east to west)—formed a triangle with the Leipziger Strasse that converged on a plaza simply called *Rondell*. In 1815 this round square was renamed Belle-Alliance-Platz to commemorate the battle perhaps better known as Waterloo in Anglo-American parlance, and in 1947 it was given its present name Mehringplatz. Because of reconstruction after World War II the three streets no longer quite make it to the plaza, but it is still easy to see that they *should* end there. Friedrichstrasse, long disrupted by the Berlin Wall, is now once again a center for tourism and commerce, though it is hardly a good traffic route because it is so narrow, has many traffic lights, and ends at an impractical T-junction. Mehringplatz is large, blighted by the ugly architecture of 1960s social housing and has obviously lost its original purpose (for military exercises), so it is currently an awkward space. There are, however, attempts to revive it with projects like the Path of Visionaries, a series of plates with quotations from famous Europeans.

There had always been farmers in the areas around Berlin, many of whom had built residences, for instance to the south of Cölln. This particular area was originally known as Myrica and had been purchased by Berlin as far back as 1261. In total, 108 buildings were torched in 1641 during the Thirty Years' War so that they could not provide shelter for the approaching Swedish army. More buildings were in the way of the Fortification, but after the southern portion was completed around 1665 a new suburb quickly developed known alternately as Cöllnische Vorstadt or Köpenicker Vorstadt. Also settled predominantly by the same Huguenots who built their church at the Gendarmenmarkt, its citizens were recognized as Berliners in 1701. A century later, in 1802, the settlement was renamed Luisenstadt after the popular wife of Prussian King Friedrich Wilhelm III. Luisenstadt included several important bridges over the Spree (like the Oberbaumbrücke) and became prominent through various gates into the city when the next Berlin wall, the Akzisemauer, was built in 1734–36 (see below). Since it was divided between the newly formed districts of Mitte and Kreuzberg in 1920, the name disappeared from maps—and the Wall ended up passing straight through the former Luisenstadt.

The inhabitants of Dorotheenstadt, Friedrichstadt, and Luisenstadt all quickly became citizens of Berlin. In contrast, the Stralauer Vorstadt to the east of Berlin and along the Spree to the southeast, which developed after 1690, was never recognized in this fashion. The main street in this area was a large thoroughfare for troop movements that was laid out in 1708 and baptized Frankfurter Chaussee (now Frankfurter Allee). Near Strausberger Platz in the Stralauer Vorstadt was a place of execution for Berlin, the Rabenstein; Hans Kohlhase, the horse dealer and fighter for justice whom Heinrich von Kleist immortalized in *Michael Kohlhaas*, was executed here in 1540.

North of the Stralauer Vorstadt, another suburb grew up outside the Oderberger Tor. This gate in the Fortification was also known as Georgentor (because the Georgenhospital, one of Berlin's oldest hospitals—first mentioned in 1272—was situated outside the city walls here) or Königstor (because Friedrich I made his entrance into the city through the gate when he became King in Prussia in 1701), so the suburb was also known as Georgenvorstadt or Königstadt. From the gate, the Prenzlauer, Bernauer, and Landsberger Strassen fanned out towards those destinations. Thus, important Berlin landmarks like Alexanderplatz and the Friedrichshain park were in the Königstadt. A skyscraper near Alexanderplatz was recently dubbed Königstadt-Carrée to commemorate the old name. In 1689 the Georgenkirche (destroyed in World War II) in this suburb was declared the parish church for both the Stralauer Vorstadt to the south and the Spandauer Vorstadt to the north.

The Spandauer Vorstadt had long been used by citizens of Berlin and Cölln to grow food for personal consumption, but in the eighteenth century it developed into Berlin's largest and most important suburb. The Great Elector Friedrich Wilhelm gave this area to his second wife Dorothea at the same time as she received Dorotheenstadt, and starting in 1699 streets were constructed. A new bridge across the Spree connected the Spandauer Vorstadt and the Dorotheenstadt to make traffic easier along what is now Friedrichstrasse. Dorothea had a summer residence here, the Monbijou Palace, rebuilt in the late baroque style in 1703–06 (it was destroyed in an air raid in 1943), and she had the road to her palace straightened and widened (today's Oranienburger Strasse). In the northwest of the Spandauer Vorstadt, Elector-turned-King Friedrich

III/I founded the Charité hospital in 1710—originally a home for victims of the plague, after 1810 the university hospital of the new Berlin University, and today one of Europe's leading research clinics. In the early twentieth century the tenements known as the Hackesche Höfe were built here in an attempt to combine living space, gastronomy, cultural institutions, small business, and even factories (see p.56).

The eastern part of the Spandauer Vorstadt is famous as the Scheunenviertel, the home to many of Berlin's Jews. *Scheunenviertel* literally means "barn quarter," and since barns were forbidden within the city, they were built outside the city walls (in this case, the Akzisemauer). For some reason, there was a concentration here to the north of the old twin cities, and the area has kept its name almost into the present. In 1737 King Friedrich Wilhelm I commanded all Berlin Jews to move to this district and only permitted them to enter the city through the two northern gates. Of course, the resulting concentration of Jews meant that those new to the city tended to move there as well, so the Scheunenviertel remained an area with heavy Jewish cultural and religious influences. For instance, Jewish cemeteries and synagogues (like the nineteenth-century Neue Synagoge on Oranienburger Strasse—see pp.161–62) were located here. Not entirely unexpectedly, the Scheunenviertel witnessed several pogroms, such as the one in 1923 when the Jews were irrationally held responsible for a rise in the price of bread.

Akzisemauer

By the beginning of the eighteenth century, only about twenty years after the completion of the Fortification, it became clear that Berlin had outgrown its walls. The new conglomerate of Berlin, Cölln, Friedrichswerder, Friedrichstadt, and Dorotheenstadt was officially united in 1710 and declared *Königliche Haupt- und Residenzstadt Berlin*, Royal Capital and Residence Berlin (so technically, it is only correct to speak of "Berlin" from this point on). This "new" city had an area of approximately fifteen acres and about 55,000 citizens. In 1705 King Friedrich Wilhelm I had ordered the construction of a palisade fence around the larger city area—the semi-wall mentioned

Berlin: Early Development of the City

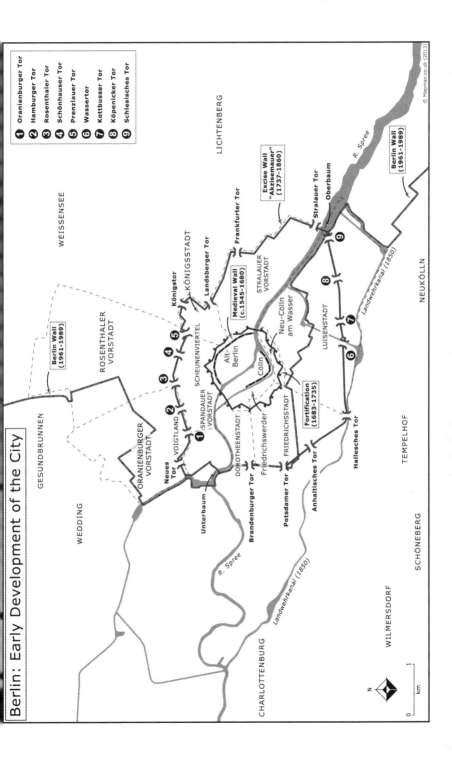

Legend:

1. Oranienburger Tor
2. Hamburger Tor
3. Rosenthaler Tor
4. Schönhauser Tor
5. Prenzlauer Tor
6. Wassertor
7. Kottbusser Tor
8. Köpenicker Tor
9. Schlesisches Tor

Berlin Wall (1961–1989)

Excise Wall "Akzisemauer" (1737–1860)

Medieval Wall (c.1545–1680)

Fortification (1683–1735)

Districts / Areas:
GESUNDBRUNNEN, WEDDING, WEISSENSEE, CHARLOTTENBURG, WILMERSDORF, SCHÖNEBERG, TEMPELHOF, NEUKÖLLN, LICHTENBERG, ROSENTHALER VORSTADT, ORANIENBURGER VORSTADT, VOIGTLAND, SPANDAUER VORSTADT, SCHEUNENVIERTEL, KÖNIGSSTADT, DOROTHEENSTADT, Friedrichswerder, FRIEDRICHSTADT, Alt-Berlin, Cölln, Neu-Cölln am Wasser, STRALAUER VORSTADT, LUISENSTADT

Gates / Places:
Neues Tor, Unterbaum, Brandenburger Tor, Potsdamer Tor, Anhaltisches Tor, Hallesches Tor, Königstor, Landsberger Tor, Frankfurter Tor, Stralauer Tor, Oberbaum

R. Spree

Landwehrkanal (1850)

N

0 1 km

© Mapman.co.uk (2013)

at the beginning of this chapter—even beyond his royal capital. (This structure is remembered in street names like Linienstrasse—Line Street—and Palisadenstrasse.) In 1734–37 Friedrich Wilhelm I replaced this fence with the *Akzisemauer*—Customs or Excise Wall—which Helmut Zschocke in the subtitle to his brilliant book (written in German) on this edifice calls *The Capital's Penultimate Wall*.

The Akzisemauer had four main functions. Nominally, it was still intended for military protection, though the few times an army appeared before Berlin in its lifetime it proved more or less useless. In 1757 an Austrian force easily overwhelmed the Berlin garrison, and in 1760 the local government bought off the Russian army that had occupied the city for four days. In 1806 a ragtag French force entered through the Hallesches Tor, followed a few days later by Napoleon Bonaparte, who chose the Brandenburg Gate for symbolic reasons. Secondly, the wall was supposed to keep soldiers from deserting the Prussian army. Military service was extremely unpopular even in peacetime because of inhumane conditions in the army, and many soldiers were pressed into service anyway. The army represented a surprisingly large percentage of the Berlin population: in the first decades of the eighteenth century ten percent of Berliners were soldiers, and by the 1730–50s that figure had risen to over twenty percent. Of course, desertion was rampant, with over a thousand cases per year—until the construction of the Customs Wall, when the number dropped by about a half.

Then, its purpose was to control the growth, size, and behavior of the population. For instance, as mentioned above, Jews were only allowed to enter the city through two gates (Rosenthaler and Hallesches Tor) and had to register with the authorities. In the 1848 rebellion (see p.74), Berliners gathered at a popular destination outside the walls, and one of the rebels' first strategic goals was to secure the city gates. Finally and most importantly (since this gave the wall its name), the *Akzisemauer* was used to control the flow of goods into Berlin, and specifically to levy taxes on most items entering the city. In this sense, it was most successful, allowing the king's customs officers to collect significant revenue. The economic impact of this policy was debatable, however, since some historians argue that the taxes raised prices in the city and formed an obstacle to the development of free trade and industry.

In practical terms, the Excise Wall was nine miles long and enclosed about 85,000 people in an area of over five square miles. Approximately every half mile there was a gate, and in most places there was a walkway on the inside of the wall called the *Communikation*; the city could be circumambulated on the *Communikation* in about four hours. Berlin now included almost all of the suburbs described above as well as several undeveloped fields such as the Tempelhofer Feld and the Köpenicker Feld in the south. The wall was generally built of brick (which could hardly withstand a serious military attack) and stood a little over ten feet high. At the end of the eighteenth and beginning of the nineteenth centuries, under Kings Friedrich Wilhelm II and Friedrich Wilhelm III, it was reinforced and heightened by about a third. At that time many of the gates were reconstructed by prominent architects.

The course of the *Akzisemauer* is still fairly easy to trace on the Berlin urban map. To start with the most obvious landmark, the Brandenburg Gate was one western entrance. The famous current structure, designed by Carl Gotthard Langhans and built from 1788 to 1791, replaced an earlier, smaller gate. It is difficult to visualize today that—in both incarnations—this was literally a guarded entrance to the city: gatekeepers lived in the small houses to the left and right of the structure, kept ledgers of each individual entering and exiting the city, and collected taxes when appropriate. (The gate was topped by a statue of the goddess Victory in an open carriage drawn by four horses known as the Quadriga. When the Quadriga was abducted as plunder to France by the Napoleonic army in 1806 and then returned in the wake of Napoleon's defeat, Berliners nicknamed it *Retourkutsche*, "witty retort.") The city limit later formed the border of the Mitte district, which meant that the Wall ran along here during the Cold War. Slightly south of the Brandenburg Gate was the Potsdamer Gate between the Leipziger Platz in Friedrichstadt and the Potsdamer Platz right outside the wall. The Anhalter Tor even further south was added in 1840, when the Anhalter Bahnhof (train station) was built right outside the wall. Askanischer Platz now occupies the site of the gate, while the remaining façade of the train station, bombed in 1943 and 1945, stands as a memorial to the devastation of World War II. From here, the Customs Wall followed the border of Friedrichstadt south and turned east at Hallesches Tor. The foundation was excavated along today's Stresemannstrasse, and a small portion of the wall was reconstructed in the 1980s. Somewhat more authentically, a section of the wall at Hannoversche Strasse 9 (north of the Brandenburg Gate) was integrated from 1835–36 into a contemporary building and is now historically protected.

The southern route of the *Akzisemauer* is just as easily identifiable because the names of some of the gates are preserved in underground stations: Hallesches Tor, Kottbusser Tor, and Schlesisches Tor. Actually, the U-Bahn is elevated here and built more or less along the route of the wall. As in the case of the Anhalter Bahnhof, most railway lines to Berlin had to stop outside the wall, and to the chagrin of the rail companies, the lines thus could not connect, resulting in significant travel complications. When the Excise Wall was razed in the late nineteenth century, the land seemed the obvious place to build the junction—as was the case here.

After crossing the Spree at the Oberbaumbrücke, the *Akzisemauer* turned north to form Berlin's eastern edge past Stralauer, Frankfurter, Landsberger, and Königstor. The wall had finally been pushed onto the Barnim plateau, so these gates were all versions of earlier entrances that were further away from the center. The new Königstor was named after the gate through which King Friedrich Wilhelm III returned after fleeing from Napoleon, and the Frankfurter Tor—the only place where a railway line made it inside the wall—is still the name of an U-Bahn station.

At the Prenzlauer Tor, the Customs Wall turned west along what is now Torstrasse (Wilhelm-Pieck-Strasse during GDR times). A new building (1995) marks the former Schönhauser Tor, while the Rosenthaler Tor, which plays a major role in Döblin's novel *Berlin Alexanderplatz* (see pp.97–99), was where the present U-Bahn station Rosenthaler Platz is now located. Further west, Oranienburger Tor is now an U-Bahn station as well. The sandstone memorials that used to decorate the top of that gate were moved to the estate of the Borsig family in Gross Behnitz in Brandenburg when the gate was taken down in 1867. The Neues Tor (new gate) of 1836 was supposed to facilitate traffic towards Hamburg, and in 1846 the Hamburger Bahnhof was built here. Though this train station was taken out of service after only 37 years, the building was preserved and is now the only remaining nineteenth-century railway station in Berlin and today serves as a museum for contemporary art. From here, the *Akzisemauer* turned south, crossed the Spree at the Unterbaum, and skirted the eastern edge of the Tiergarten to join the Brandenburg Gate.

Greater Berlin

Once again, as with the Fortification, the Akzisemauer was almost immediately exposed as a hindrance rather than an improvement. There were still suburbs like the Rosenthaler Vorstadt and the Oranienburger Vorstadt that were outside the walls (both to the north), and these suburbs grew more quickly (in population) than the city within the walls. In 1860 the customs arrangement was suspended, and between 1866 and 1869 most of the Excise Wall and its gates were demolished.

Even by then the city had grown much larger. The Rosenthaler Vorstadt was added to Berlin in 1829–31. Also known as Voigtland, this area became notorious for its dreadful social conditions and was described by Bettina von Arnim in imaginary dialogues between the king and the mother of Johann Wolfgang von Goethe in *Dies Buch gehört dem König* (*This Book Belongs to the King*, 1843). The Oranienburger Vorstadt was also incorporated into Berlin in 1831, and by 1841 the city had grown to about thirteen square miles. In the following decades the process of swallowing up surrounding villages began in earnest. The expansion of 1861 contributed more than nine square miles to Berlin by adding parts of Schöneberg (first mentioned in 1264) and Tempelhof (1290) in the south, and Wedding (1251) in the north. Wedding had a long history as a village, but it had come to prominence more recently when a medicinal spring (Gesundbrunnen) was discovered there around 1748. After 1861, Berlin covered almost 23 square miles. The incorporated villages did not add much in terms of population, but industrialization had massively increased the numbers of inhabitants: approximately 172,000 people in 1800; 202,000 in 1820; 330,000 in 1840; and about 525,000 in 1861.

At this point the government tried to address the city's problems head-on by asking a commission led by urban planner James Hobrecht to develop a plan for Berlin's future development. The resulting Hobrecht-Plan of 1862 was heavily criticized and was out of date very quickly, but it determined the form and direction of growth for the following decades. Hobrecht projected that Berlin would have between one and a half and two million citizens within fifty years and would encompass the surrounding towns such as Charlottenburg, Wilmersdorf, Rixdorf (Neukölln), Weissensee, and Lichtenberg. Incorporating earlier city plans by worthies such as Schinkel and Lenné, the recent redesign of Paris, and the wishes of the Prussian king, Hobrecht wanted to widen the main streets in the old town and imagined a huge ring road around all of Greater Berlin. Rather than design specific streets within the ring road, he simply devised rules like a uniform height of 66 feet and a minimum size for inner courtyards (so that fire engines could turn around). Hobrecht believed that all classes could live in the resulting housing together: the bourgeoisie in the lighter and larger front apartments, workers in the cheaper and smaller back flats. While he was (and is) correctly criticized for doing nothing to prevent the construction of unhygienic and almost inhumane tenements where the poor lived in squalor, his rules did create the typical urban image of Berlin, with four- or five-story blocks along straight streets with inner courtyards. Hobrecht also designed a new sanitation system where refuse, rather than being dumped into rivers, was pumped to irrigation fields outside the city with the help of *Radialsysteme*, or radial pump stations. One of these *Radialsysteme* (in Friedrichshain) is now an event center for contemporary art.

By the early twentieth century Berlin had effectively merged, as Hobrecht predicted, with the surrounding towns, especially Charlottenburg, Schöneberg, Wilmersdorf, and Neukölln. In 1877 the population of Berlin had passed one million, and by 1905 it had doubled to over two million. As early as 1875, Mayor Arthur Johnson Hobrecht (James' brother) suggested uniting the towns and cities, but encountered resistance for two main reasons: because the more rural areas were worried they would be overwhelmed by the city, and because conservative political forces were concerned that the more progressive Berlin majority would prevail.

In addition, each of these towns had their own history and identity. As Lietzow (preserved in today's Lietzensee), Charlottenburg had been around since the thirteenth century. It was re-founded by Elector Friedrich III's wife Sophie Charlotte in 1695, and a baroque palace was built here in the first years of the eighteenth century. In the nineteenth century Charlottenburg was a favorite place for Berliners to escape the city, though by 1910 there were over 300,000 citizens. Schöneberg was not nearly as large (95,000 in 1900), but it was also a city in its own right. Its town hall was later incorporated into Berlin, but gained its own fame when John F. Kennedy gave his famous "Ich bin ein Berliner" speech here in 1963. In addition, the town hall has one of Berlin's few still functioning paternosters. Wilmersdorf was mentioned for the first time in 1293, and after a few uneventful centuries it became the place for rich Berliners to build summer villas. After World War II, the district was supposedly home to the "*Wilmerdorfer Witwen*," the widows of soldiers who had died in the war. In other words, it was a sleepy district where elderly women protected an old way of life from the new Berlin.

Neukölln was first mentioned as Rixdorf in 1360. In 1737 it became home to a large group of immigrants from Bohemia, who built their own church (in the Moravian denomination) and populated the area around today's Richardstrasse. The Bohemian and German parts of Rixdorf did not unite until 1874, by which time the area was known for frivolous entertainment. In the early twentieth century, after being renamed Neukölln to alter its image (and in memory of Neu-Cölln am Wasser, see above), the town turned into a working-class district. During the Cold War, Neukölln was close to the Wall, which hindered its development, and many immigrants settled here, so it maintained its image as home to both foreigners and proletarians—or real Berliners, depending on one's perspective. Today, Neukölln is one of the few districts in which you are likely to hear true Berlin dialect, as well as the new multiethnic *Kiezdeutsch* dialect spoken by inner-city youth (see p.177).

In the end, however, the proponents of unification won out, and in 1920 *Grossberlin* was created. This Greater Berlin incorporated the seven surrounding cities of Charlottenburg, Schöneberg, Wilmersdorf, Neukölln, Spandau, Lichtenberg, and Köpenick as well as 59 rural municipalities and 27 manorial districts, doubling the population of the city from 1.9 million to about 3.8 million in one fell swoop. Greater Berlin was divided into twenty districts, each named after the largest town, village, or manor in its area. These inadvertently determined the cityscape for almost a century, since the twenty districts were used as the basis of the division of the city after World War II and hence decided the route of the Wall. In addition, they continue to define the character of the city up to this very day since the historical identities of the towns and villages are still very much recognizable. In 1920 Greater Berlin covered almost 340 square miles, though only fifteen percent of that area was built up. Depending on the method of counting, *Grossberlin* now came in somewhere between first and fifth (in population and/or size) of cities worldwide—by 1925, the population passed four million for the first time.

The Wall and Beyond

After the medieval city wall, the Fortification, and the *Akzisemauer*, Berlin was (partly) surrounded by a wall for the fourth and—it is to be hoped—last time between 1961 and 1989 (see pp.82–83). This Wall ran between the sectors of the city occupied by France, Britain, and the United States in the west, and Russia in the east. Thus (from north to south), Reinickendorf, Wedding, Tiergarten, Kreuzberg, and Neukölln formed the eastern border of West Berlin. On the other side, Pankow, Prenzlauer Berg, Mitte, Friedrichshain, and Treptow constituted the western limits of East Berlin. For obvious reasons, West Berlin could not grow in size during this period, and the population shrank slightly as the city lost its industrial base and was increasingly considered a backwater. Some areas were developed, like

Gropiusstadt, but the closer to the Wall a district was the fewer improvements took place. East Berlin added Marzahn (1979), Hohenschönhausen (1985), and Hellersdorf (1986), but these soon earned a bad reputation because of their ugly *Plattenbauten* (highrises made from prefabricated concrete), lack of infrastructure, and social problems.

After the fall of the Wall and the reunification of Berlin, new concepts have been articulated for development in the twenty-first century. According to *Zukunftsfähiges Berlin* (Sustainable Berlin), the 2001 report of a government commission, the city is supposed to consider economic productivity, social justice, and ecological compatibility in any future plans. In practice, this means balancing factors such as the renovation of old and the construction of new buildings; improving public transportation while making the city more navigable for cars; preserving green areas and avoiding more high-rises; and globalizing Berlin while maintaining its unique charm. Most current large projects—like the old palace in the center of the city reimagined as the Humboldtforum or the new Berlin airport south of the city—are running horribly over budget and schedule, but this is arguably not all bad in the sense that it allows for more discussion about how the urban map will look in the new century.

Standing on top of the Wall (with the Brandenburg Gate in the background) to celebrate its opening in November 1989—with a sign in front that says, "Caution, you are leaving Berlin," and has "Well, how?" ("Wie denn?") spray-painted on it. (Sue Ream/Wikimedia Commons)

3 Landmarks
Buildings and Styles

In contrast to other European cities like Rome, Paris, or London, Berlin has a fairly short architectural history—only about eight hundred years. The historical origins of Berlin lie in the Nikolaiviertel (Nikolai Quarter), where the Nikolaikirche was erected in the thirteenth century (see p.152), but apart from the church there are no significant remnants of Berlin's early days. In addition, the city has not been gentle with its heritage: various rulers—absolutist, fascist, or democratic—have tried to impose their urban vision by razing old parts of the city and building new ones, and of course World War II and the separation of Berlin did their part. On the one hand, this history makes it difficult to identify coherent styles of architecture beyond individual buildings; on the other, it means that different looks can interact with and play off each other, giving the cityscape a unique fluidity and vibrancy.

For the same reason, perhaps the most emblematic building ensemble in Berlin is the Jewish Museum in Kreuzberg, which is actually two buildings, one from the early eighteenth century and the other from the late twentieth, with an attached memorial garden. Also in typical Berlin tradition, the museum almost did not materialize. The West Berlin government had decided to build a Jewish Museum and held a design competition that the German-American architect Daniel Libeskind won in 1988. Yet after reunification Berlin's budget collapsed, and in 1991 the project was earmarked to be discontinued. An international outcry arose—over Berlin, of all places, deciding not to honor Jewish history and culture—and fortunately the government quickly relented. Libeskind's structure was built between 1992 and 1999, and the new museum opened in 2001.

The entrance to the museum is through the two-story Kollegienhaus of 1734–35, the last remaining baroque palace in the old Friedrichstadt. The building housed a lower court for most of its history—the author and composer E. T. A. Hoffmann worked here. Constructed after designs by Philipp Gerlach (1679–1748), the Kollegienhaus is typical of its time period: symmetrical, with straight lines, few curves, and ornamental details above the entrance and some windows. The pediment shows the Prussian coat-of-arms and allegorical figures of Wisdom and Justice. The main building and two perpendicular wings at the back form three sides of a square courtyard that is now covered with a glass ceiling. The Kollegienhaus was almost completely destroyed during World War II, but reconstructed in the 1960s as a museum for local (Berlin) history, later including a few rooms with exhibits on Jewish history.

This straightforward, subdued, venerable, and monumental structure is paired brilliantly with Daniel Libeskind's new, deconstructive, shiny, and challenging Jewish Museum—the two are subtly connected through their equal height. Today, visitors come into the old building, where they buy tickets, leave their coats, and perhaps grab a coffee (or visit special exhibitions) before descending a slate staircase and walking along a slanted tunnel into the new building. This structure is certainly important because of the artifacts it exhibits, but for the present purpose it is more significant how marvelously it embodies its mission in architecture—350,000 visitors came before the first exhibition even opened. Seen from above, the two principles of design become easily visible: on the one hand, there is a straight axis running through the entire building; on the other, the floor plan is like a huge zigzag or lightning bolt. Actually, the straight axis is empty space, or void, symbolizing the destruction of Jewish life in Berlin—in the museum visitors can only cross it on bridges—while the zigzag is a broken Star of David. From the inside, these design principles and their significance are intentionally more difficult to decipher, challenging the visitor to make sense of a confusing world.

Inside, the building is organized along three axes. The tunnel that leads in and out of the museum between the Kollegienhaus and Libeskind's structure is the axis of continuity, which reminds visitors that there was a long history of anti-Semitism that led up to the

Holocaust—and that Germans (and other nationalities) need to remain vigilant. Secondly, the axis of Holocaust ends in the Holocaust Tower, a tall, empty, dark, concrete space which was apparently not intended as an evocation of a gas chamber, but is perceived as such by many visitors. Finally, the axis of exile ends in the Garden of Exile, where stelae at an odd angle create the unsettling impression that the surrounding buildings are about to collapse onto the garden. Thus, visitors experience some aspects of Jewish life and culture not just in the exhibits, but also in the very architecture of the Jewish Museum.

There are many other places in Berlin where old and new are juxtaposed in similarly interesting ways: the ruins of the Kaiser-Wilhelm-Gedächtniskirche at Breitscheidplatz (known as *Hohler Zahn*, "hollow tooth," because of the gaping top of the church tower) with the 1960s Europacenter; the ancient Marienkirche in the shadow of the TV Tower at Alexanderplatz; the Deutsches Historisches Museum in the baroque armory with a contemporary extension by Ieoh Ming Pei on Unter den Linden; the Brandenburg Gate with the new embassy buildings at Pariser Platz; the preserved *Kaisersaal* (emperor's dining room) amidst the postmodern designs of Potsdamer Platz; and of course the nineteenth-century Reichstag with Norman Foster's iconic contemporary glass dome (mocked by some Berliners as *Eierwärmer*, "egg warmer," or *Denkbeule*, "thought bump"). Almost anywhere you turn in the city you will find that the architectural heritage is not ossified, but a living part of the cityscape.

Baroque

Still, for the purposes of description it is perhaps easier to focus on areas where individual structures or ensembles of buildings have survived and provide examples of specific periods in Berlin's architectural history. (Much more detailed lists and descriptions can be found in books such as Rainer Haubrich's *Berlin: The Architecture Guide* or Arnt Cobbers' *Architecture in Berlin*.) In many cases, these groupings are associated with one architect and with one sponsor (a person, a company, or a political system).

For instance, the Forum Fridericianum on Unter den Linden is named after its sponsor Frederick the Great and was designed to a large extent by Georg Wenzeslaus von Knobelsdorff (1699–1753)—though Frederick himself contributed ideas and sketches for most structures. Frederick wanted to build an ensemble that represented in architectural terms his modern conception of monarchy, including encouraging the arts and sciences. A large plaza was supposed to be created between a new palace on one side and an opera and a kind of gymnasium on the other, with the busy Unter den Linden thoroughfare running straight through the middle to symbolize the monarchy's closeness to its citizens. However, one of the residents on the site (a Hohenzollern relative) refused to sell his property, so plans had to be changed. The result was not as unified as Frederick would have liked, but the four buildings still nicely interact with each other (architecturally) and with the still-popular Unter den Linden.

The first structure to be completed was Knobelsdorff's opera (1741–43). This was the first free-standing opera building in Germany, and the first not directly connected to a royal house. Home to music as well as masques, the opera was intended to represent the grandeur and importance of the Berlin bourgeoisie and serve as a counterpart to similar institutions in Rome, Paris, or London. Indeed, it was opened with the Italianate opera *Cleopatra e Cesare* by local composer Carl Heinrich Graun on 7 December 1742 (before construction was even finished). The most remarkable architectural feature of the building (actually an addition after the opera burnt down in 1843) is the grand entrance, a hexastyle (six-column) Palladian portico with narrow staircases to either side. The pediment shows mythological and literary figures from antiquity, is crowned by three sculptures, and sports the dedication *Fridericus Rex Appolini et Musis*, "from Frederick to Apollo and the Muses." Important musicians such as Giacomo Meyerbeer, Richard Strauss, and Wilhelm Furtwängler were musical directors here, and Herbert von Karajan was the main conductor from 1939 to 1945, which led to accusations of collaboration with the Nazis. The building was bombed twice in World War II, in 1941 and 1945, but rebuilt in 1952 mostly following the original plans (at least on the outside). Under the current team of artistic director Jürgen Flimm and musical director Daniel Barenboim, the inside is being renovated to improve the acoustics.

After the opera, St.-Hedwigs-Kathedrale (St. Hedwig's Cathedral, 1747–73) was the second structure on the Forum Fridericianum. With this building—the first Catholic church in Prussia since the Reformation—Frederick wanted to signal his religious tolerance, especially to the newly conquered territory of Silesia, whose patron saint was Hedwig. (At the same time, he hardly contributed to the expenses of construction, so the Catholic community had to collect money from all over Europe. At one point, when the Catholics were so short of money to even be able to close the roof, the Jewish community offered to buy the building, which would have made for an interesting presence in the center of Berlin.) Originally designed by Knobelsdorff and completed by Johann Boumann (1706–76), the beautiful round structure is based on the Pantheon in Rome and divided into twelve sections like a clock. The entrance—at an angle to the opera—is topped by a pediment supported by six Ionic columns and with images from Christ's life. This frieze was added in the nineteenth century when more money became available. When Berlin was turned into a bishopric in 1930, the church was elevated to the status of cathedral. Over its lifetime, St.-Hedwigs-Kathedrale has had various domes and towers; the current reinforced concrete version, comprising 84 segments, is lower than the original and crowned with a plain cross.

The third structure of the Forum Fridericianum, Prince Heinrich's Palace across Unter den Linden, was begun in 1748 for Frederick's younger brother by Boumann, based on plans by Knobelsdorff, and completed in 1766. Designed to complement the opera (especially with another six columns), the three-story squat baroque palace has three perpendicular wings around a large courtyard opening onto the street. The fourth side is marked by an iron fence and an entrance with two tiny gatehouses, just big enough for one soldier each. After Heinrich died, the palace was given to the university, and to this day it is the main building of the Humboldt University.

The Forum was completed from 1775 to 1780 when the next-door relative finally relented and Frederick was able to construct a new library (now known as the Old Library). Frederick wanted to use a design he had seen for the Vienna Hofburg Palace, but because of space constraints he was unable to make the curvature of the architecture as deep as intended. (The original design had in fact not been built in Vienna at the time, but was only realized over a century later.) With a rather ornate façade, the library was nicknamed the *Kommode* (dresser). To the GDR's great joy, Lenin used the facility in the late nineteenth century, so a reading room was named after him.

Thus, the Forum combines the representative opera, the angled church with its round dome, the square palace (university) set back with the courtyard, and the curved library—not exactly consistent in form, but an eclectic mix of slightly different takes on baroque architecture. The plaza between the three sides of opera, church, and library is now called Bebelplatz and is used for temporary and permanent art exhibitions. Visitors will often wonder about groups of people clustered around one spot, staring intently at the ground. There is a subterranean monument by the Israeli artist Micha Ullman commemorating the burning of books that took place here in 1933. A glass square in the ground opens into a small library with empty white shelves symbolizing the absence of the 20,000 books destroyed by the Nazis. A plaque next to the glass square carries prescient verses by Heinrich Heine: "That was merely a prelude; where they burn books, they will eventually burn people as well."

Neoclassicism

Originally older than the Forum Fridericianum, the Gendarmenmarkt was refashioned only slightly later as Berlin's foremost neoclassical square. Many observers consider the Gendarmenmarkt Berlin's most beautiful plaza. The market square was first designed in 1688 as part of the new Friedrichstadt development (named after Friedrich III, later Friedrich I, King in Prussia, grandfather of Frederick the Great—see pp. 71–72), but received its current form after 1780. A crack troop of Prussian cavalry known as the *Gens d'armes* had their barracks here in the mid-eighteenth century, and the square was named in memory of their presence in 1799. The Gendarmenmarkt has three major buildings (two churches and a theater) with a statue of the German author Friedrich Schiller in the middle. The two churches were originally built after 1701, and a comedy theater was added between them in 1773. This theater was replaced in 1800–02 by a structure that burned down in 1817. The replacement for that structure was the Schauspielhaus (theater) by Karl Friedrich Schinkel (1781–1841).

Schinkel's importance for Berlin and its architecture can hardly be overstated. Born in Neuruppin, Schinkel experienced the impact of new architecture and urban planning at a young age when that entire city was rebuilt in 1787 after a fire (to which the young man lost his father). In 1794 Schinkel's family moved to Berlin, where he was inspired by and became a student of the father-and-son architect team of David and Friedrich Gilly. From 1803 to 1805 Schinkel went on a grand tour of Italy and absorbed the classical architectural design that for a while became his trademark. On his return to Berlin, he could not find work in an economy depressed by the Napoleonic Wars, so he turned (successfully) to painting and stage design—for instance, the famous set for Mozart's *Magic Flute*. The Prussian King Friedrich Wilhelm III recognized Schinkel's talent and appointed him as an official architect, and for the rest of his life Schinkel was torn between his duties as a state employee and his passion for art and architecture. The list of buildings he designed and executed in Berlin is long and varied: from the Humboldt-Schloss in Tegel (1821) to the bridge next to the castle in the center of Berlin (1822); from the Friedrichswerdersche Kirche (1824–31, now the Schinkel Museum) to the Old Museum (1824) in the museum quarter; from a new building for the Architectural Academy he had attended himself (1831) to a new observatory (1835).

For the Gendarmenmarkt, Schinkel was required to recycle the foundations and the columns left from the previous structure after the fire of 1817, yet he still managed to build something entirely new. The Schauspielhaus (see p.119), built 1818–21, is basically a raised structure of three cubes, the middle (and largest) one housing the main theater (now concert hall), the left one a chamber music concert hall, and the right one offices. The façade towards the Gendarmenmarkt offers the six recycled columns in a portico elevated high above ground level, with a grand open staircase leading to the doors. On either side of the staircase, bronze sculptures by Christian Friedrich Tieck (1776–1851) show music taming wild animals, while not one but two pediments depict the Muses and other mythical figures. The interior originally had seats arranged in a half-circle with two balconies above. Destroyed in World War II, the structure was entirely rebuilt, preserving Schinkel's exterior but changing the main interior space into a large concert hall. The old chamber music hall was recently reconstructed and opened in 2003 as the Werner-Otto-Saal (named after its sponsor, the founder of an extremely successful mail-order company).

One of the two baroque churches on the Gendarmenmarkt was built for a German congregation, the other (the Friedrichstadtkirche) for the French Huguenots who had recently migrated to Berlin in large numbers (see pp.170–71). Frederick the Great decided he wanted to improve the plaza along the lines of Piazza del Popolo in Rome or the Royal Naval College in Greenwich, so he ordered Carl von Gontard (1731–91) to build two large domed towers next to the churches (1780–85). Oddly, the towers have no interior connection with the churches, but the structures are still called Französischer (French) and Deutscher (German) Dom respectively. Both were destroyed in the war and rebuilt in the 1980s and 1990s. The French church was reopened in 1987 with a carillon that competed with its western counterpart in the Tiergarten for Berlin's 750th birthday. Today, both towers house museums, while the plaza between them hosts open-air concerts and an annual upscale Christmas market.

Historicism

After baroque and neoclassicism, the next eighty to a hundred years in Berlin's architecture were characterized by the mixture of influences known as historicism. In this period, until the beginning of the twentieth century, architects took elements from styles across time and space—from Gothic and Renaissance to the Orient—and came up with individual and eclectic combinations. In Berlin historicism found its most typical expression in the four-story tenement buildings called *Altbau* that still shape the cityscape in most districts (at least where the old buildings were not destroyed during World War II).

Since historicism is such a mixture, it is difficult to pinpoint one particular representative ensemble. However, many of Berlin's best-known structures are examples of this style. City Hall, known as Rotes (Red) Rathaus for its distinctive red brick (and more recently occasionally as Rosarotes Rathaus, Pink City Hall, because of the openly gay mayor), was built between 1861 and 1869. Rather than opting for monumental classicism, Hermann Friedrich Waesemann (1813–79) imitated municipal architecture from Italy and Flanders with rounded windows and a seemingly unfinished main tower. Along all four sides of the building, a frieze of sandstone and terra-cotta shows scenes from Berlin's history. The monumental Reichstag (1884–94) by Paul Wallot (1841–1912) combines elements of antique architecture (another hexastyle portico) with the Italian Renaissance (the square towers on the corner). The emperor was not happy with the cupola on the building since it competed with the dome on his palace, and the inscription "For the German People" was not installed until 1916.

Various museums were built during the historicist period as well. An Arts and Crafts Museum (1877–81) was designed by Martin Gropius (1824–80), whose name the building now carries. Gropius' style is reminiscent of Schinkel's late works, with tripartite windows sporting small pediments and a massive façade, but the building also shows the influence of the Italian Renaissance in the overhanging roof, the terracotta upper story, and the frieze depicting various arts and crafts. The building was bombed in World War II and then long abandoned because it was right next to the Wall. It only escaped demolition because the original architect's more famous great-nephew, Walter Gropius (1883–1969), came to the rescue. Restored as Martin-Gropius-Bau (with the main entrance moved away from the Wall), the museum appropriately opened with a Schinkel exhibition in 1981 and then offered a seminal show on Prussia. Today there is no permanent collection, but a series of visiting exhibitions. The Bode-Museum (1897–1904—originally called Kaiser-Friedrich-Museum and later renamed after one of its directors) is neo-baroque but also integrates elements (and even actual examples) of Italian and Dutch architecture. Built in an unusual triangular shape at the north end of the Schlossinsel in the Spree, the museum required the construction of bridges from both shores to grant access to the main entrance.

Historicism served both religious structures and secular temples. The Berliner Dom (Berlin cathedral, 1893–1905—see pp.155–56) is sometimes characterized as "Wilhelminian baroque" due to its ornate façade and over-decoration. On a more secular note, the Theater des Westens (1895–96) has been offering light entertainment for over a hundred years—so its name is in relation to the development of Berlin rather than the separation of the city during the Cold War. This building presents an exuberant mixture of styles: the French Renaissance appearance of the façade, which also has some Art Deco influences, and a half-timbered look combined with a medieval castle for the stage area. A Latin inscription on the façade translates, "This structure was built for the support of the arts." A different kind of temple, the KaDeWe (Kaufhaus des Westens) department store (see pp.196–97), is also a historicist building from 1907.

Historicism contributed to more utilitarian architecture as well. The U-Bahn station Wittenbergplatz (1910–13) by Alfred Grenander (1863–1931) at the KaDeWe was considered an eyesore when it was built: apparently it blocked the view between the streets on either end and negatively affected property prices in the area. Today the cross-shaped, garlanded structure is considered an architectural gem. The iconic Oberbaumbrücke (1895), which takes pedestrians, cars, and subways across the Spree (and seems to be a required location for every movie filmed in Berlin), imitates the northern German Gothic style. The tall brick turrets are intended to recall the original function of the bridge as a customs office, while the level for the subways is supposed to remind the viewer of a medieval cloister walk.

Altbau

All over Berlin, historicism is alive and well in the typical tenement buildings. These were mostly thrown up quickly in the late nineteenth century in two or three squares of four high-ceilinged stories behind each other, accessible through arched entrances and with tiny inner courtyards. In typical historicist mixing, the buildings might have Gothic, Renaissance, baroque, or neoclassical façades. The tenement houses allowed for unique social mixing: better-off and upper-class citizens lived in the front houses, often with balconies and large "Berlin Rooms" that connected the front with the side or back wings. The latter were inhabited by the servants or lower classes. In the front, the apartments were airy and beautiful; in the back, they were small, dark, and dank. The inner courtyards were required to be 17 feet in diameter so that fire engines could turn around, but that size hardly provided enough light or space for children to play. Of course, sanitation was not up to modern standards: there were no bathrooms in the contemporary sense, and toilets were usually in the staircases between the floors. These conditions gave the houses their nickname *Mietskasernen*, "rental barracks."

After the war the tenement buildings were attacked under the misguided notion that their façades were ugly, and the stucco on many of them was simply removed. They were now considered *Altbau* (old structures) as opposed to the new post-war architecture. However, since the 1970s tenement buildings have enjoyed a renaissance of their own, especially in West Berlin. For a long time they offered cheap housing, and many students and immigrants of my generation found their first apartments within them, complete with the original tiled coal ovens and shared toilets in the staircase. My own first apartment, in Neukölln, still had a coal oven, though mercifully an inside toilet. In the 1960s many owners simply let these buildings fall into disrepair, in the hope that they could then tear them down and build new structures in their place. At the same time, house prices in West Berlin were booming, so a squatters' movement developed that took over entire tenement buildings and simply renovated them independently, updating sanitation, adding lifts, turning attics into loft apartments, and restoring interior and exterior decoration. In the 1980s squatters and owners mostly came to arrangements, so today the middle-aged middle class lives in beautifully renovated tenement apartments with high ceilings, hardwood floors, plenty of light, and all the modern conveniences. This process happened at least once in the West (mainly in Kreuzberg, for instance around Chamissoplatz and Marheinekeplatz) and once in the East (mostly in Prenzlauer Berg at Kollwitzplatz), and today most Berliners look for *Altbauwohnungen.*

While it is of course difficult for tourists to get into such apartments, there are certainly places where the structures can be visited. Riehmers Hofgarten (1891–99) in Kreuzberg, named after the architect Wilhelm Riehmer (1830–1901), is a kind of upscale version of a tenement house. Instead of being directly connected, the 24 buildings (with 270 apartments) are separated by a private interior road, now a cobblestone walkway with a grass corridor and the occasional tree. The buildings show elements of Romantic, Renaissance, and baroque. As usual, the smaller apartments are grouped around the courtyards, while the larger ones face the streets. There are two main entrances to the complex (Yorckstrasse and Grossbeerenstrasse) with massive sculpted human forms or Atlantes "carrying" the balcony above. With all this attention to quality and detail, Riehmers Hofgarten was originally an expensive place to live. After the war, which the buildings survived almost without damage, intellectuals like Heinz Ohff (long-time arts editor at the local *Tagesspiegel* newspaper) and author Jurek Becker lived here; today they could probably not afford the rent.

Another unusual but accessible example of the tenement is the Hackesche Höfe (1905–07) at the S-Bahn station Hackescher Markt. Here are nine courtyards between Rosenthaler Strasse and Sophienstrasse designed by Kurt Berndt (1863–1925) and August Endell (1871–1925). In contrast to other tenement buildings, this one was always intended not just for apartments, but for restaurants, stores, workshops, and even two ballrooms. (One survives and is used by the Chamäleon variety theater.) One of the courtyards has an *Ampelmännchen* store, where you can buy all kinds of paraphernalia associated with East Berlin's traffic light pedestrian (see p.199). If all this sounds too commercial, the Sophie-Gips-Höfe right up the road are similar but much quieter. As spectacular examples of Art Deco, the outside façade and the first courtyard (from Rosenthaler Strasse) point to the next phase of Berlin architecture.

Modernism

Like historicism, Art Deco and modernism are not represented by one particular ensemble in the Berlin cityscape. Indeed, there are at least two important incarnations of this style with very different aesthetic and ideological associations: modernism proper and national socialist architecture.

In the wake of World War I one of Berlin's biggest problems was providing housing for the rapidly growing population. To this end, the government often worked with charitable organizations rather than private investors, the former being more interested in humane living than profit. Exponents of the modernist movement thus found themselves designing large residential developments with more space, light, and greenery than the earlier *Altbauten*. To achieve their goal of maximum and affordable housing in the shortest time possible, the modernist architects had to make their designs simpler, more accessible, and cheaper, which they did so successfully that some 140,000 units were built just in the period between 1924 and 1930. For the same reason, the most prominent buildings of modernism are these residential developments. (Of course there are also individual examples like the Titania film theater, the Erich Mendelsohn building that is now the Schaubühne theater, or the Berolina building at Alexanderplatz.) Six of the housing estates were considered architecturally important enough to be declared UNESCO World Heritage sites in 2008, and these are described in detail in Markus Jager's *Siedlungen der Berliner Moderne*.

In Treptow-Köpenick, Bruno Taut (1880–1938) wanted to develop a large estate with 1,500 apartments for his charitable investors. Because of the outbreak of World War I only 128 apartments were ultimately built on a hillside in the Gartenstadt (Garden City) Falkenberg (1913–16), the earliest of the six World Heritage sites. In contrast to Berlin's earlier tenement buildings, Taut's eighty individual or semi-detached houses (imitating British models) and six apartment buildings were state-of-the-art in terms of sanitation and insulation, so even today their upkeep is easy. The estate is known as the "Paint-Box Settlement" because the houses were painted in bright and varied colors, with accents in the doors, windows, and balconies—and restored to their original color schemes a few years ago. Taut imagined urban and rural living integrated, so every apartment had its own garden plot. In order to preserve the estate's aesthetic integrity, there is an approved list of flora that can be planted, even today. In spite of these restrictions, residents love living in the Gartenstadt Falkenberg, and many are second- or even third-generation tenants.

Taut was also responsible for the Siedlung Schillerpark (1924–30) in Wedding and the Wohnstadt Carl Legien (1928–30) in Prenzlauer Berg, two of the other World Heritage sites. However, his most famous work is probably the Hufeisensiedlung (1925–33) in Britz, a southern part of the Neukölln district. The settlement takes its name from the central building, a 1,150-foot repetition of the same three-story structure 25 times over—curved in the shape of a horseshoe around a small pond. Originally, all residents of the horseshoe even had allotments for flowers, vegetables, and fruit trees around the pond. To achieve simple and cheap housing, Taut based the over 1,000 apartments in the Hufeisensiedlung on only four different layouts. He employed tricks like changing the exterior surface and employing color schemes to avoid monotony. The original investor owned the settlement until 2000, but since then the apartments and houses have also been sold to individuals among the 3,100 residents.

The two remaining modernist residential estates recognized by UNESCO are the Siedlung Schillerpromenade (1929–31) in Reinickendorf and the Ringsiedlung Siemensstadt (1929–31) in Spandau. Urban planner Martin Wagner (1880–1957), who was the driving force behind most of Berlin's improvements between World War I and the rise of the Nazis (who fired him since he was a Social Democrat) and had worked with Taut on the Hufeisensiedlung, was involved in both. In Siemensstadt, Wagner worked with Hans Scharoun (1893–1972), who was to remodel important parts of Berlin after World War II (see below).

In the meantime, unfortunately, the Nazis did their best to shape Berlin to their own aesthetic and ideology. Under the megalomaniac

Albert Speer (1905–81), in close cooperation with Adolf Hitler, they developed plans to reorganize the entire city and rename it Germania. Traffic was to be diverted into rings circling the city, and two monumental axes were supposed to dissect it. At their intersection, a Great Hall with a 1,050 x 1,050-foot foundation and a 950-foot high dome was intended as a symbol of German superiority. (By comparison, St. Peter's Basilica in Rome would have fit into the Great Hall seventeen times.)

Fortunately, Speer and Hitler did not get very far with their plans, which would have destroyed the fabric of the city and required the removal of some 150,000 residents. One curious remnant of their activity does, however, survive. On the corner of Papestrasse and Loewenhardtdamm in Tempelhof, Speer decided to test the carrying capacity of the Berlin ground for the monumental triumphal arch he planned. To that end, he had French prisoners of war build an enormous cylinder of reinforced concrete that reached over 60 feet underground, stood 45 feet above the surface, had a diameter of 70 feet, and weighed over 12,000 tons. Rumor has it that this *Schwerbelastungskörper* (heavy load-bearing structure) was simply too large to demolish after the war, though perhaps it was not removed because it was located in a residential area. Subsequent plans included turning it into a rock-climbing wall or putting a café on top. As one of the few reminders of the Germania plans, the *Schwerbelastungskörper* was protected as a historic monument in 1995, and today there is a small exhibition and stairs to the top. Ironically, the very measurements that Speer initiated showed, but only after the war, that the Berlin ground would not have been strong enough to bear his monumental architecture.

Yet the Nazis did manage to put their stamp on Berlin in one place, the Olympic Park in Charlottenburg. The Olympic Stadium is the most prominent building of the ensemble, but there are actually many more: the Maifeld parade ground (where up to 250,000 people can congregate) with the 250-foot bell tower, the Sports Forum with the Swimming Stadium (today a popular public outdoor swimming pool), the Hockey and Equestrian Stadiums, and the Waldbühne amphitheater. The entire complex was built at record speed to host the 1936 Olympics and principally functioned as a propaganda tool to present the Nazi regime as a successful, modern, and normal member of the family of nations. The project, which required other infrastructure improvements across the city like the new Tempelhof airport (at the time the largest continuous building in the world) and the electrification of the S-Bahn, was a complete success in terms of propaganda and probably contributed to the rest of the world's taking so long to recognize the evil of the Nazis. When I was growing up in 1970s and 1980s Berlin, the road leading to the Olympic Stadium at the center of the park was still—unbelievably—called Reichssportfeldstrasse, the original Nazi name. In 1997 it was finally changed to Flatowallee, commemorating two Jewish gymnasts persecuted by the Nazis.

Like the rest of the Olympic Park, the design of the Olympic Stadium itself was based on models from antiquity—and aligned according to the plans for Germania. Built in concrete, it was covered in natural stone to make it look more authentic. The elliptical stadium had 100,000 seats, and the ground in the middle was lowered forty feet so that spectators could enter at ground level (on the outside) and flow easily into the various sections. On the east side, the Olympic Gate led visitors into the stadium, and on the west the Marathon Gate let runners in and opened a view towards the bell tower. After the war the stadium was soon renovated (it had not been too badly damaged), and in 1963 the football club Hertha BSC started using it as its ground. Since 1985 the final of the German football league cup (DFB-Pokal) has always been played here. The stadium was renovated in 2000 in two significant ways: it received a roof covering the spectators (but not the athletes), which also meant that the number of seats had to be reduced to 75,000, and the track was re-laid in Hertha's blue team colors. Other sports take place here, like the annual international ISTAF track meet, together with events such as a mass celebrated by Pope Benedict in 2011. However, football is still the stadium's most important attraction: the final of the 2006 World Cup took place here (with Zidane's famous head-butt), as did the final of the 2011 Women's World Cup.

International Style

Between repeated aerial bombardment during World War II and the Battle of Berlin at its end, about one-fifth of the city's buildings were either destroyed completely or damaged so comprehensively that it was easier to demolish than to rebuild them. The Mitte and Tiergarten districts were particularly hard hit—here about half of the urban fabric was ruined. On the one hand, this situation meant that almost half the population abandoned Berlin; on the other, the empty spaces opened up all kinds of possibilities for urban planners and architects. During this time, the International style which had emerged in the 1920s and 1930s dominated design. Each political system tried to demonstrate its superiority in architecture: for instance, the West's authorities built the Corbusier House in Charlottenburg and the Hansaviertel north of Tiergarten, while the East embodied Socialist Realism in the Karl-Marx-Allee parade route and in the Palast der Republik (Palace of the Republic), the GDR's parliament by Heinz Graffunder (1926–94), which has recently been torn down. (This building had received more than one nickname: to some it was known as *Erichs Lampenladen*, "Erich's lamp store," because it was gaudily lit during the rule of Erich Honecker; to others simply as *Palazzo Prozzi*, "show-off palace.") While some horrible architectural decisions were made (such as removing the stucco from *Altbau* façades and building monotonous apartment complexes all over the city), one architect managed to revive his career and give Berlin some of its most iconic landmarks: Hans Scharoun.

Scharoun was born in the port city of Bremerhaven in northern Germany in 1893, and throughout his career maritime motifs such as waves and ships characterized his designs. After briefly studying architecture in Berlin, he served in World War I and ended up in East Prussia and later Breslau, refusing offers enticing him back to Berlin since they did not guarantee him sufficient independence. A member of various artistic cooperatives, Scharoun finally returned to Berlin in 1930 when one of the first major projects of which he was part, the Ringsiedlung Siemensstadt, came to fruition. As a matter of fact, Scharoun lived in an apartment of his own design in Siemensstadt for many years. During the Nazi period he was excluded from major projects, but survived with smaller commissions like single-family residences and bunkers. After the end of the war Scharoun was appointed building commissioner for Berlin. This gave him the opportunity to take advantage of the unique situation of a widely destroyed city that in many places had to be rebuilt from scratch. Yet Scharoun's plan for an organic city following the contours of the natural landscape was rejected, and he went back to the private sector. His greatest architectural triumphs came late in life, when he designed the buildings that came to be known as the Kulturforum, Berlin's showcase of the International style.

The first piece in the Kulturforum was the Philharmonie (concert hall). Scharoun won the competition for this building in 1956, and it was finally built between 1960 and 1963. The hall was planned for the center of Berlin, but in the middle of construction the erection of the Wall turned its site into a (West) Berlin backwater—for which the quality of the orchestra fortunately more than compensated. Eschewing straight lines and right angles and embracing irregularity, the outside shape is reminiscent of a ship's bow (or a tent) in spite of the yellow tiles (which were not added until later). Inside, a maze of staircases and hallways encourages mingling rather than quick movement towards the seats. In a revolution of concert hall design, Scharoun decided to group the audience around the performers rather than in front of them, arguing that spectators naturally gathered around improvising ensembles that way. The stage is surrounded by terraced seats in three levels of pentagons set at different angles, so each area feels right next to the stage and there is no bad seat in the house. Of course, it helps that the Berlin Philharmonic Orchestra, currently under the leadership of Sir Simon Rattle, is considered by many to be the best classical orchestra in the world. The orchestra gained its status under the conductor Herbert von Karajan, and the main entrance is now on a street that bears his name. (Berliners have also nicknamed the concert hall *Zirkus Karajani*, the "Karajan Circus," in reference to its tent-like form.) The Kammermusiksaal (chamber music hall) next door was completed in 1987 in a similar style, but with alterations made to Scharoun's sketch design by his student Edgar Wisniewski (1930–2007).

The Staatsbibliothek (national library, 1967–78) on the other side of Potsdamer Strasse—known to most Berliners simply as Stabi—was groundbreaking in a number of ways, not least because it was built right on top of where the old street had run before World War II and because there were no windows at all in the side turned towards the east. With this building, the architects Scharoun and Wisniewski and the city planners moved away from the idea of a unified Berlin and symbolically asserted the independence of West Berlin. The outside of the library mirrors the yellow tiles of the Philharmonie across the street, but inside it is a much lighter and airier space. Rather than having clearly defined floors, the architects designed open levels that vary across the floor plan and make the building a favorite for students from all disciplines.

Postmodernism

After the Cold War new possibilities once again opened up in Berlin—culturally, financially, and architecturally. The world's most famous architects wanted to work here, new ownership structures especially in (former) East Germany allowed for innovation, and of course the narrow strip of the city that had been sacrificed to the Wall needed to be rebuilt entirely. In some cases this led to fast and unimaginative construction, in others to careful restoration and renovation, and in a significant number of cases to the innovative combinations of new and old architecture described at the beginning of this chapter. The government district is certainly interesting (with buildings like the Bundeskanzleramt by Axel Schultes and Charlotte Frank popularly known as the "Washing Machine"), as is the nearby new Hauptbahnhof. But the most significant showcase of the city's new architecture was constructed in the old center of Berlin which had lain fallow for the duration of the Cold War because it was right along the Wall: Potsdamer Platz.

In 1902 Potsdamer Platz became the final stop on Berlin's first U-Bahn line, and in 1924 the first traffic light was set up here—where a replica stands today. Potsdamer Platz became one of the city's busiest squares with crowds of pedestrians (drawn by many attractions including a red light district), trams, and, increasingly, cars.

Many buildings were destroyed in the course of World War II, and the rest (with two exceptions) were demolished by the GDR, but since the reunification of Germany the square has experienced an amazing renaissance. Reconstructed according to a master plan designed by architects Renzo Piano and Helmut Jahn, Potsdamer Platz has become one of the landmarks of twenty-first century Berlin, even as it integrates various elements and examples of its (architectural) past. Yet in contrast to most other places in Berlin, Potsdamer Platz did not grow organically, but was entirely designed, and perhaps for that reason it feels somewhat cold and is visited by tourists more than Berliners. The place is unnaturally clean, unlike the rest of Berlin, where graffiti is ubiquitous. Security personnel roam the area and put a quick stop to anything that distracts visitors from consumerism. The only time Berliners congregate here is when important football matches are shown on gigantic screens.

South of Potsdamer Strasse—which bisects the area—is Daimler City, constructed to resemble an old city with a tree-lined street between higher buildings. The street in question is, in fact, the old Potsdamer Strasse. One side of the quarter is mostly in yellow terracotta, the other in red brick. The entrance from Potsdamer Platz has a triangular twenty-story red brick highrise by Hans Kollhoff and Helga Timmermann on the right, meant to evoke early twentieth-century Art Deco US skyscrapers. To the left is one of Piano's buildings, with a glass V-shaped façade (actually, there are two façades in front of each other, to conserve energy) pointing towards Potsdamer Platz. Behind this nineteen-floor skyscraper is the 1912 Huth Winehouse, a typical turn-of-the-century commercial structure and one of two remaining original buildings on the site.

The center of Daimler City is Marlene-Dietrich-Platz, named after the famous actress who was unfortunately long a *persona non grata* in her hometown Berlin because she supported US troops in their fight against the Nazis. At the far end of Daimler City from Potsdamer Platz is the Debis-Haus, Berlin's fourth-highest building at almost 350 feet. The square on top of the tower is the Debis (Daimler-Benz Interservices) logo—and serves as an air vent for the tunnel under the Tiergarten beneath the building. The atrium of the

Debis-Haus, which is open to the public, is supposedly the same size as the cathedral of Notre Dame. In the same direction but closer to the current Potsdamer Strasse is the Hyatt Berlin, designed for function rather than fashion with a red sandstone façade. Finally, Daimler City is home to the Potsdamer Platz Arcades, a covered shopping mall with over 120 stores that has become popular with Berliners.

On the north side of Potsdamer Strasse is Helmut Jahn's Sony Center (1996–99), the European headquarters of that corporation. The glass and steel buildings are triangular and house stores, cinemas, offices, restaurants, and apartments. In the middle is a large open forum with a fountain, covered 200 feet in the air with tent-shaped glass. Beneath the glass, canvas sheets are fastened to the roof as well as the surrounding buildings and can be opened and closed depending on the climate and atmosphere that is supposed to be created. One of the most interesting details of the Sony Center—and an example of how old and new architecture are juxtaposed in Berlin— is the *Kaisersaal* (emperor's grand room) and the *Frühstückssaal* (breakfast room). These "rooms" are all that is left of the former Grand Hotel Esplanade (1907–08), which was bombed in 1944. The 1,300-ton *Kaisersaal* was moved to its current location inside the Sony Center in a spectacular process by which the entire structure was lifted on a kind of pillow and transported 250 feet. The *Frühstückssaal* was cut up into about 500 pieces and reassembled at Café Josty in the Sony Center.

Thus, even the most modern of Berlin architecture incorporates the old, constructing a seamless continuity from the baroque to the present. And as long as Berlin remains the capital of Germany and (arguably) the cultural, political, and financial heart of Central Europe, architects will certainly continue their attempts to offer new and exciting buildings here.

Part of the Reichstag, c.1905, with the statue of Otto von Bismarck (dedicated in 1901 and moved to the Tiergarten in 1938), but without the slogan "Dem Deutschen Volke" ("For the German People") under the

4

Rulers and Ruled
A Brief Social and Political History

B erlin's history over the last eight hundred years has usually been driven by the competition between two opposing forces: the rulers promoting their stately agendas, and the ruled pursuing their own interests. This division, however, should not be confused with conservative and progressive stances: absolute rulers could be enlightened and far-sighted enough to support new developments, while democratically elected governments were perfectly capable of initiating atrocities, and populations of committing public acts of violence. Also, rulers and ruled might come from different religious, ethnic, tribal, or regional groups that might or might not be in conflict. Still, the basic competition between them can be traced through centuries and millennia.

Prehistoric hunters left traces of their presence in the Berlin region—today's state of Brandenburg—some 50,000 years ago, and hunters and gatherers traversed the area after the last Ice Age retreated around 10,000 BCE. Parts of today's Berlin were finally settled some time between 4000 and 2000 BCE at the beginning of the Bronze Age. Remains of Iron Age settlements from between 600 BCE and 200 CE have been found in various parts of Berlin such as Rudow and Marzahn. On the grounds of the Heimatmuseum Reinickendorf, a farmstead has been reconstructed from this period, specifically based on what is known about the Germanic indigenous Semnones. The main building on a typical farmstead served as living quarters for humans and animals; a secondary house with a lowered floor (to preserve humidity and warmth) was used for textile production; and a granary in the middle was raised to protect the grain from vermin.

At the beginning of the first millennium, Central Europe was still socially and politically in the orbit of the Roman Empire. That empire fell in the fifth century, partly due to the westward migration of Germanic tribes. As part of that migration, Germanic groups left the Brandenburg region and were replaced fairly peacefully by two Slavic tribes. The Hevellians constructed forts on the locations of today's Schlossinsel and the Spandau Citadel in the eighth and ninth centuries (so they had probably arrived in the preceding centuries); the Sprewans had their center in the district now known as Köpenick. The Slavs took over names of landmarks and rivers such as Havel and Dahme from their Germanic predecessors and probably absorbed whatever Germanic population might have been left.

The centuries after the fall of the Roman Empire are often called the Dark Ages and witnessed constant conflict between smaller groups as well as the traumatic invasions by the Huns and their successors. Stability returned to Central Europe with the formation of the Holy Roman Empire by Charlemagne (800) and later Otto the Great (962), and with the subsequent establishment of the German Kingdom, made up of various smaller duchies, in the tenth and eleventh centuries. Holy Roman Emperors were invested by the pope and expected to spread Christianity, so in addition to the Crusades to the Holy Land these emperors supported an eastward expansionism of rulers in the German heartland that promoted both territorial acquisition and attempts to Christianize the heathen Slavs.

In the tenth century German dukes battled Slavic armies, but were repulsed and retreated behind the Elbe river. Over the next two hundred years, though, the Germans were more successful in both of their endeavours. In 1157 the Ascanian (German) Albrecht the Bear succeeded in the first project, territorial expansion, by subduing the region and was named Margrave (border ruler) of Brandenburg. A legend around Albrecht's nemesis Jaxa of Köpenick, a chieftain of the Sprewans, symbolizes the second western victory: supposedly, Jaxa was escaping from Albrecht through the Havel river when his horse was so exhausted that it was about to drown. In desperation, Jaxa lifted his shield over his head and prayed to the previously despised Christian god to be saved. According to legend, Jaxa converted to Christianity on the spot (after being rescued) and nailed his shield to an oak tree on the Havel shore. There is a small derelict tower built at the beginning of the twentieth century marking the spot where Jaxa went into the Havel on the east side, while his arrival on the western shore and conversion are commemorated by the Schildhorn memorial erected in 1845.

Medieval Berlin

The Ascanians ruled Brandenburg for about a century and a half (1172–1320) and were followed by the houses of Wittelsbach (1323–73) and Luxemburg (1373–1415). These rulers mostly used the city of Brandenburg as their residence—if they even bothered to reside in the state they were supposedly governing. In the meantime Berlin was a backwater town—actually comprised of the two twin cities on either side of the Spree river, Berlin-Cölln. A pastor from Cölln is documented in 1237, which is often taken as the year Berlin was "born," though obviously the city must have existed for some time to have garnered a church and pastor. Berliners are apparently happy to appropriate this first reference to Cölln, but conveniently ignore that Spandau became a city in 1232. Cold War politics are probably partly to blame here: if Berlin celebrated birthdays according to the Spandau date, East Berlin would have been celebrating a part of the city enclosed by the Wall, and West Berlin did not press the issue. For their part, West Berliners celebrating anniversaries based on the 1232 date would have put them out of sync with the East, which in turn would have been an admission that these were two separate cities rather than one temporarily divided. In any event, Berlin celebrated its 750th birthday in 1987 (see below). The name of the city probably derives from a Slavic word meaning "dry spot in a swamp," but this origin was forgotten or repressed and replaced with a popular etymology relating to bears, which appeared in the city shield by the end of the thirteenth century.

Medieval Berlin-Cölln was a city of about 175 acres and a population of 5–8,000 surrounded by one wall—a wall *between* the cities was considered unnecessary because of the river. Two-thirds of its area was in Berlin to the north and east of the Spree, the rest in Cölln to the south and west. The city was located on an important trade route and was a center of commerce rather than industry or production. From the beginning, the population struggled with its rulers, entering a confederacy with other towns in the area to coordinate dealings with the margraves, whose representatives were called *Schultheiss*—now the name of one of Berlin's most popular beers. The revenues from customs, taxes, and trade were bandied back and forth, with cities trying to maintain sources of income and rulers attempting to assert their authority. For a while, Berlin-Cölln joined the Hanseatic League, an organization of merchant cities such as Hamburg, Gdansk, and Riga around the Baltic Sea. On the other hand, the city definitely needed the protection of its rulers for a period when robber barons terrorized the Brandenburg countryside.

Matters came to a head when new rulers took over at the beginning of the fifteenth century, the house of Hohenzollern. The Hohenzollern ruled Berlin, Brandenburg—and later Prussia and all of Germany—for an astounding five hundred years from 1415 to 1918, but the start of their tenure was rather inauspicious. In 1432 Berlin and Cölln had officially united, but some of the guilds were not happy with this development. In 1442 the city government asked its Hohenzollern ruler Friedrich II "Irontooth" to intervene and resolve the situation. Friedrich obliged, but only in order to weaken the city by several measures: separating it into two again, reserving the right to confirm and dismiss city officials, and seizing land within the city limits to build a fortress. Friedrich's repression increased to the extent that it caused a rebellion in 1447–48 known as the Berliner Unwille (unwillingness). In the course of these protests documents were burned and the construction site for the fortress was flooded. Things did not end well for the Berliners—the leaders of the protests were punished with fines, loss of property, and banishment—and a pattern of tension between rulers and ruled was established.

Over the next two centuries Berlin slowly developed and grew, but more dramatic changes happened when religion and politics mixed with the Reformation. Berliners were quick to embrace the new denomination of Lutheran Protestantism, and Hohenzollern ruler Joachim I ran into problems of his own when his wife *and* his mistress converted from Catholicism only a decade after Luther initiated the Reformation. By 1539 Joachim's son had also become a Protestant. Of course, there were denominational struggles within Protestant Christianity as well. In 1613 the Hohenzollerns became Calvinists, and in 1615 they cleared the Berlin cathedral of images and crosses. Afraid for their Lutheran faith, Berliners rioted and ransacked the house of the court preacher. The Hohenzollern knew they were in the minority as Calvinists and sensibly refrained from punishing the rioters (most of whom had fled anyway).

The Enlightenment

Berlin was comparatively lucky during the Thirty Years' War (1618–48), which also had its origins at least partly in religious struggles. The city was occupied by various foreign armies, and there were outbreaks of plague that reduced the population, but there was no actual fighting in the city. Nevertheless, by the end of the war Berlin's population had shrunk to around 6,000, half to two-thirds of what it had been before the conflict. Yet with a series of four formidable Hohenzollern rulers over the next century and a half—starting with Friedrich Wilhelm, known as the Great Elector, who ruled from 1640 to 1688—the city bounced back quickly with a population of around 50,000 by 1709 and around 100,000 by 1740.

At the same time, the linguistic, religious, and ethnic make-up of the city experienced changes from above and below. As early as the sixteenth century, the Hohenzollern instituted an early form of High German as the official language, but this High German merged with the Brandenburg dialect that was more common among the population to form a unique mixture. In the eighteenth century various religious and ethnic groups came to Berlin to add to the mix. First, Friedrich Wilhelm had allowed Jews back into Berlin. After 1685, he invited French Huguenots who had been persecuted at home—officially in order to protect them from the French king and government, but certainly also because they were skilled laborers.

A few years later, Friedrich III's main goal was to turn Berlin into a center of European culture. (Since Friedrich's father had acquired parts of adjacent Prussia, which lay outside the borders of the Holy Roman Empire, Friedrich added King in Prussia to his previous titles of Margrave and Elector of Brandenburg—"in" because other parts of Prussia lay within the Polish kingdom.) To this end, he pursued a large number of prestigious and expensive public and personal projects. For instance, the Academy of Arts was founded in 1696 (the third in Europe after London and Paris) and the Charité hospital in 1710 (where medical teaching and practice were combined). Both of these institutions still exist. Friedrich had castles built at Oranienburg, Niederschönhausen, and Charlottenburg (only the first is now still outside Berlin's borders), but his main project was a reconstruction of the castle in the center of Berlin. Various structures previously stood on this island in the Spree, but Friedrich added a magnificent castle first under the architect Andreas Schlüter (c. 1660–1714) starting in 1698, and then (when one of Schlüter's buildings collapsed) under Johann Friedrich Eosander von Göthe (1669–1728). Eosander had grand plans for the site, but after Friedrich's death most of them were shelved—not least because he died leaving a twenty million-thaler debt.

Friedrich was succeeded by his son Friedrich Wilhelm I, aka the Soldier King. Where Friedrich had spent enormous amounts of money on prestige projects and the arts, his son was more interested in consolidating and expanding Prussia's military power. To achieve that goal, Friedrich Wilhelm had to improve the country's financial situation, which he did by firing most of his father's court and ending work on projects like the Berlin castle. Instead, he expanded his army to 83,000 soldiers, promoted the textile industry because he needed uniforms, constructed drill grounds to train his soldiers, and improved the roads around Berlin so he could move his army more quickly. (He also built the *Akzisemauer*, or Excise Wall, described on pp.34–39.) On a more personal note, King Friedrich Wilhelm I created a special regiment, the *Lange Kerls* ("tall guys"), in which each member had a height requirement of at least six-and-a-half feet. The *Lange Kerls*, who were recruited from all over Europe, must have been quite intimidating in battle, and in addition were able to handle longer and hence more accurate rifles.

As king, Friedrich Wilhelm I was his father's opposite. His son Friedrich II (Frederick the Great) was in turn quite different. (Under his reign, the title of Prussian rulers changed to King *of* Prussia when they acquired large parts of Poland.) Where Friedrich Wilhelm I pursued the martial life, his son was interested in music and the arts. Because of contemporary accounts and some of his own remarks in letters, little doubt remains that Friedrich II was gay. When he tried to escape to England with his friend (and probably lover) Hans Hermann von Katte, and the two were caught, Friedrich Wilhelm I had Katte executed and forced his son Friedrich to watch. Friedrich's valet Michael Gabriel Fredersdorf was definitely a very close associate, and probably more than that. Friedrich was interested in the well-being of his subjects, supporting trade, and instituting freedom of religion, but he also engaged in three expensive wars: the two Silesian Wars (1740–42 and 1744–45), where he claimed victory (he received his epithet "the Great" for his strategic brilliance), and the Seven Years' War (1756–63), where he did less well. During this war, Berlin was occupied briefly by Austrian (1757) and Russian troops (1760). The growing influence of the bourgeoisie, even within Friedrich's monarchy, can be seen in the fact that a merchant, rather than the government, negotiated the withdrawal of the Russian army.

Occupation, Reform, and War

Friedrich was succeeded in 1786 by his nephew King Friedrich Wilhelm II, who was followed in turn by his son King Friedrich Wilhelm III in 1797. These rulers seem to have been more interested in their private pursuits than in governing, so it came as no surprise that they were unable to resist Napoleon's armies, and in 1806 Berlin was occupied by a French force. Napoleon himself stayed in Potsdam and at Schloss Charlottenburg, entered Berlin in a parade through the Brandenburg Gate, and took up residence in the castle in the center of town—the Prussian royal family had fled. The two years of French occupation (until December 1808) were traumatic for the city: Berliners had to house and feed the troops, they were forced to form a new administration headed by a French officer, they built barracks for 25,000 French soldiers, and ultimately they had to pay a huge sum to convince the army to leave. By early 1809 Berlin had been reduced to a shell of a city, more of an overgrown village than a metropolis.

Yet surprisingly there was little resistance to the French—maybe replacing one autocratic ruler with another was not so bad after all. Berliners did not appreciate that King Friedrich Wilhelm III had gone into exile rather than put up a fight, and only his wife Luise was adored and beloved for her dramatic flight (in winter-time, in spite of typhoid fever) and her subsequent negotiation with Napoleon in Tilsit (though she did not have much success in gaining any concessions). After the two returned to Berlin, they had to support political reform and agreed to the first freely elected city parliament—though of course only wealthy citizens were allowed to vote. Berliners still embraced the institution, which was interrupted one more time when the French came back in 1812. This time around, there were more protests and resistance, and Berlin celebrated when the French were defeated in early 1813.

For the next fifty years (at least), rulers and subjects in Berlin remained in conflict over the significance of their respective roles. The Prussian rulers continually promised, or at least suggested, that they would write a constitution, and just as regularly they refused to draft any such document and insisted on their god-given right to govern. Every so often politically motivated individuals (or just crackpots) tried to assassinate the king (Friedrich Wilhelm IV after 1840), but never with any success. The situation escalated in 1848 in the context of revolutionary movements all over Europe. In Berlin, thousands of citizens drafted a letter to the king demanding equal votes, independent courts, freedom of the press, and participation in a German parliament. On 18 March the military tried to intercept a demonstration of 10,000, who built barricades and engaged the army in pitched battles. After three days and almost two hundred dead, the king capitulated and promised a constitution as well as press freedom. However, the reforms were half-hearted: for instance, a three-class franchise was introduced in which votes counted according to the voters' tax burden, so that the richest Prussians had much more influence in elections than their workers. After the failed 1848 revolution, many Prussians went into voluntary exile, including a young man named Karl Marx.

Liberal reformers had demanded the formation of a German state—Germany was still divided into many different statelets and a few free cities—but in the end the country was unified around conservative and nationalist ideals rather than liberalism. In 1870 the prime minister Otto von Bismarck provoked the French king into declaring war against Prussia, and immediately most other large German states declared their support for Prussia. The Germans won the war quickly and decisively, and in the immediate aftermath a previously existing loose federation was strengthened into the *Deutsches Reich*. Literally the "German empire," this was the second *Reich* after the Middle Ages and was to be followed by Hitler's Third Reich in the twentieth century. Wilhelm was crowned German emperor in the Hall of Mirrors at Versailles, a location chosen to rub the German victory into French faces (in a hall where the ceiling depicts French victories over Germans). Because Prussia was the most powerful state in the new empire, Berlin was selected as the empire's capital.

Berlin grew dramatically during this period: the population doubled from 408,000 in 1846 to 826,000 in 1871, and then again to almost 1.7 million in 1895. With this growth came a stronger workers' movement and the foundation of left-wing political parties, which every once in a while were banned. Social conditions slowly improved in many ways—tenement housing was built, sanitation established, public transportation introduced, working hours limited, etc.—but the well-being of the general population was rarely at the top of the agenda of the rulers in palaces and parliaments.

Instead, the new ruler, Emperor Wilhelm I, was more interested in strengthening Germany's position within Europe, especially vis-à-vis Britain and Russia. Inevitably, these politics led to military confrontation in World War I (1914–18) under Emperor Wilhelm II. The war had an immediate impact in Berlin, where rationing was introduced and museums and theaters were closed. Industry was reorganized to supply the war effort, and women entered the workforce since men were fighting in the army. The war was initially supported by almost all politicians, regardless of party, but by 1916 the "home front" was falling apart with strikes and protests. A poor harvest that year, including potatoes, meant food shortages, and the following winter came to be known as the "turnip winter" since the dreary yellow turnip replaced almost every kind of food: there was turnip soup, turnip bread, turnip jam, and even turnip steak.

Weimar Republic

After the end of World War I Berlin witnessed a series of political revolutions never seen before by Germany. On 29 October 1918 Emperor Wilhelm II fled to Belgium, hoping that the army and navy would support his rule, but neither proved entirely loyal. On 8 November, one of the social democratic parties in Berlin called for a general strike to demand the emperor's abdication, and the following day there were demonstrations all across the city. Two political futures seemed possible for Germany at this moment: representative democracy or socialist republic. When the SPD (Social Democratic Party of Germany) heard that the KPD (Communist Party of Germany) was about to declare a socialist republic, the SPD's leader, Philipp Scheidemann, hastily announced the "German republic," a representative democracy, from the Reichstag (even though the emperor had not yet resigned). Less than two hours later, and less than two miles down the road in the Lustgarten at the Hohenzollern castle, communist politician Karl Liebknecht proclaimed a free socialist republic—so suddenly there were two competing systems. Later in the day, Liebknecht repeated his proclamation from a window of the castle. Integrated into a newer building, this window was preserved by the GDR as a memorial to what they considered the first socialist republic on German soil.

While the parties on the left, center, and right of the political spectrum (though of course those designations are inevitably subjective) tried to organize some kind of constitutional convention, the parties on the far left attempted to establish a workers' republic. The communists managed to arrange elections for the very next day, but the SPD countered with a quick and successful effort to win that vote. For several weeks, workers' councils and a federal government existed side by side, but when a national assembly convened in December, it was also dominated by the SPD. By now, however, the

SPD were resorting to unsavory tactics: they had collaborated with the army, and they violently repressed a communist rebellion in January 1919. When Karl Liebknecht and his fellow communist Rosa Luxemburg were murdered on 15 January the communist revolution was over and the uneasy coalition of SPD and army was firmly in power.

The following elections to a constitutional convention in 1919—which met in Weimar, hence the name of the republic—were the first in which women could vote and where each vote counted equally, but they hardly resolved political tensions. As a matter of fact, many historians argue that the unresolved situation (or rather its violent and repressive resolution) was directly responsible for the rise of the Nazis fifteen years later. Even though the SPD were clearly dominant in Berlin, political violence continued. An attempted coup in 1920 tried to resist the reduction in the size of the army, a condition imposed on Germany in the Treaty of Versailles, which had ended World War I and had been signed at Versailles to remind Germans of their hubris in crowning Emperor Wilhelm I there. In 1922 the liberal politician Walter Rathenau was assassinated in an attempt to spark a civil war in Germany, and in 1923 hyperinflation hit Berlin: a ride on the tram was 150,000 Marks, and on 15 November 1923 a stamp for a domestic letter cost a cool ten billion Marks.

Rise and Rule of the Nazis

By 1932—partly due to the after-effects of the 1929 global economic crisis—about 630,000 workers were out of work in Berlin, a disastrous unemployment rate of thirty percent. In 1929 the National Socialist Workers' Party of Germany (NSDAP) entered the city parliament with 5.8 percent of the vote, the communists (KPD) taking 24.6 percent. Even though the SPD remained the strongest party with 28.4 percent, political discourse was dominated by the confrontations between Nazis (led by Joseph Goebbels) and communists (led by Wilhelm Pieck), often carried out in pitched battles in the streets and in public places like dance halls. In 1930 the Nazi functionary (and thug) Horst Wessel was killed by a communist activist, and Goebbels turned Wessel into a martyr and a song Wessel had written into the official Nazi hymn. Over the next few years, the city became increasingly polarized, and in 1932 the totalitarians between them took the majority—though not in the same way as in the country as a whole. In the national elections of July 1932 the NSDAP won 37.4 percent of the vote and the KPD 14.6 percent; in Berlin the respective percentages were 28.6 and 27.3 percent. Some apologists argue that these figures show that Berliners were less disposed than other Germans to Nazi sympathies, and certainly they demonstrate the continuing strength of the workers' movement, but still the NSDAP was now the strongest party even in Berlin.

After the national elections of November 1932, in which the NSDAP actually lost some votes, various parties unsuccessfully tried to form coalitions. In response, the German president, the elderly Paul von Hindenburg, swore in Adolf Hitler as chancellor on 30 January 1933. That evening, the Nazi paramilitary *Sturmabteilung* (SA) and *Schutzstaffel* (SS) along with Nazi sympathizers celebrated the occasion with a torchlight procession through the Brandenburg Gate. The German term *Machtergreifung* (literally "power grab") nicely captures the ambiguous situation: rather than actually being voted into office—they were still a minority party—the Nazis had seized power strategically, though not illegally. Hindenburg immediately dissolved parliament, and during the following election campaign the Nazis used atrocious violence to intimidate (or simply kill) their political opponents. This wave of terror was intensified when they blamed the burning of the Reichstag on 27 February on a former communist—the actual authorship of the fire remains uncertain to this day. The Nazis were still unable to capture a majority in the parliamentary elections of 5 March 1933, and even though they had banned all other political parties by July 1933, their ambivalence towards the Reichstag can be seen in the fact that they only ever repaired the damage from the fire in a perfunctory manner. The *Machtergreifung* was completed when the Nazis handily won a referendum in August 1934 that united the offices of president and chancellor in the person of Adolf Hitler.

During this period, and for the rest of the 1930s, the Nazis persecuted anyone who disagreed with their politics, as well as entire other groups for irrational ideological reasons. Members of other political parties were first on the list, the lucky ones simply being removed from office and beaten up. The less fortunate ended up in Berlin's predecessors to concentration camps like the former barracks in the General-Pape-Strasse or the unsupervised prison in the Hedemannstrasse, where they were kept without trial and often eventually killed. On 10 May 1933 Nazi activists burned "un-German" books by authors such as Heinrich Heine, Karl Marx, Sigmund Freud, Erich Kästner, and Thomas Mann at the Forum Frediricianum (see p.50). Around the same time, museums were purged of what the Nazis called *entartete Kunst*, "degenerate or abnormal art." The Nazis started a "boycott" of Jewish businesses in 1933, and in 1935 they passed laws prohibiting intermarriages between Christians and Jews, and banning Jews from public office. In the *Reichskristallnacht* (Night of Broken Glass) on 9 November 1938, nine of Berlin's twelve synagogues (including the biggest one on Oranienburger Strasse, see pp.161–62) were torched, and 1,200 of Berlin's remaining Jews were deported to concentration camps. Other marginal groups like Roma and homosexuals fared little better. Sadly, the Berlin population by and large acquiesced to these changes and the concomitant violence.

One of the reasons the Nazis were able to get away with these horrors was that they simultaneously celebrated economic and political successes. Unemployment fell dramatically, partly because the Nazis started up the German war machine (and simply refused to pay the reparations determined in the Treaty of Versailles). The Olympic Games of 1936 were a huge international hit, blinding many critics to the atrocities that were being committed only a few miles from where they were watching events. A buoyant film industry produced popular fare that celebrated Aryan values, while musicians and painters who had remained in Berlin—some with the idea of opposing the Nazis from the inside, others as collaborators—provided a veneer of respectability.

Life in Berlin changed immediately and dramatically with the

RULERS AND RULED

beginning of World War II, when Germany invaded Poland on 1 September 1939. A curfew was introduced in anticipation of air raids, the use of cars was limited, and food was rationed. Most green areas within the city were used to raise crops: most famously, potatoes were planted at the Gendarmenmarkt. The first air raid did not happen until 1940 (in response to Germany's attack on London), and regular bombing only commenced in 1943. That year, Goebbels declared "total war," which meant that all men between 16 and 65 years of age were drafted to serve in the military. When the fortunes of war turned against Germany in 1944, air raids of two types became constant features: attacks by the high-speed wooden de Havilland Mosquito bombers, which caused little damage but had a bad effect on morale, and heavy assaults by four-engine Avro Lancasters. In all, Berlin experienced over 350 air raids, which ultimately destroyed about twenty percent of the city's buildings (and fifty percent in the center)—though only about a third of industrial capacity, which raises questions about the usefulness of the tactic.

During the final struggle for Berlin from February to April 1945, the Nazi propaganda machine convinced many Berliners that they were fighting for their lives. So-called traitors who wanted to surrender or had deserted from their units were strung up from trees and lampposts. By April, Berlin was surrounded by the Red Army, but capitulation was unimaginable for the Nazi leadership, who disappeared into underground lairs and continued to command military forces that no longer existed. Above ground, adolescents as young as fourteen as well as elderly men over 65 were drafted into the army, but with only about a million German "soldiers" against the Red Army's two and a half million (not to mention constant air raids, diminishing resources, and crumbling morale), they stood no chance. In the last days of the war, the German and Russian armies fought for every street, destroying even more of the city in the process. On 30 April, surrounded in their bunker in the middle of the city, Hitler and Goebbels committed suicide, and on 2 May the city commander officially surrendered. The Soviet flag had first been raised on the Reichstag on 30 April, though the iconic photo of the event was not taken until 2 May (and then doctored to hide evidence of looting and to generally look more impressive).

Cold War Years

At the conference of Yalta in early 1945, the Allies—the US, Great Britain, France, and the Soviet Union—had decided to divide all of Germany into four sectors. Similarly, they agreed to split Berlin into four parts (not geographically connected to the other four sectors). After the end of the war all four Allies moved their armies out of any areas that were not "theirs," and in Berlin the Red Army made room for US, British, and French forces. In general terms, the Soviets occupied the eastern part of the city, while the western two-thirds became the French, British, and US sectors (from north to south). For a short time immediately after the war Berlin was ruled by a Control Council made up of all four powers, but this soon proved untenable, and in 1948 the Soviets refused to allow elections for the city parliament. Instead, a parliament of the newly formed Socialist Unity Party of Germany (SED) declared itself to be in power and "elected" a new mayor.

Of course, in all of these developments Berlin was simply a pawn in the greater struggle of the Cold War. The Allies had fallen out, and the US and the Soviet Union were trying to establish world-wide supremacy by any means possible. Specifically, the Soviet Union attempted to extend its sphere of influence as far west as possible. Since the three western parts of Berlin were an island within the Soviet sector that was to become East Germany, one strategic option was to try to expel the western powers. To this end, Soviet forces cut off all roads, waterways, and railways leading into Berlin on 24 June 1948, hoping that the US, Britain, and France would abandon the city. The isolation indeed led to serious problems: Berlin hardly produced any food or energy of its own, so the city depended entirely on imports. Yet rather than cave in, the Allies organized one of world history's most impressive rescue operations: the Berlin Airlift. For the next eleven months, until May 1949, Berlin was supplied entirely through the air, where the Soviets had not disrupted the flight corridors that had been dedicated to the three western allies in the Treaty of Yalta (so that they could fly between their larger sectors and their parts of Berlin).

The scale and logistics of the Berlin Airlift are hard to imagine today. Since France was involved in its next war (in Asia), only US and British airplanes participated. The northern and southern flight corridors (from around Hamburg and Frankfurt, respectively) were used as one-way routes into Berlin, while the planes flew out of Berlin only along the middle corridor towards Celle. While there were some hydroplanes that could land on lakes and rivers, the vast majority flew into Tempelhof airport, where a plane landed every two to three minutes. Over the course of the Airlift, almost 280,000 flights arrived in Berlin (two-thirds US, one-third British), carrying over two million tons of essential supplies. This load consisted of 1.6 million tons of coal, 537,000 tons of food, and over 200,000 tons of other items—such as building materials to maintain the airport runways. The pilots made friends with Berlin children by dropping chocolate bars and chewing gum with tiny hand-made parachutes, and the airplanes came to be nicknamed *Rosinenbomber* (raisin bombers). On 9 September 1948 Mayor Ernst Reuter gave a famous speech to 300,000 Berliners at the Reichstag, appealing: "Nations of this world, look at this city, and realize that you can and should never abandon this city and its people!"

Obviously the Soviet strategy to isolate western Berlin had not succeeded, and on 12 May 1949 the blockade was lifted. In the following decade the two parts of Berlin lived under an uneasy truce, with easy traffic between them (especially from East to West) but different political systems developing. The western sectors of Germany had become the Federal Republic of Germany (FRG), while the Soviet sector became the German Democratic Republic (GDR). Technically, the four parts of Berlin were not part of either state, but in practical terms the Soviet part became the capital of the GDR and was even provocatively called "Berlin (Hauptstadt der DDR)." The western parts of Berlin were referred to as "West Berlin" in common parlance, but West Berlin did not send any representatives to the parliament of the FRG, and West Berliners (such as myself) did not have to do military service. While the FRG supported West Berlin with large financial subsidies, the GDR denied its very existence by leaving the area white on many maps.

The separation of the city, and the political systems, was reinforced on 13 August 1961 when the GDR began to construct the infamous Wall. East Berliners (and other East Germans) had been "voting with their feet" by leaving their country via West Berlin, and the GDR had to stop this drain on its workforce and the associated propaganda damage. Of course, the reason given officially was quite different: the Wall was intended to protect East Berlin from the threat of capitalism and other reactionary forces, and it was given the convoluted title of "Anti-fascist Protective Barrier." The Wall ran between East and West Berlin for 26.8 miles and a further 69.6 miles around the other parts of West Berlin. In its final form (achieved around 1975), the Wall was 11.8 feet high and consisted of various "layers": the concrete wall itself (which was actually 6.6 feet inside the East German border), a "death strip" that was supposedly mined, a series of control towers with floodlights to illuminate the area, and a hinterland where all vegetation had been removed and structures demolished.

Since the Allies' access to Berlin remained unchanged by the construction of the Wall, they hardly protested, and Berlin's reality was changed for the next thirty-odd years. The brutality and inhumanity of the Wall is beyond discussion, but at the same time it has often been fetishized in historical and political writing, and attempts to cross it have taken on almost mythical status. A shocking number of East Germans were killed trying to escape across, or under, the Wall (about two hundred), but these escapees were often economic emigrants rather than political protestors. In any case, the Wall shaped Berlin for the next decades, starting with John F. Kennedy's famous speech in which he declared, "Ich bin ein Berliner" ("I am a Berliner"), to underscore that any citizen of what he termed the free world should support this city enclosed by a wall.

At the same time (and for most of the 1960s, 1970s, and 1980s), many West Berliners hardly conceived of themselves as champions of democracy and the capitalist economic order. On the contrary, the city took a political turn to the left for various reasons. Berlin's leftist tradition had been driven underground by the Nazis, but never destroyed. Since Germans living in West Berlin could not be drafted, many left-leaning young men fled the FRG to Berlin to escape the army. The student movement at the Free University in the late 1960s challenged not just university hierarchies, but the entire social structure, and encouraged Germans to come to terms with their Nazi past. The students demanded the end of the Vietnam War and opposed nuclear arms and energy. In 1967 demonstrations turned violent, and one student (Benno Ohnesorg) was killed by a police officer during a confrontation. Another (Rudi Dutschke) died as a consequence of an assassination attempt by a neo-Nazi.

The left subsequently divided into more or less two wings. The more violent went underground and embraced terrorism, murdering a judge in 1974 and kidnapping a right-wing politician in 1975. More peacefully, the other part of the protest movement tried to address social injustice as squatters, especially in Kreuzberg and Wedding. They invented the term *Instandbesetzung*—approximately "repair-squatting"—to describe their tactic of squatting in derelict buildings and renovating them (see pp.55–56). By the mid-1980s many of these squats were retroactively legalized, and suddenly the squatters found themselves owning valuable properties. Around the same time, the peaceful wing of the leftist movement founded the Green Party (first under a different name), which entered city parliament in 1981 and achieved thirty percent of the vote in Kreuzberg in 1985.

On the other (East) side of the Wall, hope briefly bloomed when Erich Honecker became leader of the GDR in 1971. In the previous decade Berlin mayors and FRG chancellors had become more accepting of the GDR, and travel and trade had been much simplified and improved under mayors Willy Brandt and Heinrich Albertz (a former pastor). In 1972 the two German states signed a treaty in which both gave up their claim to be the sole representative of the German people, though they never quite recognized each other's existence. For that reason, they had what were called "Permanent Representations" rather than embassies in one another's capitals. However, the opening under Honecker's early rule was short-lived, and by 1976 a number of dissidents had been put under house arrest or forced to leave the country. Several of these—like the singer Wolf Biermann, the actor Manfred Krug, and the punk rocker Nina Hagen—moved straight to West Berlin.

In the 1980s the two halves of the city competed to put on the most impressive displays. In 1987 Berlin celebrated its 750th anniversary, which was commemorated with various building projects and concerts. In East Berlin, the historic Nikolai Quarter was reconstructed (or rather re-imagined), while in the West parts of Kreuzberg were rebuilt for the International Architecture Exhibition. Provocatively, West Berlin located a three-day rock extravaganza in June, with artists such as Genesis, Eurythmics, David Bowie, and New Model Army, in front of the (still fairly derelict) Reichstag. Since the Reichstag was right next to the Wall, the concert could be heard from the East side as well, and many East Berliners gathered to listen—and had to battle with East German security forces trying to keep them away.

By 1989, when GDR rulers tried to celebrate its fortieth anniversary, the regime was already falling apart. East German dissidents had long been congregating at churches in East Berlin and occasionally demonstrating for their ideals. Mikhail Gorbachev's policy of *glasnost* had led to some opening of the Soviet Union, but the East German leadership resisted change. On 12 June 1987, US President Ronald Reagan demanded (in a speech near the Brandenburg Gate that I attended with my mother), "Mr. Gorbachev, tear down this wall!" In early 1989 Hungary opened its borders to the West, and East Germans started going there to travel to West Germany—in September 1989, over 30,000 fled that way. When the East German government responded by making it virtually impossible to travel to Hungary, East German citizens sought refuge in the West German embassies in Warsaw and Prague instead, and the West German government negotiated the emigration of almost 5,000 from Warsaw and 800 from Prague. An increasingly panicked East German leadership deposed the ailing Honecker and replaced him with a series of increasingly inept figureheads, but to no avail. The reasons and motivations behind the events of 9 November 1989 remain unclear, but in a press conference that day the leader of the East German government announced that the border to West Berlin could be crossed without visa, leading to an almost immediate stampede—the Wall was open.

In the following days and weeks, hundreds of thousands of East Germans visited West Berlin. Of course, West Berliners were thrilled about the political developments, but in practical terms the situation was often chaotic. East Berliners drove their noisy and smelly Trabant cars very slowly through the streets, honking in celebration—and holding up traffic. At this time, any East German coming to the West was given a "welcome payment" of 100 DM by the government, which was paid out at banks—leading to long queues. Some food items, like bananas, were hard to come by in the East— so they were sold out in West Berlin shops for weeks on end. It took a long time for life in West Berlin to return to normal—and then the "new normal" was not at all what long-time residents of West Berlin were used to.

Berlin since 1989

To some critics, the history of Berlin since the fall of the Wall is a story of globalization and decline. For decades, West Berlin's budget had relied on subsidies from the West German government, so when those fell away, the city faced huge deficits—which have not really been recovered to this day. Arguably, the standard of living has dropped in terms of cleanliness, transportation, social services, and landscape maintenance since the end of the Cold War. Klaus Wowereit, mayor since 2001 (Berlin's first openly gay mayor, a member of the SPD, and now the longest-serving mayor since World War II), tried to turn this into a virtue by calling Berlin "poor, but sexy," but that notion was scant consolation for most Berliners.

At the same time, the city became the national capital again when Germany was unified in 1990. Over the next decade, it also became the official seat of parliament and government, so ministries and members of parliament moved from Bonn to Berlin. This meant huge construction projects, paralyzing the city center. In a ripple effect, major German and then international companies came to Berlin, leading to higher rents, especially in the central districts. New developments like Potsdamer Platz and the many buildings on Friedrichstrasse are often impressive in architectural terms, but just as frequently they are neither loved nor embraced by Berliners—no locals go to Potsdamer Platz except for public screenings of impor-tant sporting events. In most major shopping areas, local business is steadily being pushed out by multinational conglomerates, so in that sense the city is losing its unique character.

Of course, these new developments are not entirely pervasive nor entirely bad. Berlin politics still lean to the left: the three parties left of the center—SPD, Green Party, and Die Linke (Left Party)—between them received almost sixty percent of the popular vote in 2011, and that is not even counting the Pirates protest party (who now fortunately seem to be imploding). There are certainly some benefits to modernizing developments in Berlin: parts of this book were written (during the heat waves that have become regular summer features in the new century) in an international coffee shop, the only place with both air-conditioning and free wifi. The basic fabric of the city certainly needed some updating (even if that meant more expensive apartments); rents in trendy districts continue to be cheaper than elsewhere in Germany, attracting aficionados of counter-culture and idealists from Germany, Europe, and the rest of the world; more international exhibitions and concerts cannot be thought of as a bad thing—and, most importantly, the freedom of East Berliners has no price (to embrace a cliché). Berliners continue to be stubborn and contentious, and they will criticize their govern-ment at the drop of a hat, but now at least all of them can choose their own rulers.

Carl Breitbach's portrait of Theodor Fontane (1819–98), perhaps the archetypal Berlin author (though born in Neuruppin), contributing journalism, travel narratives, poetry, and novels about the city from the eighteen residences he lived in during his career.
(zeno.org/Wikimedia Commons)

5

The Written Word
The City in Literature

A ll authors dealing with Berlin have had sophisticated, complex, multi-layered relationships with their city. One way to introduce a selection of these writers would be to group them by the ways they represent Berlin. To some, it was a vibrant, exciting metropolis of opportunities; to others, a threatening behemoth of danger and corruption. In the past, Berlin was often portrayed as the quintessential German city; more recently, it has been depicted as the site of international and multicultural conflict, communication, and connection. Some West Berliners during the Cold War saw their city as a symbol of freedom in a world of antagonistic political systems; for some East Berliners it shone as a beacon of hope for a glorious socialist future. These, inevitably, are all simplifications.

Alternately, authors who have lived in and written about Berlin could be introduced by traversing the city geographically. A writer from bourgeois Wilmersdorf will arguably see the city differently from his or her counterpart in working-class Wedding; an author stuck in the high-rise flats of Hellersdorf will have a different point of view from one in a comfortable villa in Wannsee. At the same time, it is dangerous to assume too much about literary and ideological positions according to zipcodes, especially since many writers have traditionally moved all over the city. For instance (and perhaps most extremely), the realist novelist and journalist Theodor Fontane lived in at least eighteen different apartments during his long, illustrious, and successful career. For that reason, it is perhaps best to approach Berlin literature chronologically—not because every period had its own view of the city (which is not the case) but because this offers the most coherent overview of this vast topic. (Throughout this chapter, titles given in German first are only available in the original; titles given in English are available in translation.)

Enlightenment

One of the centers of Berlin's literary culture in the Enlightenment was the bookshop of publisher Christoph Friedrich Nicolai (1733–1811), who also owned a private library of 16,000 volumes. Nicolai was a freemason and a passionate proponent of reason over religion, which got him into trouble on a regular basis. His home in the Mitte district was a meeting place for the Berlin intelligentsia and is still used by the book trade. Nicolai's *Beschreibung der königlichen Residenzstädte Berlin und Potsdam* (*Description of the Royal Residences of Berlin and Potsdam*, 1769) already offers a cosmopolitan version of Berlin, as he divides the population into six groups: military, expatriates, French and Bohemian colonists, Jews, and citizens (*Bürger*).

Nicolai's colleague and friend Gotthold Ephraim Lessing (1729–81)—a poet, dramatist, critic, librarian, and theologian who lived in Berlin most of the time between 1748 and 1767—is most famous for plays such as *Minna von Barnhelm* (1767) and *Nathan the Wise* (1779). There are several memorials to Lessing in Berlin, and the Lessingbrücke in Moabit is decorated with scenes from his plays. The model for Lessing's Nathan was Moses Mendelssohn (1729–86), who lived his entire life in a precarious position because of his Jewishness. He apparently suffered a nervous breakdown at one point, and his membership of the Prussian Academy of Sciences was held up by Frederick the Great himself. Known in intellectual circles as the "German Socrates," Mendelssohn became an influential critic and founded a dynasty that included the sibling composers Felix and Fanny Mendelssohn. The family established a bank in 1795; the Mendelssohn Depot where it was housed in Jägerstrasse in the late nineteenth and early twentieth centuries now offers an exhibition on the family. Nicolai, Lessing, and Mendelssohn were part of the Monday Club, which met to discuss artistic and scientific subjects. Another member of the club, Karl Wilhelm Ramler (1725–98), apostrophized his home town in the poem "Ode an die Stadt Berlin" ("Ode to the City Berlin"), praising the Spree over all other German rivers and calling Berlin the "crown" of German cities.

Enlightenment Berlin was also remarkable for its many journals and newspapers. Nicolai, Lessing, and Mendelssohn co-edited the *Briefe die neuste Literatur betreffend* (*Letters Concerning the Latest Literature*, 1759–65) and were involved in the *Allgemeine deutsche Bibliothek* (*General German Library*, 1765–1806), which reviewed an amazing 80,000 books in its forty-year run. The *Berlinische Monatsschrift* (*Berlin Monthly Magazine*, 1783–96) remains famous to this day because of Mendelssohn's contributions and because it published Immanuel Kant's seminal essay, "What is Enlightenment?" and the ensuing philosophical debate. From 1617 Berlin had supported a newspaper that was published under various titles but is known overall as *Vossische Zeitung*. Lessing reviewed books for the *Vossische Zeitung*, and later authors who worked on it before the Nazis forced the paper to shut down in 1934 included Theodor Fontane and Kurt Tucholsky (see below). Back in the Enlightenment, the Prussian King Frederick the Great wanted to promote intellectual, political, and economic competition, so he encouraged the founding of another newspaper in 1740—the *Berlinische Nachrichten* (*Berlin News*), which stayed in business until 1874.

Romanticism

Salons where the literati met played an important part in the Romantic era as well. The Humboldt brothers Alexander and Wilhelm, Heinrich Heine, Ludwig Tieck, Georg Friedrich Wilhelm Hegel, Bettina von Arnim, and even Prince Louis Ferdinand of Prussia met at the salon of Rahel Varnhagen (née Levin, 1771–1833). Doubly at a social disadvantage for being a woman and having Jewish heritage, Varnhagen was most active as a letter writer. The poet, dramatist, novelist, and critic Heinrich von Kleist (1777–1811), another member of Varnhagen's salon, is one of Germany's most important Romantic authors. The title character of his play *The Prince of Homburg* (1807) wins an important battle, but against the orders of his commanding officer, the Elector of Brandenburg. Sentenced to death because of his insubordination, the prince struggles with duty on the one hand and his will to survive on the other. The death sentence is pronounced at the castle of the Elector in Berlin, which thus stands for the rule of order over the subjective intuition of the individual. Kleist himself had to close down one of the newspapers he founded in Berlin because of censorship. Impoverished and depressed, he committed joint suicide with his companion, the terminally ill Henriette Vogel, on the shore of the Wannsee. Since suicides could not be buried in cemeteries, Kleist and Vogel were interred where they died. The publicist Ruth Cornelsen donated €500,000 to renovate and update the site for the bicentennial of Kleist's death in 2011.

Another regular at Varnhagen's salon, Heinrich Heine (1797–1856), studied and lived in Berlin in the 1820s. Heine's *Briefe aus Berlin* (*Letters from Berlin*, 1822), originally published in weekly installments, introduce an early prototype of Walter Benjamin's urban *flâneur* (stroller) and co-opt the reader into walking around the city with the narrator. Critics disagree as to whether the *Letters* are simply tiresome or offer a proto-modernist political and cultural sensibility. Heine's view of Berlin is not always flattering; for instance, he writes: "No town in the world has so little local patriotism as Berlin. Berlin is no real town, but simply a place where many men, and among them men of intelligence, assemble, who are utterly indifferent as to the place; and these persons form the intelligent world of Berlin."

Another group of literati, the Serapion Brethren, met less formally, and with much more alcohol involved, at the Lutter & Wegner champagne bar. The group included Ernst Theodor Amadeus (E. T. A.) Hoffmann (1776–1822), the poet Friedrich de la Motte Fouqué, and the novelist Adalbert von Chamisso. The original Lutter & Wegner was destroyed during World War II, but was revived in 1997 on the Gendarmenmarkt on the site of a building where Hoffmann lived between 1815 and his death. Hoffmann, a Renaissance man who trained as a lawyer, wrote literature in many genres, drew caricatures so revealing that they almost cost him his administrative career, and actually wanted to be a conductor and composer. He immortalized his friends in a four-volume collection of stories called *The Serapion Brethren* (1819–21), where a group of young men meet for eight evenings and tell each other tales. Hoffmann's double-edged homage to Berlin is his short story "Ritter Gluck" ("Knight Gluck," 1809). Here, the narrator meets an eccentric stranger who shares his love of the composers Mozart and Christoph Willibald Gluck (1714–87) and his dissatisfaction with the contemporary music scene in Berlin. The stranger plays a Gluck opera for the narrator on his piano, and it turns out that this stranger is an apparition of Gluck himself. In "A New Year's Eve Adventure" (1815), the protagonist wanders through the center of Berlin (Unter den Linden, Jägerstrasse), stops at the Restaurant at the Sign of the Golden Eagle on Dönhoffplatz off Leipziger Strasse, and meets similarly eccentric characters.

Naturalism and Realism

For much of the nineteenth century the Berlin literary world was dominated by another club, the so-called *Tunnel über der Spree* (Tunnel over the Spree). More official than the groups and salons of the Enlightenment and Romantic eras, this club was founded in 1827 and met until at least 1898. The name was ironic—Berlin did not get its first tunnel *under* the Spree until 1895—and contrasted Berlin with London, where the construction of a tunnel under the Thames had started in 1823 (though it was not completed until 1843). The club counted 214 writers, painters, composers, musicians, historians, and scholars as members. These included Paul Heyse (the first German novelist to win the Nobel Prize for Literature, in 1910), the painter Adolph Menzel, the writer Theodor Storm, and the composer Johann Nepomuk Hummel (as an honorary member).

Another member, Theodor Fontane (1819–98), spent most of his life in Berlin (he was born in Neuruppin) and worked as an apothecary before becoming a professional writer. He was a foreign correspondent in London and Paris and wrote columns and reviews for various Berlin newspapers. One of Fontane's most successful works was the *Wanderungen durch die Mark Brandenburg* (*Walks through the Mark Brandenburg*, 1862–89), five volumes of description of Brandenburg's history, culture, architecture, and nature. Fontane used his experience writing the *Wanderungen*, and his knowledge of Berlin from living in many different apartments over the years, to create the milieu for many of his novels.

In *The Poggenpuhl Family* (1895–96), Fontane traces the decline of that family. The Poggenpuhls—a widowed mother, two sons, and three daughters from the aristocracy—have to come to terms with the decline of a society that upheld aristocratic values and the victory of the capitalist system in the newly unified Germany (after 1871). Though members of the family travel widely, the Poggenpuhl home is in Grossgörschenstrasse in Kreuzberg, and Fontane's realist description of the family's dilemmas extends to the Berlin setting of the story. The same backdrop of 1870s Berlin informs *Delusions, Confusions* (1887–8, also translated as *On Tangled Paths, Trials and Tribulations* and *Entanglement*). Here, an officer falls in love with a young working-class seamstress who lives in a garden plot near the zoo. Typically for Fontane, the two realize the impossibility of their love and marry other, more socially acceptable partners. One of the most famous scenes of this novel is the outing to a place called *Hankels Ablage* (Hankel's Deposit) just south of Berlin. Here, the rural landscape serves to characterize the female protagonist as simple and honest, in contrast to superficial socialite women. In *Mrs. Jenny Treibel* (1892), Fontane contrasts two Berlin families: that of the successful entrepreneur Treibel and the petit bourgeois Schmidt family. Schmidt's daughter and Treibel's son want to marry, but the relationship fails because of the interference of the Treibel matriarch Jenny, who many years previously had chosen Treibel's wealth over love with Schmidt. Once again, Fontane's Berlin is a place where the classes mix and where that mixing usually ends in tragedy, or at least disappointment. Fontane also evokes the complexities of class as he describes the Treibel residences, the earlier presumably designed by a famous architect and the later situated next to his factory:

The Treibel villa was situated on a large property that extended spaciously from the Köpenick Strasse to the Spree. Here in the immediate vicinity of the river there had once been only factory buildings in which every year uncounted tons of potassium ferrocyanide, and later, as the factory expanded, not much smaller quantities of Berlin blue dye had been produced. But after the war of 1870, as billions poured into the country and the newly founded empire began to dominate the views of even the soberest heads, Kommerzienrat Treibel found his house in the Old Jakobstrasse no longer suited to his times nor his rank—though it was supposed to have been the work of Gontard, and according to some, even that of Knobelsdorff. He therefore built himself a fashionable villa with a small front yard and a parklike back yard on his factory property. The house was built with an elevated first floor, yet because of its low windows it gave the impression of a mezzanine rather than a *bel étage*. Here Treibel had lived for sixteen years and still couldn't understand how he had been able to endure it for such a long time in the Old Jakobstrasse, un-fashionable and without any fresh air, just for the sake of a presump-tive Frederickan architect.

Fontane's *Effi Briest* (1894–95) is the unhappy story of the eponymous heroine. At the young age of sixteen, Effi is married to a Prussian civil servant who loves his wife but is unable to recognize, much less fulfill, her needs. Effi's husband is posted near the Baltic Sea, where she meets a dashing officer who makes advances to her—though Effi manages to resist the temptation. Effi is ecstatic when her husband is relocated to Berlin, where they spend a few happy years until the husband accidentally finds out about the officer. Compelled by the Prussian code of ethics, he duels with (and kills) the officer and divorces Effi, who lives out the rest of her life in shame. During her good times in Berlin Effi resides in the beautiful Keithstrasse in Tiergarten; after her divorce she lives in small apart-ment in Königgrätzer Strasse (now Ebertstrasse). In *Effi Briest* Fontane portrays Berlin both as the bustling new German capital, the city of culture and society, and as a heartless urban jungle where those who do not conform are mercilessly cast aside.

Fontane's contemporary Wilhelm Raabe (1831–1910) offered his most complete image of Berlin in the novel *Die Chronik der Sperlingsgasse* (*Sparrow Lane Chronicle*, 1856), which explores the lives of the denizens of that short street. Raabe also deals with the tensions between social classes: a working-class female character is raped by an aristocrat, and towards the end of the novel the male protagonist meets the aristocrat's impoverished daughter, who now also lives on Sparrow Lane. But most importantly, *Chronik der Sperlingsgasse* narrates the triangular relationship between two men who love the same woman, and the child of that relationship. There is a good deal of death and misery in the novel, but ultimately the Berlin community in the street transforms such experience into happiness and tranquillity. Towards the end of the novel, Raabe writes, "What was dead is alive; what was a curse has become a blessing." In an example of life following art, the Spreegasse, where Raabe lived and on which he based his novel, was renamed Sperlingsgasse in 1931. Almost all of the buildings in the street, however, were demolished in the 1960s.

Gerhart Hauptmann (1862–1946) lived long enough to experience World War II and was tolerated by the Nazis, but by then he was an old man, and his work was not influenced by Nazi ideology. On the contrary, his most important drama *The Weavers* (1892) expressed almost Marxist ideas about class and exploitation, and he should certainly be numbered among the realist writers. Hauptmann lived in the eastern district of Erkner from 1885 to 1889 (his home is now a museum) and in Charlottenburg from 1889 to 1891. His most Berlin-oriented work, the drama *Lonely Lives* (1891), is set in an estate on the Müggelsee in southeastern Berlin and explores the triangular relationship between the married couple Johannes and Käthe, and a visiting artist, Anna. Johannes and Anna fall in love, but realize that their relationship has no future. The drama ends with Anna leaving town and Johannes rowing out onto the Müggelsee to drown himself.

Adolf Glassbrenner (1810–76) took his subjects from even lower down the social scale than Raabe and Hauptmann, contributing to the stereotype of the quarrelsome, mischievous, and witty Berliner. His most famous and enduring character was Eckensteher Nante (Nante on the Corner), based on a real-life lowly servant who worked from the corner of Königstrasse and Neue Friedrichstrasse and spent much of his time at the nearby Eulner distillery. From the 1820s to the 1840s Glassbrenner published a series of journals and pamphlets—most famously the *Berliner Don Quixote* and *Berlin, wie es ist und—trinkt* (*Berlin as it is and—drinks*)—that were politically progressive and often censored. Glassbrenner's poems, stories, and dialogues are almost impossible to translate because of their brilliant use of Berlin dialect.

The 1920s and 1930s

Berlin in the first decades of the twentieth century was an exciting place to be—and soon a very tense one during the short-lived Weimar Republic. Writers took both sides in the conflict between communists and Nazis in the 1920s and early 1930s, but only those opposing the Nazis tend to be remembered. These included world-class novelists, dramatists, philosophers, and journalists such as Walter Benjamin, Ernst Bloch, Bertolt Brecht, Lion Feuchtwanger, Siegfried Kracauer, Erich Maria Remarque, and Carl Sternheim, all of whom lived and wrote in Berlin at some point in their careers. However, none of them made Berlin a major setting in their oeuvre.

Writing nonsense poetry and using cinematic and collage techniques, Joachim Ringelnatz (1883–1934) was a member of a different generation (in literary terms). His progressive artistic and political tendencies were not appreciated by the Nazis, who prohibited the publication and performance of his work and burned his books as "degenerate" in 1933. Barely staving off poverty with some work in Switzerland, Ringelnatz died in 1934. Even the title of his homage to Berlin, *...liner Roma...* (*[Ber]lin Nov[el]*, 1924), proclaims his view about the metropolis: incomplete, disjointed, and incomprehensible. The "novel" does not have a straightforward narrative, but offers disconnected vignettes of powerless characters controlled by the inhuman will of the city they live in. Like Ringelnatz, the journalist and poet Kurt Tucholsky (1890–1935) had no sympathy for the Nazis. In the characters Mr. Wendriner and Lottchen (apparently based on his partner Lisa Matthias), who appeared in various short stories and collections, Tucholsky created a satirical portrait of what he considered typical Berliners, even if he was writing not so much for working-class Berliners as for the Berlin intelligentsia. Afraid of what he believed was going to happen in Germany, Tucholsky emigrated to Sweden in 1930.

Arguably the most famous novel set in Berlin is *Berlin*

Alexanderplatz (1929) by Alfred Döblin (1878–1957), who fled Germany between 1933 and 1945. The story begins in 1920s Tegel, where the protagonist Franz Biberkopf, a small-time criminal, is released from prison. Franz tries to leave his life of crime, but begins a downward descent by associating with the Nazis. On the one hand, he picks a series of underworld companions who get him into more and more trouble; on the other, he gets involved with a number of prostitutes who seem to return his love but only create more difficulties for him. Franz loses an arm in a car accident, spends time at a mental institution, and ultimately appears to have escaped into a better life. All of this happens against the backdrop of a dark, uncaring, and dangerous city that has no interest in the well-being of the individual and where nothing is as it seems—and against the looming threat of the Nazis. Alexanderplatz in particular is both an alluring and exciting locale (with bars that are more home to some characters than their apartments, and pulsating public life through newspapers and popular songs) and a center of chaos (with crazy traffic, ever-present burglary and violence, and constant construction). In one instance, Döblin describes that chaos in short, staccato sentences and lists:

> On the Alexanderplatz they are tearing up the road-bed for the subway. People walk on planks. The street-cars pass over the square up Alexanderstrasse through Münzstrasse to the Rosenthaler Tor. To the right and left are streets. House follows house along the streets. They are full of men and women from cellar to garret. On the ground floor are shops.
>
> Liquor shops, restaurants, fruit and vegetable stores, groceries and delicatessen, moving business, painting and decorating, manufacture of ladies' wear, flour and mill materials, automobile garage, extinguisher company.

Later, Alexanderplatz is the nexus of the many narratives intersecting in the metropolis:

> People hurry over the ground like bees. They hustle and bustle around here day and night, by the hundreds.
>
> The street-cars roll past with a screech and a scrunch, yellow ones with trailers, away they go across the planked-over Alexanderplatz, it's dangerous to jump off. The station is laid out on a broad plan, Einbahnstrasse to Königstrasse past Wertheim's. If you want to go east, you have to pass police headquarters and turn down through Klosterstrasse. The trains rumble from the railroad station towards Jannowitz Brücke, the locomotive puffs out a plume of steam, just now it is standing above the Prälat, Schlossbräu entrance a block further down.

Berlin Alexanderplatz is remarkable for its epic sweep, its departure from realism (Franz encounters angels and Death), and its use of the Berlin dialect. The enduring power of the novel is demonstrated by various radio, television, and film adaptations, culminating in Rainer Werner Fassbinder's fifteen-hour movie of 1980.

The counterpart of *Berlin Alexanderplatz* in terms of young adult novels set in Berlin is *Emil and the Detectives* (1929) by Erich Kästner (1899–1974), which as book or film (1931) must be familiar to every Berliner. Kästner came to Berlin in 1927 and soon became one of the city's most prominent writers and critics. During the Nazi period he stayed in Berlin, supposedly to take care of his mother and to be a witness to German history. Kästner was interrogated by the Gestapo, and his books were burned in 1933. At the same time, the Nazis used his literary talent by allowing him to contribute dramas and screenplays under a pseudonym. Before all of that, *Emil* describes the experiences of a twelve-year-old boy who comes to Berlin from the provinces. On the train, the money he is supposed to bring his grandmother is stolen, but once in Berlin he is able to stalk the thief and ultimately recover his money with the help of a gang of children. Emil gets off the train at Zoo station, catches a tram to Bundesallee at the corner of Trautenaustrasse (to follow the robber), and rides a taxi with his new friend Gustav past Prager Platz, Motzstrasse, and Martin-Luther-Strasse to Nollendorfplatz. There, the children observe the culprit from the theater (now Metropoltheater) before they corner him as he tries to change the money into smaller notes at a bank on Kleiststrasse. In *Emil*, Berlin is dangerous (Emil is robbed), but also redeems itself by demonstrating community and wit (in the shape of the children who help Emil). Kästner's adult novel, *Fabian* (1931), paints a more depressing picture of the city. The protagonist moves from detached observation of the shenanigans of communists, Nazis, prostitutes, and pimps to moral engagement—the novel is subtitled "The Story of a Moralist"—and enters a relationship with a rising film star, but ultimately retires to the countryside.

During this period, several important writers from English-speaking countries also spent time in Berlin and wrote about the city. Christopher Isherwood (1904–86) is most famous for his *Berlin Stories* (1945), which combine the novella *Mr. Norris Changes Trains* (1935) and the episodic novel *Goodbye to Berlin* (1939). In *Mr. Norris*, Isherwood follows the fortunes of the title character, a masochist, communist, and spy who is involved in various shady dealings. The novel is set in the 1930s (Isherwood was in Berlin from 1929 to 1933) and in places such as the Friedrichstrasse station and around the Reichstag. The stories in *Goodbye to Berlin*, which are largely based on Isherwood's own experiences, introduce characters such as a typical landlady and a Jewish heiress. One story deals with the homosexual relationship of Peter and Otto. (Isherwood was gay, came to Berlin to explore the gay scene—"For Christopher, Berlin meant boys," he wrote in a later memoir—and was himself involved with a man named Otto.) The book is most famous for the character of Sally Bowles, however, who came to be the main character in the musical *Cabaret* (1966). The poems that Isherwood's some-time lover W. H. Auden (1907–73) wrote when the two were in Berlin are less about the city and more about his sexuality. Isherwood and Auden were regulars at bars such as Noster's Restaurant zur Hütte (which Isherwood named Cozy Corner in his fiction) and the Kleist-Kasino (finally closed in 2002). Both of them warned directly and indirectly against the coming Nazi catastrophe.

The US author Thomas Wolfe (1900–38) went through an interesting transformation with regard to Berlin and Germany, which he visited six times. Until the early 1930s he seems to have celebrated Berlin and German culture—and was in turn fêted by the Berlin intelligentsia. After returning to watch the 1936 Olympics, however, he took a very different and much more critical view. In the short story "I Have a Thing to Tell You" (1937), later part of his posthumous novel *You Can't Go Home Again* (1940), Wolfe gives a sympathetic view of a German Jew and paints a picture of the Nazis as evil, barbaric, and dangerous. The character George Webber senses the aggressive militarism of the Nazis in the Olympic Games, revives his memory of a better Germany on Kurfürstendamm, and witnesses the arrest of a heroic Jewish lawyer at the German-French border. Unsurprisingly, the Nazis proceeded to ban Wolfe's works.

The Divided City: East and West Berlin

After 1945, literature continued to be produced in and about both parts of Berlin. There are some authors who were clearly West or East Berlin writers, but there were also many who started out in the East and fled, emigrated, or were exiled into the West. All of them dealt with themes of entrapment and marginality (both in the moral and physical senses), whether that meant being trapped behind the Iron Curtain or behind the Wall.

One writer who remained in East Berlin was Ulrich Plenzdorf (1934–2007). His novel *The New Sufferings of Young W.* (1972) has been translated into more than thirty languages, so it clearly strikes a chord beyond just Germany. The title is a reference to Goethe's novel *The Sorrows of Young Werther* (1774), one of the most influential books of the proto-Romantic *Sturm und Drang* movement. In Plenzdorf's book (which started out as a play), the protagonist moves to East Berlin, where he experiences both love and loneliness. When his application to art school is rejected, he takes a job as a house painter and dies in a work-related incident. This tragic character is clearly a creative individual who feels marginalized by his conflict with a society that does not value individualism, but the novel never comes out openly against the GDR regime. Plenzdorf himself stayed in East Berlin until the Wall came down.

In imitation of Plenzdorf's homage to Goethe, the West

German writer Leonie Ossowski, who moved to Berlin in 1980, wrote *Wilhelm Meisters Abschied* (*Wilhelm Meister's Farewell*, 1982). Goethe's novels *Wilhelm Meister's Apprenticeship* (1795–96) and *Wilhelm Meister's Journeyman Years* (1821–29) were examples of the *Bildungsroman* in which the protagonist learns to become a productive member of society. In contrast, the Wilhelm of Ossowski's novel gives up his apprenticeship, consciously joins the margins of the Berlin squatter scene, and learns that alternatives to traditional society are possible.

Another author who chose to stay in East Berlin was Christa Wolf. Her novel *Divided Heaven* (1963) is perhaps the quintessential text about the divided Germany, and it exerted significant cultural influence through the film version of 1964. The narrative is presented on two levels by Rita: she recounts her life story in the past tense while she is in a hospital in the present, having woken up from a coma. From the East German countryside, Rita falls in love with the city boy Manfred. Manfred slowly loses confidence in the East German system and flees to the West. Rita follows him, but does not feel at home in the West and returns to East Germany. When Manfred is permanently trapped in the West by the building of the Wall, Rita tries to commit suicide and falls into a coma. Perceived in the West as a critique of East Germany, *Divided Heaven* was still tolerated in the GDR, perhaps because the narrator ultimately rejects the West. For instance, she introduces West Berlin:

These houses all looked alike. They were the same in both parts of Berlin, built for the same kind of people, with the same joys and sorrows. And they would be the same in other cities, too, she was sure. Of course, there was more glass and more glitter in the shop windows in West Berlin, and there were things to buy which she had never even seen before. But she had known that already. She had liked all that, too, and had thought it would be fun to go shopping there.

But after Rita's return, she is not as certain:

"Have you ever been in West Berlin?" she asked Schwarzenbach.

> "Yes, years ago."
> "Then you know what it's like. Lots of things are fine, but they're no fun. There's always the feeling that there's something wrong. And it's worse than being in a foreign country, because people talk the same language. It's like being in a foreign country, familiar, yet horrible."

On the Western side of the Wall, contemporary author Günther Grass, who won the Nobel Prize for Literature in 1999, lived in Berlin for most of the 1950s and 1960s and set two of his most important works there (one after reunification). *Local Anaesthetic* (1969) deals with the Berlin protests against the Vietnam War. One of the key figures is a student who has come to the conclusion that Berliners are so hardened to human suffering, and to the atrocities of napalm in particular, that the only way he can shock them is to burn a dog in front of the respectable cake-eating ladies at the famous Kempinski café on Kurfürstendamm. "If my dog burns," the cynical Scherbaum says, "the cake will fall out of their faces."

In *The Wall Jumper* (1982), Peter Schneider makes the attempt to construct fiction about a divided Berlin the raison d'être of his book as the narrator recounts a mix of stories, memoirs, and essays about his topic. The main characters of all the vignettes are border-crossers of some kind, trying to avoid being trapped: the narrator's landlord finances his West Berlin apartment by buying cheap food in East Berlin; three young men leave East Berlin through a house right on the Wall to go to the cinema in West Berlin; another character (with the archetypal Berlin name Bolle) is an agent who switches allegiances between West and East so often that he loses his identity; another (East Berlin) writer is punished because his work is published in the West. The novel even opens with a border crossing:

> In Berlin, the prevailing winds are from the west. Consequently a traveler coming in by plane has plenty of time to observe the city from above. In order to land against the wind, a plane from the west must cross the city and the wall dividing it three times: initially heading

east, the plane enters West Berlin airspace, banks left in a wide arc across the eastern part of the city, and then, coming back from the east, takes the barrier a third time on the approach to Tegel landing strip. Seen from the air, the city appears perfectly homogeneous. Nothing suggests to the stranger that he is nearing a region where two political continents collide...

On a clear day the traveler can watch the plane's shadow skimming back and forth across the city. He can track the plane closing in on its shadow until it touches down right on top of it. Only when he disembarks does he notice that in this city, the recovered shadow signifies a loss. After the fact, he realizes that only the plane's shadow was free to move between the two parts of the city.

Again and again, *The Wall Jumper* emphasizes that the antagonisms and propaganda of the divided city weaken Berlin—both sides have their physical and moral limitations. This concept is exemplified in repeated descriptions of contrasting TV broadcasts, where each system relies on only one source and presents only one view. Harking back to the montages and surrealism of Ringelnatz and Döblin, the short novel suggests that Berlin is incomprehensible and schizophrenic—a city trying unsuccessfully to come to terms with its past and present.

The Nazi period and the Cold War offered settings for non-German writers as well. John Le Carré set various scenes in his Smiley novels in Berlin, and in *Fatherland* (1992) Robert Harris imagined an alternative version of history in which Germany had won World War II. In a more literary vein, *The Innocent* (1990) by Ian McEwan combines espionage with a love story. Leonard Marnham goes to post-war Berlin in 1955 as a technician to help the US and British forces tap phone lines linking East Berlin and Moscow. Leonard starts an affair with the divorced German typist Maria and accidentally kills her ex-husband. Complications ensue that separate Leonard and Maria. The novel concludes with a coda in 1987 and a reunion that shows how much the characters and the city have changed. Thus, the novel—turned into a film in 1993—explores themes of innocence and corruption, love and sex, and freedom and responsibility against the backdrop of the divided city.

Berlin after Reunification

Since the reunification of Berlin (and Germany), the city has been trying to find the novel that definitively captures its voice. The fact that readers and critics have not been able to agree on such a novel is perhaps testament to two underlying issues. First, it is difficult to concur on what criteria should be used to identify such a text: does it have to cover (former) East and West Berlin? Must it address the immigrant experience? Should it be "literary," or can it be popular literature? Can the author be young, or must there be some historical perspective? Katharina Gerstenberger's *Writing the New Berlin* (2008) grapples with these and many other questions. Secondly, it is probably a mistake even to think that a city as diverse, multi-layered, self-contradictory, and complex as Berlin could ever be encapsulated in one text. Nevertheless, there are important, substantial, and humorous books that deal with different aspects of the late-twentieth- and early twenty-first-century city.

Many writers who had been active in the post-war years tried to come to terms with the newly reunited city in literature. Günter Grass' *Too Far Afield* (1995) is perhaps the ultimate novel about German unification. The two protagonists are Theo Wuttke, who calls himself Fonty in admiration for Theodor Fontane (the title of the novel itself is a quotation from Fontane), and Hoftaller, a half real, half imaginary spy who seems to be immortal. In the time between the fall of the Berlin Wall and German reunification, the two explore parallels between the German present and the past of the 1848 revolution and Fontane's Berlin. Much of the action revolves around the building in central Berlin at the corner of Wilhelmstrasse and Leipziger Strasse—once the biggest office building in Europe— which served as the Nazi Ministry of Aviation, the GDR's House of Ministries, and reunified Germany's Trust Agency, which was tasked with privatizing East Germany's state-owned industry. Now renamed Detlev-Rohwedder-Haus after the assassinated leader of the Trust Agency, it is home to the Finance Ministry and for a long time had one of Berlin's last functioning paternosters (which makes an appearance in the novel). *Too Far Afield* ultimately (and controversially) calls the GDR a "comfortable dictatorship" and suggests that the Berlin (and German) character has not much changed across history.

Christa Wolf's *In the Flesh* (2002) is almost a mirror image of her earlier *Divided Heaven*. Again, the protagonist is a woman in a hospital who is sometimes conscious and sometimes seems to be hallucinating. This time, it is her male counterpart who has committed suicide. Much of the novel is set at the Friedrichstrasse station and border crossing, where East and West meet. Wolf plays with the word *Mauerdurchbruch*, which literally means "break in the wall," historically refers to access between air-raid shelters in the basements of adjoining apartment buildings, and metaphorically hints at the fall of the Berlin Wall. The protagonist's dangerous illness can be read as a symbol of the diseased GDR, but the book ends on a happier note with the narrator healed and looking over the panorama of the city.

Peter Schneider revisited Berlin in *Eduard's Homecoming* (1999), where the protagonist returns after almost a decade in the US. Eduard is doubly homeless: the Berliners he meets think of him as American, but his US wife considers him German. His wife's Jewish heritage adds to the historic depth of the narrative. Eduard has inherited a building in Friedrichshain (East Berlin), but cannot take possession of it because of squatters—an ironic allusion to Schneider's own association with the 1960s student movement and 1980s squatters' movement in West Berlin. Schneider uses biblical and medical metaphors to emphasize how Berlin is completely reinventing itself, and to suggest how easy (and dangerous) it would be to forget the past in the process.

In contrast to such serious and literary works, a number of young writers are trying to cope with the new Berlin in comic and satirical texts. In *Heroes Like Us* (1996), Thomas Brussig's protagonist Klaus Uhltzscht claims he has brought the Wall down by exposing himself to the GDR border guards, who flee in amazement at the size of his penis. He captures the haphazardness of the situation:

You know the pictures: champagne parties at the Brandenburg Gate, horse-riding on top of the Wall, happenings with hammer and chisel. Everyone was ecstatic, no one grasped what had really happened. The late-comers and the ones at the back felt sure they *would have* pushed the gate open if they'd been at the front, and the ones at the front thought they *had* pushed it open because it really had opened. If I had claimed sole credit at the time, no one would have believed me...

I wanted to get away, I was frightened, and when another camera was thrust in my face I blurted out a word that emanated from the deepest quagmires of my soul: "Germany!" I half croaked, half whispered it—out of fear. The West Germans took it literally, of course, though they subjected it to a small but vital distortion: they behaved as if all who said "Germany" meant "the Federal Republic." How unimaginative! All they lacked in their spick-and-span republic, where even the rivers have been straightened out, was the feeling that they led a life for which others envied them. What's so good about the Federal Republic, aside from the fact that it produces the best BMWs in the world?

Brussig's *Am kürzeren Ende der Sonnenallee* (*At the Shorter End of the Sonnenallee*, 1999) is set in the 1970s on the short section of this street that remained in East Berlin—most of it was in the Neukölln district of West Berlin. The young East Berliners in this novella, which was turned into a popular film, are constantly confronted with the Wall, but its effects are often entertaining rather than threatening. In other words, Brussig argues that even in the face of a monstrosity such as the Wall individuals (especially teenagers) developed almost normal patterns of existence.

Berlin Blues (2001) by Sven Regener, founder of the band Element of Crime, is set in the autumn of 1989. The protagonist is less than pleased by the fall of the Wall, responding "Oh shit" in anticipation of the hordes of semi-barbaric East Berliners about to descend on his quiet and quaint West Berlin refuge. Wladimir Kaminer is one of those semi-barbaric Easterners—in fact, he was born in Russia and did not arrive in Berlin until 1990. In short story collections like the 2000 *Russian Disco* (his only book currently available in English, with which I am somewhat dissatisfied since it misrepresents activities at my brother's church), *Ich bin kein Berliner* (*I Am No Berliner*, 2007), and *Meine kaukasische Schwiegermutter* (*My Caucasian Mother-in-Law*, 2010), which he writes in German and turns out on an almost annual basis, Kaminer observes the comedy of everyday life in Berlin, especially the life of recent immigrants. He is not always sanguine about developments since the fall of the Wall, as this excerpt shows, where a friend is trying to write a travel guide about Potsdamer Platz:

> We couldn't think of a thing to say about Potsdamer Platz. 'A superb future in the old heart of the city?' I suggested in desperation. The last time I was there, I was approached three times in half an hour by security officers. The first time my shoelace had come undone and I had knelt down to tie it. The next second he was standing next to me: 'What's the problem?' 'Thanks, everything's just fine,' I answered, and went on my way. Looking for a toilet, I went into one of those superb residential and recreational developments that are all over the place there. Instantly another officer was at my side: 'What's cooking?' 'No sweat,' I said, and was out of there. 'Be sure to visit Potsdamer Platz, the realm of the rich. In the bars and casinos here you are sure to be rid of your hard-earned money in next to no time and without the slightest effort.' That, as things turned out, was what we ended up with.

Earlier immigrants to Berlin, especially from Turkey, have their own literature as well. Most of the novels by Emine Sevgi Özdamar, who was born in Turkey and writes in German, are semi-autobiographical. *Life Is a Caravanserai—Has Two Doors—I Came in One—I Went Out the Other* (1992) is set in Turkey between 1945 and 1963 and ends with the family emigrating to Germany. Like the heroine in *The Bridge of the Golden Horn* (1998), the author came to Berlin as a young woman for several years in the 1960s to work in a factory, a typical experience for Turkish immigrants (though Özdamar went back to Turkey). The protagonist occasionally reflects on the differences between her homeland and Berlin:

> When we walked along the Berlin streets, I was astonished at how few men were to be seen on the streets, even in the evenings there were not many men to be seen. I was also astonished that the men whom I saw didn't scratch themselves between the legs, like many Turkish men on Turkish streets. And some men carried the bags of the women they were walking beside and looked as if they were not married to these women, but to these bags.
>
> They walked along the streets as if at that moment they were being filmed for TV. To me the streets and people were like a film, but I didn't have a part in this film. I saw the people, but they didn't see us. We were like the birds, who flew somewhere and from time to time came down to earth, before flying away again.

The subtitle of Özdamar's *Seltsame Sterne starren zur Erde* (*Strange Stars Stare towards Earth*, 2003), *Wedding—Pankow 1976/77*, indicates the focus of the book, the years the author spent moving between West and East Berlin when she was an assistant director at the Volksbühne theater in East Berlin. The novel is partly written in diary form, and some of the characters are recognizable as important members of the Volksbühne, such as director Benno Besson. In all of her texts, Özdamar embraces the Turkish dialect of German as a valid form of expression.

In *Selam Berlin* (2003: the Turkish title means "Greetings, Berlin"), Yadé Kara explores the complications that arise from the overlay of German-Turkish and East-West relationships. Hasan, the nineteen-year-old protagonist of *Selam Berlin*, shuttles back and forth between Berlin and Istanbul and returns to Berlin on the day the Wall falls. Subsequently his family life is disrupted when his father's East German mistress and illegitimate child suddenly turn up. Hasan drifts through his days in Kreuzberg, trying to construct an identity from all the influences to which he is exposed. These Turkish-German authors have been embraced by the literary mainstream; Kara won the German Book Prize in 2004 for *Selam Berlin*, while Özdamar has won many distinctions, including the Kleist Prize in 2004 and the Fontane Prize in 2009.

In the last few years two books about Berlin in particular have been very successful and will certainly soon be translated. *Walpurgisnacht* (*Walpurgis Night*, 2011) by Annett Gröschner is set on 30 April, the night for celebrating the rites of spring—and the night before Berlin regularly experiences riots on 1 May. Gröschner follows the intersecting paths of a small group of Berliners from all walks of life throughout the day. The epigraph to her novel is a quip by Fontane: "Before God, all humans are really Berliners." In *Gehwegschäden* (*Damages to the Sidewalk*, 2012) by Helmut Kuhn, the main character is a journalist and historian who is trying to get a grip on his crumbling home city Berlin. A love story seems to offer hope, but in the end the novel exposes how most of us have acquiesced to the status quo. The title is a metaphor for imperfect situations that are simply accepted as natural.

Berlin continues to be both a home and an inspiration for authors of many different backgrounds and circumstances. The more international the city becomes, the more multicultural a flavor its literature takes. Still, the city's history is difficult to ignore, and each generation—and each author—constructs a different version and vision of Berlin out of the past and present.

6 | Visual Images
Art, Drama, and Cinema

Innumerable images of Berlin have been painted and engraved since the earliest (known) painting was composed in the first half of the seventeenth century. In an excellent exhibition in 1987 called *Stadtbilder* (a pun on "pictures of a city" and "cityscapes"), with an equally impressive catalogue, some three hundred of these images were brought together. Yet, in a way, the unified metaphor implicit in the term(s) Stadtbilder is misleading. Throughout the history of visual images of Berlin there have been fruitful tensions between artists concentrating on the man-made environment and others focusing on nature, between painters offering realistic depictions and those presenting personal interpretations, between images of static architecture and of people in movement, and between representations of the higher and lower strata of the city's population.

The best-known engravings from the eighteenth century are those by Johann Georg Rosenberg (1739–1808) from the 1770s and 1780s, but these were more representational than interpretive. Personal artistic takes on Berlin—often disguised as exact depictions of real scenes—started in the nineteenth century and have proliferated ever since. Here, it is only possible to mention a few artists (among many described by Matthias Pabsch in *Berlin und seine Künstler*) and sketch their contribution to images of Berlin, literal and metaphorical.

Like many of his contemporaries, Johann Heinrich Hintze (1800–61) traveled all over Europe (or at least Germany) and created some of his most important paintings in Berlin. His *View from the Kreuzberg* (1829) has Schinkel's monument celebrating the victory over the French in the left foreground. A path lined by restaurants snakes down the hill and towards Berlin in the distance. Several buildings there are clearly discernible such as the churches at the

Heinrich Zille's *Hof im Scheuneviertel* (*Tenement Courtyard in the Scheunenviertel*, 1919) with old and new(er) buildings, a water pump, laundry hanging out to dry, boards laid over the mud, children fighting, and possibly World-War I veteran in a wheelchair.
(http://www.bassenge.com)

Gendarmenmarkt, the dome of the St.-Hedwigs-Kathedrale, and the Siegessäule (Victory Column) in its original position. Hintze's painting emphasizes the juxtaposition of rural and urban, old and new, traditional and modern: there are wide open green spaces between the Kreuzberg and Berlin; the Kreuzberg monument is a new structure as opposed to some of the old churches in Berlin; and windmills on the outskirts of town stand next to new factories.

Like Hintze, his contemporary Eduard Gaertner (1801–77) is best known for his paintings of Berlin buildings. Gaertner produced his classicist oil paintings in the early part of his career, before he turned to Romanticism. Both Hintze and Gaertner worked on the first illustrated guide to Berlin's architecture, *Berlin und seine Umgebung* (*Berlin and its Environment*), which was published by Samuel Heinrich Spiker in 1833. Probably for use in this volume, Gaertner worked on a panorama of Berlin as seen from the Friedrichswerdersche Kirche starting in 1832 (just a year after the church was completed). In this work Gaertner tried to transfer the popular entertainment of paintings in the round to the two-dimensional canvas. By incorporating the roof of the church and individuals walking around the platform—including himself with wife and child—Gaertner created an artistic unity and a more successful perspective.

Friedrich Wilhelm Klose (1804–c.1874) also worked on the volume *Berlin und seine Umgebung* and also often painted Berlin architecture. Yet he was less interested in representative buildings and instead offered images of more plebeian culture in Berlin. For instance, his *View from the Dorotheenstrasse* (c.1835) shows the old observatory with a new optical telegraph at the top and other details like a guard's hut, a water fountain, and street lighting. Klose gave the individuals in his paintings more life than his contemporaries; here a milkmaid plies her trade at the bottom edge of the painting, while officers prance around in the street. Similarly, Johann Wilhelm Brücke (1800–74) populated his paintings of popular places with soldiers, bourgeois citizens, children, and dogs. In *View of the Tower of the Former City Hall* (1840), the ostensible object of the painting is upstaged by a group of tradespeople waiting for business. On one side a woman is selling pottery, while opposite is a fruit stall; a woman in a pink dress walks in the middle of the street behind a black-clad matron, while a girl is feeding her pet poodle.

Adolph Menzel (1815–1905) went through an interesting development in the course of his career. Pabsch calls him "the inventor of Frederick the Great," and indeed Menzel is most famous for his *Flute Concert of Frederick the Great at Sanssouci* (1850–52, see pp.236–37). An ambidextrous autodidact who was only four and a half feet tall, Menzel had to provide for his family from the age of sixteen when his father died. Menzel was commissioned to produce the illustrations for a history of Frederick and drew some four hundred well-researched and well-documented sketches. In contrast to some of the hagiographic art of the period, Menzel portrayed Frederick and his court as real individuals in *Flute Concert*. When political circumstances no longer allowed Menzel to show a human Frederick, he turned to industrial images such as a group of bricklayers and the inside of a steel mill (in a painting subtitled "Modern Cyclops," 1872–75). In the latter picture, Menzel contrasts the horizontal and vertical lines of the building with the round wheels of the machinery. The steel itself is the pulsing center of the composition, surrounded by a crowd of workers, a young woman bringing food, and in the background what seems to be the owner of the factory inspecting the building. Menzel's funeral was a state occasion attended by none other than Emperor Wilhelm II, but by the end of his career he was recognized for much more than his apotheosis of the old Prussian king. Menzel's motto, "No day without drawing a line," had served him well.

Heinrich Zille (1858–1929) took representations of Berlin in an entirely new direction, eschewing architecture altogether, depicting officers and gentlemen mostly as foils, and portraying instead the lower classes of the city. During the first thirty years of his career (apart from two years in the military) Zille worked for the Photographic Society of Berlin, so his own art was at first only a hobby. Around the end of the nineteenth century he turned increasingly to sketches, drawings, and paintings of proletarian Berliners in their natural habitats of streets and *Altbauten*. To his dismay, he was fired from the Photographic Society for his art, some of which (they claimed) verged on the pornographic in its vulgar postcard forms. Fortunately, his images, displayed in exhibitions and distributed in cheap magazines, were immensely successful, so he never experienced the poverty he portrayed. Zille was not political in the sense that he supported a particular party, but his images were clearly a critique of the society he lived in, and he achieved this critique not by satire or exaggeration, but simply by portraying his subjects as realistically as possible—dirty, hard-working, proud, cheeky, sick, funny, and sad. Many of his sketches were combined with captions or stories in which he liberally used Berlin dialect, another departure from high art. Zille became a well-known figure throughout Berlin, easily recognizable with his wide-rimmed hat and full beard, and was given affectionate nicknames such as "Paintbrush-Heinrich" and "Raffael of the Backyards." The artistic establishment took its time, but eventually acknowledged Zille's accomplishments. Today, two streets, a park, and a school in Berlin are named after him, and there are at least two monuments and four plaques—besides a museum devoted exclusively to Zille. Zille was supported throughout his career by Max Liebermann (1847–1935), another beloved Berlin artist who did not paint the city, but only a few beautiful images of the trees outside his villa on the Wannsee, now a museum dedicated to his art and memory.

Expressionism

In the early twentieth century, the impressionist and expressionist movements made inroads in the Berlin art scene. While impressionism offered scenes of common life, often including movement, and tried to capture reality with heightened colors and seemingly unfinished compositions, expressionism aimed to impose the individual artist's subjective vision on the world, often by employing techniques like distortion and exaggeration. Impressionism was dominant throughout European art in the last decades of the nineteenth century; expressionism developed in Germany in the first decade of the twentieth. The latter movement came to a violent end because the Nazis objected to it as "degenerate art," and many im-

portant expressionist artists—like Kirchner, Beckmann, and Grosz—
had to flee Germany.

The expressionist artists' collective "Die Brücke" (The Bridge)
was founded in Dresden, but by the early 1910s most members had
moved to Berlin. Today, the Brücke Museum in Dahlem exhibits a
constantly changing selection of the group's work. Ernst Ludwig
Kirchner (1880–1938), one of the founders, painted his Berlin
images between 1911 and 1915 and committed suicide (in
Switzerland) in despair over the political situation in Germany.
Kirchner's *Nollendorfplatz* (1912) does not set out to be an exact representation of the square, but expressionistically adapts lines and
colors: the entire painting is dirty yellow or blue (with some black),
and all buildings, streets, and even two trams (which seem to be
crashing into each other) point towards a narrow intersection. Thus,
Kirchner perhaps expresses what he sees as Berlin's aggressive movement and confrontational attitude.

Max Beckmann (1884–1950) lived in Schöneberg in the periods
1904–14 and 1933–37 before he had to flee to the US from the
Nazis. His early work, like a painting of a tenement house in the
middle of a rural area (*Berlin Suburban Landscape*, 1906), still shows
the influence of impressionism, but he soon turned to expressionism.
In *Tauentzien Street* (1913) Beckmann chooses a perspective that
puts him at a level with the pedestrians, conveying a claustrophobic
atmosphere to which the gathering clouds, the tram rushing by, and
grey tones of the entire painting contribute. Even more dramatically,
the dark-red and brown colors in *Street at Night* (1913), punctuated
by bright street lights, seem to suggest that Berlin is hell. The curved
lamp on the right could be a serpent, the figure in the foreground
Charon, and the wheelbarrow on the left a canon. The crowded street
car seems to be ferrying condemned souls to the bright red vanish-
ing point of the composition. Like Kirchner and Beckmann, George
Grosz (1893–1959) was heavily influenced by the two World Wars—
he, too, fled to the US. Born in Berlin as Georg Gross, Grosz moved
away as a child, lived and worked back in the city between 1912 and
1933, and finally returned one year before his death. In contrast to
Kirchner and Beckmann, his main works are from between the wars,

excoriating the excesses and hypocrisy of the Weimar Republic, and attacking the rising Nazi movement. On the one hand, Grosz participated in the flamboyant culture of the 1920s, dressing in a smart suit, his face made up in white with bright red lips, wielding a cane topped by an ivory skull, and Anglicizing his name. On the other hand, he recognized that the politics of the era were rotten to the core. Grosz first flirted with the Dada movement and then embraced the artistic style of New Objectivity, which allowed him to become politically engaged in his art. In one famously disturbing painting, *The Pillars of Society* (1926), the heads of the three foremost figures summarize Grosz's view of society: legal paragraphs sprout from the skull of the bourgeois, a journalist wears a chamber pot as his hat, and a supposed social democrat has a pile of feces instead of a brain. The bourgeois is perhaps most frightening, wielding in one hand a rapier that seems splattered in blood, carrying a half-empty beer glass in the other, with gashes on his cheek that mark him as a member of a conservative fraternity, and a tie with a swastika. In his pictures of Berlin, Grosz portrays similar chaos and violence. *The Metropolis* (1916–17), a scene near Friedrichstrasse, is painted in apocalyptic red tones; individuals and trams rush in diagonals towards the center of the painting, where they meet in a crash or battle. The entire composition, as well as details such as what seem to be coffin, a skeleton, and collapsing buildings, suggests a vision of Berlin as a site of madness reinforcing humanity's basest instincts. The Nazis confirmed that vision of humanity, and in addition to the other atrocities they committed they had a catastrophic impact on all of the visual arts: painters, authors, actors, and directors left the country in droves, and many of those who remained behind were second-rate artists producing mediocre work.

The Post-War Period

After World War II Berlin was a haven for all kinds of artists because of its cheap rents and because it was a focal point for political and cultural developments—but it is still fairly early to assess what art from the last sixty-odd years will stand the test of time. In his old age, the Austrian-born Oskar Kokoschka (1886–1980) was commissioned to make a painting for the headquarters of the Axel Springer AG (see pp.189–90) near the Wall and produced the beautiful *Berlin—13 August 1966*. The title is a reference to the fifth anniversary of the erecting of the Wall, but the only obvious connection in the picture is a marching regiment of soldiers. It is difficult to make out specific buildings in the colorful painting, which seems to hold out some hope in the blue sky and an airplane crossing the border. Karl Oppermann (b.1930) painted some seventy images of Berlin, mostly of the Eastern part, but no longer lives in the city. In *Gendarmenmarkt* (1964), the theater and German church are white ruins contrasted by the fire- or blood-red French church, while a green bush in the foreground suggests either God speaking from a burning bush or the return of life after destruction. According to the exhibition catalogue *Stadtbilder, At Potsdamer Platz* (1973) allows Oppermann to "represent the city in the style of Dutch landscape painters of the seventeenth century"—while portraying the Wall and the heavily mined "death strip" behind it. More recently, Oppermann has painted *Berlin auf Achse* (1999)—Berlin on the go. Hans Stein (b.1935) focuses on construction sites, high-rises, and train stations, especially in Charlottenburg. In *S-Bahnhof Witzleben* (1964), the functional architecture of the train station is presented as more important than the more famous Radio Tower, which is cut off at the top edge of the composition. In *Highway Intersection Radio Tower* (1973), from the perspective of the same tower, the autobahn in light blue looks more like a river and is contrasted with a red sky. Stein's *Construction Site at the Reichstag* (1999) shows the building with Norman Foster's glass dome, but still under construction—certainly a symbol of Germany's continuing reinvention. Of course, that reinvention will inspire a whole new generation of Berlin artists to imagine their city in new ways.

Drama

In Berlin—as in most other Western cultures—a distinction arose early on between "high" and "low" drama. High drama had named authors, treated serious subjects, was often composed in strict rhyme and meter, and was usually performed at court theaters for select audiences. (Since there were so many different principalities before the nation-state of Germany was founded, Berlin theater did not have any real prominence. For most of the eighteenth and nineteenth centuries, this kind of drama in Germany was focused almost entirely on Weimar. Today, the annual Theatertreffen festival presents the best of high drama from across the country in Berlin.) In contrast, low drama was by and for the people, pursued entertainment as much as moral edification, was rarely even written down, and was most frequently performed at fairs or in drinking establishments. In the eighteenth and early nineteenth centuries, both forms became institutionalized and moved closer to each other: high drama might now include more comedy, and low drama was put on for paying audiences in purpose-built theaters. In a corresponding overlap, the Friedrich-Wilhelmstädtisches Theater was opened in 1850 for popular dramas including farces and operettas—and transformed in 1883 into the Deutsches Theater, which concentrated on a traditional and serious repertory. Many famous directors such as Max Reinhardt and Gustaf Gründgens worked here, and new dramatic movements were introduced. The building survived both World War II and the Cold War and is once again one of Germany's leading theaters.

Several other famous theaters in Berlin are exemplars of particular artistic and dramatic movements. The classicist Schauspielhaus at the Gendarmenmarkt (see pp.51–52) was built at the behest of the Prussian kings, so it was still close to the ideal of court theater. So as not to offend the ruling family, some dramas such as Friedrich Schiller's *The Robbers* and Heinrich von Kleist's *Prince of Homburg*—which, though part of the canon, clearly challenged the ruling order—were either banned or quickly removed from this stage. Times had changed two hundred years later when the Schillertheater, which served as stage for the Prussian National Theatre in the 1920s and 1930s, was actually inaugurated in 1907 with *The Robbers*. Destroyed in 1943, this theater was rebuilt after the war. Directors like Samuel Beckett, Hans Neuenfels, and Peter Zadek worked here, and such actors as Bernard Minetti, Will Quadflieg, Erich Schellow, and Katharina Thalbach performed on its stage. Eventually, however, the Schillertheater fell victim to Berlin budget cuts and was closed in 1993. Today, the building mainly serves as a site for visiting ensembles, and the Staatsoper Unter den Linden is currently using it while its own theater is renovated.

The Volksbühne (people's stage) took up the tradition of popular theater, but tried to transform it by offering avant-garde drama to the people at affordable prices. The 2,000-seat modernist building in Mitte was constructed in 1913–14 and financed by donations from workers. Until World War II, the phrase *Die Kunst dem Volke* ("Art to/for the people") was inscribed on the façade, and the structure still presents an imposing bowed front of high columns to the visitor. Early directors who challenged conventional theater included Max Reinhardt—fresh from his work at the Deutsches Theater—and Erwin Piscator, who introduced cinematic devices to the stage. Since 1992 the controversial Frank Castorf has been the artistic director of the Volksbühne.

Three important theater groups that formed after World War II were the Berliner Ensemble, the Schaubühne, and the Grips-Theater. The first was founded in East Berlin in 1948 by Bertolt Brecht, who had recently returned from exile in the US and Switzerland. With Brecht at its helm, the ensemble promoted socialist-realist theater, including many of his own works. After performing at the Deutsches Theater until 1954, the Berliner Ensemble moved to the Theater am Schiffbauerdamm (where Max Reinhardt had also been artistic director), its main stage to this day. After Brecht's death in 1956 the ensemble was led by his widow Helene Weigel until 1971. Today, it still produces exciting and controversial drama under artistic director Claus Peymann.

Oddly, Brecht's dramatic testament to Berlin was the 1928 *Dreigroschenoper* (*Three Penny Opera*), an adaptation of John Gay's 1728 *Beggar's Opera*, which had recently experienced a successful revival in London. Technically, Brecht's piece was not an opera, but a play with interspersed musical numbers by the young composer Kurt Weill, some also adapted from eighteenth-century originals but others incorporating contemporary influences from jazz and blues to Weill's own atonal music. An immediate success, the *Dreigroschenoper* became the most frequently performed German drama of the twentieth century. Even though it was set in eighteenth-century London, the play intended to expose the commercialism, social injustice, moral hypocrisy, and gender inequality of 1920s Berlin.

The Schaubühne (an antiquated word for stage) was founded in 1962 to perform politically and socially relevant theater. The troupe used a stage in Kreuzberg until 1981, when they moved into a renovated 1928 modernist cinema (by Erich Mendelsohn) at Lehniner Platz (named after the Brandenburg village Lehnin, not the Russian politician Lenin) on Kurfürstendamm. The Schaubühne was dominated by the productions of Peter Stein until the late 1980s (I saw his legendary eight-hour production of all three parts of Aeschylus' *Oresteia* in the early 1980s), and the current artistic director is the young Thomas Ostermeier. Finally, the Grips-Theater, which uses a colloquial term for intelligence or wit in its name, came into being in the late 1960s and moved into its own space in the Hansaviertel in 1974. The ensemble came from a self-avowedly leftist background and specialized in writing drama for children and young adults. With plays about sex, guest workers, squatters, multinational corporations, neo-Nazis, Rosa Luxemburg, climate change, the holocaust, and the student movement—all specifically tailored to young audiences—it comes as no surprise that the Grips-Theater was frequently criticized, especially by Berlin's right-wing tabloid press. At the same time, it had an international success with the musical *Linie 1*.

Linie 1 (1985) is named after the U-Bahn line that traversed most of West Berlin. The musical, with some twenty songs, tells the story of a young girl, pregnant from a one-night stand, who comes to Berlin. On and off the U-Bahn, she gets to know a cross-section of the city's people, from conservative Wilmersdorf widows to Kreuzberg punks and pimps to guest workers, and finally finds a suitable partner. Of course, some stereotypes are invoked in the play, but it is still an interesting snapshot of a particular time in Berlin's history. (The 1980 song "Wir stehn auf Berlin"—"We're into Berlin"—by the band Ideal starts on the same subway line and captures the same era and atmosphere.) The play was turned into a film in 1988 and has been adapted all over the world. When Berlin's underground lines were reorganized after reunification, Linie 1 largely retained its designation because of the fame of the musical.

Cinema

Berlin's involvement in the film industry stretches back to even before the beginning of the twentieth century. The first silent film was shown at a Berlin variety theater in 1895, and the first successful movie with sound premiered at the Alhambra cinema in 1922. Oskar Messter opened the first film theater in Friedrichstrasse in 1896 and was shooting short films in Berlin in the late 1890s. Studio Babelsberg, where recent films such as *The Three Musketeers, Hanna, Anonymous,* and *Inglourious Basterds* were shot, was founded in 1912—and recently celebrated its centennial. The local celebrity Artur Brauner (b.1918), known universally as Atze—the Berlin dialect equivalent of "bro"—has been producing films in Berlin for over sixty years. Among his serious works, *The White Rose* (1982) dealt with a student resistance group in Munich during the Nazi period, and *Hitlerjunge Salomon* (1990), English title *Europa Europa,* won a Golden Globe. Earlier in his career, Brauner produced lighter fare including the spy caper *Es muss nicht immer Kaviar sein* (*It doesn't always have to be caviar,* 1961) and the love story *Die Spaziergängerin von Sanssouci* (*The Passerby,* 1982), the last role of the German film star Romy Schneider.

The first golden age of Berlin cinema was the late 1920s and early 1930s. Walter Ruttmann's documentary *Berlin: Symphony of a Great City* (1927) tried to capture the pulse of the city as if it was a living being. Divided into five acts or movements (rather than driven by any plot), the film portrays a day in Berlin, starting in the morning with a train moving from the countryside into the outskirts and then the center of the city. Each scene becomes shorter and the cuts faster, conveying the increasingly hectic activity in Berlin's streets, offices, and factories. Towards the evening the pace slows down, and Berliners are also shown at their leisure activities before the day concludes with a firework display. *Berlin,* which can be interpreted either as an endorsement or a critique of modernity—it displays anonymous urban life and encroaching technological developments, but also offers alternatives in proletarian solidarity and pastimes—was a silent film (in the sense that no actors speak) with a symphonic soundtrack by Edmund Meisel. Movie and soundtrack are frequently shown and performed, and the film has inspired various imitations. *Symphony of a World City* was shot in 1930 by Leo de Laforgue and starts with a view of Berlin from the air, while in this film a voice-over comments on the scenes. Generally more positive than Ruttmann's film, Laforgue's has been accused of supporting the Nazi agenda, but it was actually not released until 1950 under the title *Berlin—As It Was.* In 2002 director Thomas Schadt shot a black-and-white film titled *Berlin: Sinfonie einer Grossstadt* (as opposed to the original *Sinfonie der Grosstadt*—symphony of *a* rather than *the* great city). In contrast to Ruttmann, Schadt is more explicitly critical of society, dwelling on the scars left by World War II and the Cold War.

Other films of the 1920s and 1930s seem to project a dark view of Berlin. The silent movie *Metropolis* (1927) was influenced by the skyscraper modernity of New York, but also by the architecture and social situation of Berlin—and it was produced at the Babelsberg film studios. (Director Fritz Lang was another artist who left Germany because of the Nazis.) In this allegorical science fiction romance, humanity is divided into a rich class living above ground and an underclass maintaining the city in catacombs. The son of the city's leader falls in love with a young woman from the other end of the scale, and after many catastrophes, complicated intrigues, and graphic violence their romance ultimately leads to an upheaval in the social structure. *Metropolis* was immediately castigated as communist propaganda and criticized as simplistic (for instance by H. G. Wells), but over the years it has been recognized as a masterpiece of expressionist film—as a matter of fact, it was the very first film entered into UNESCO's Memory of the World Register. The film existed in many different cuts, and Lang's original three-hour version was lost until 2008. The original score is still available, but there is also a famous 1984 version produced by Giorgio Moroder with music by Adam Ant, Pat Benatar, Freddie Mercury, and others.

In *M—Eine Stadt sucht einen Mörder* (*M—A City Searches for a*

Murderer, 1931), an unnamed city that is clearly Berlin is terrorized by a serial killer of children. In the citizens' increasing anxiety, suspicion, and spying on each other, director Fritz Lang arguably portrays the political climate of the early 1930s and warns against the rise of the Nazis. Since the police prove unable to find the murderer, the *Ringvereine* (see pp.214–215) take matters into their own hands and capture the criminal through a network of beggars—raising questions about the rule of law and social action. In a macabre "trial" the murderer explains his actions through what can only be characterized as a trenchant analysis of modern alienation. He is saved from the lynch mob only to be sentenced to death in an official trial. According to at least one poll, *M* is the most important film in German cinematic history.

Kuhle Wampe (dialect for "empty belly") from 1932 begins with the suicide of a young man who has been unable to find work. His family is evicted from their apartment and moves to a tent colony on the outskirts of Berlin called Kuhle Wampe. The family's daughter and protagonist of the film, Anni, finds out she is pregnant, but breaks up with the baby's father, Fritz, when it turns out he was forced to offer to marry her. At a workers' festival, Anni and Fritz reunite, and on a train ride they have an intense discussion with (more wealthy) fellow passengers about the economy. (This scene was written by Bertolt Brecht.) *Kuhle Wampe* was banned almost immediately (partly because in the original version Anni was going to have an abortion), but soon released again (in an altered version) due to public pressure. On the one hand, the film is a scathing indictment of the Weimar Republic; on the other, it offers hope in the form of workers' solidarity.

The Nazis and Cinema

The Nazis' cinematic monument to Berlin is undoubtedly Leni Riefenstahl's *Olympia*, filmed to celebrate the 1936 Olympic Games. To an extent, the film is Nazi propaganda, glorifying the Aryan body, inciting mass hysteria (in the Olympic audiences), drawing parallels between sports and war, and, of course, showing Hitler, Göring, and Goebbels in a more than positive light. At the same time, *Olympia* is a huge aesthetic achievement, inventing new cinematic techniques like putting cameras on rails and filming under water. Towards the end of the film, a sequence showing divers practically flying through the air is the epitome of sports imagery. In addition, *Olympia* celebrates all athletes, including Jesse Owens, the African-American track star—and hardly a favorite of the Nazi regime. If nothing else, the film continues to raise questions about the relationship between aesthetics and politics.

More recently, the World War II era has been the subject of a series of moving or ridiculous contemporary movies. *Aimée and Jaguar* (1999) tells the true story of (Jewish) Felice and her love affair with (German) Lilly in 1943–44. Lilly is a mother of four whose husband is a soldier, while Felice has taken a false name (and signs her love letters as Jaguar) and works for the resistance—a fact she only discloses to Lilly under pressure. The rest of her resistance cell flees Germany, but in order to be with Lilly Felice stays in Berlin, where she is soon captured and sent to the concentration camp in Theresienstadt, where she dies. Audiences and critics were enthusiastic about *Aimée and Jaguar* both for its sensitive love story and its portrayal of wartime Berlin, and it won various prizes.

In contrast, *Valkyrie* (2008) was less successful. Starring Tom Cruise, the film told the story of the resistance movement around Claus Schenk Graf von Stauffenberg that tried to assassinate Hitler on 20 July 1944. Parts were shot in Berlin at the Bendlerblock (the site where Stauffenberg in turn was killed by the Nazis on 21 July), Tempelhof airport, and around the Funkturm. The film was controversial in Germany because of Cruise's membership of the Church of Scientology (officially designated a cult), because of its many historical inaccuracies, and because it was promoted as a mixture of *Mission Impossible* and *The Great Escape*. At least it was not as bad as *Inglourious Basterds* (2009), shot at the Babelsberg Studio outside Berlin, in which Quentin Tarantino develops an explicitly revisionist version of history in which a Jewish commando unit manages to assassinate the Nazi leadership in a Paris cinema.

Cold War and Reunification

Billy Wilder's comedy *One, Two, Three* (1961), which dramatizes the conflict between communism and capitalism, is a tribute to post-War but pre-Wall Berlin. C. P. MacNamara (James Cagney), Coca-Cola representative for West Berlin, wants to extend his operations to the East. W. P. Hazeltine, the anti-communist CEO of Coca-Cola in Atlanta, rejects the plan, but asks MacNamara to guide his daughter Scarlett around Berlin. Unfortunately, Scarlett falls in love with and marries the staunch communist Otto Ludwig Pfiffl (Horst Buchholz). MacNamara tries to drive the two apart, but relents when he learns Scarlett is pregnant. Pfiffl in turn "reforms" out of love for Scarlett and becomes Coca-Cola's head of operations for Europe. *One, Two, Three* was shot at a moment when hardly anybody could laugh at the Cold War—during filming the Wall went up, forcing the construction of a set of the Brandenburg Gate. Probably for the same reason, the film was not originally a success (in spite of the juxtaposition of the established US star Cagney and the up-and-coming German actor Buchholz), but more recently it has become a nostalgic favorite. The Coca-Cola office in Lichterfelde where parts of it were filmed still stands, though the building is now abandoned.

The Spy Who Came in from the Cold (1965), based on John Le Carré's spy novel, has a fiendishly complicated story that revolves around an MI6 plot to discredit an East German operative. Though not actually shot in Germany, much of the movie is set in Berlin, and the final climactic scene is supposed to be at the Wall between Potsdam and Berlin. More importantly, the film exposes the sordid underworld of espionage during the Cold War while also offering resonances of the more recent German past: one East German spy is a former Hitler Youth, his assistant a Jew. Again, a US-German team of actors (Richard Burton and Oskar Werner) contributed to the success of the film. Thereafter espionage and Berlin seemed to be inseparable: the film was followed by Len Deighton's *Funeral in Berlin* (1966) and *The Quiller Memorandum* (1966), inspired by a novel called *The Berlin Memorandum*. In the German production *Der Mann auf der Mauer* (*The Man on the Wall*, 1982), based on one of the episodes in Peter Schneider's *The Wall Jumper* (see pp.103–04), an

East German citizen lets himself be arrested for apparently political reasons in order to be extradited to the West. On the other side of the Wall, though, he realizes that he misses his wife (and life) and works for the Stasi so he can move between East and West at will. The film stars the German actor and singer Marius Müller-Westernhagen. More recently, the post-modern spy Jason Bourne, aka Matt Damon, visits Berlin in *The Bourne Supremacy* (2004). Scenes were shot all over Berlin at sites like Tegel airport, Alexanderplatz, Friedrichstrasse, Ostbahnhof train station, and Oberbaumbrücke. Finally, the spy drama *Covert Affairs* has an episode in Berlin, and parts of the finale of the television series *Chuck* (2006–11) about the eponymous accidental spy were set, though alas not filmed, in Berlin.

German films also dealt with Berlin's division during the Cold War, though without the drama of espionage. Arguably the best film about this period is Wim Wenders' *Wings of Desire* (1987), originally titled *Der Himmel über Berlin* (*Sky/Heaven above Berlin*). Here the angels Damiel (Bruno Ganz) and Cassiel (Otto Sander) wander through city observing the population and listening to their thoughts. In one remarkable scene, they spend time at the Staatsbibliothek near Potsdamer Platz, showcasing the subtle architecture of that building by Hans Scharoun and Edgar Wisniewski (see p.63). Since the two are invisible (except to children) and immaterial, Damiel and Cassiel can walk through the Wall and see both parts of Berlin. If the film is a reflection on the role of the past in the present, asserting that Berlin lives in the past, the disengaged angelic existence is also questioned when Damiel falls in love with a human and gives up his status as an angel to join her. In cinematic terms, the angels' perspective is in black and white, while the human point of view is in color, hinting that human interaction, as imperfect as it is, gives life its meaning. Wenders won the award for best director at the Cannes Film Festival for *Wings of Desire*, and the film regularly turns up on lists of the hundred best films of all times. Wenders shot a sequel titled *Faraway, So Close!* in 1993, which was not nearly as successful, but can boast an A-list of actors: apart from Sander and Ganz, the main roles are played by Nastassja Kinski and (a now more aged) Horst Buchholz, with supporting roles (or cameos) from the likes of William Dafoe, Peter Falk, Mikhail Gorbachev, Lou Reed, and the venerable German actor Heinz Rühmann in his last film at 91 years of age.

The legacy of the German Democratic Republic is explored in two completely different films. *Good Bye Lenin!* (2003) by German actor and director Wolfgang Becker is a comedy that lightly examines the transition from a socialist to a capitalist society. The middle-aged Christiane, a staunch supporter of the GDR, falls into a coma in the autumn of 1989. When she awakes after the fall of the Wall, the doctor says that any shock might kill her, so her son Alex tries to recreate the East within the four walls of their apartment. To that end, he hunts down old East German foods and champagne, cuts new versions of old newscasts and even dresses in old clothes. In one famous scene, a large Coca-Cola banner is hoisted outside Christiane's apartment—surely a reference to *One, Two, Three*—which Alex has to explain to his mother. Finally, Alex, his sister, and their friends enlighten Christiane, who dies shortly after. This film is probably best appreciated by Germans familiar with the cuisine, television, and fashions of East Germany, but the comedy translates into English as well—*Good Bye Lenin!* had a successful run in the UK and the US.

More seriously (though not necessarily more insightfully or engagingly), *The Lives of Others* (2006) deals with the East German regime's spying on its own citizens. Set in 1984, it follows the Stasi agent Wiesler as he stalks the playwright Dreyman, only to realize he has been told to spy on the dramatist to free Dreyman's girlfriend Sieland (who in turn collaborates with Wiesler) for the unwanted attentions of a government official. At the same time, the previously innocent Dreyman anonymously publishes an article on East German suicides in the West German magazine *Der Spiegel*, a highly punishable offense. Agent Wiesler discovers the authorship of the article, but conceals it from his superiors and is banished to a menial job. Dreyman meanwhile discovers that Sieland had informed on him, and she dies under ambiguous circumstances, either accidentally or by suicide. After reunification, Dreyman learns from his Stasi file that an agent had protected him and dedicates a novel to that agent. In the final scene, Wiesler is seen buying that very novel. Critical opinions about *The Lives of Others* differed. On the one hand, it won the Oscar for Best Foreign Film and a number of other awards, and most critics lauded director Florian Henckel von Donnersmarck's subtle portrayal of the characters. On the other hand, many former East Germans objected to a Stasi agent being made a hero, arguing that it amounted to a mystification of the past (and that no agent would actually have been able to do what Wiesler does in the film).

Perhaps the best portrayal of contemporary Berlin is in the thoughtful action movie *Run Lola Run* (1998) by director Tom Tykwer (of more recent *Cloud Atlas* fame) and starring Moritz Bleibtreu and Franka Potente (who is killed as Matt Damon's girlfriend early in *The Bourne Supremacy*). Manni (Bleibtreu) is a small-time crook who needs to find DM 100,000 quickly and is helped by his girlfriend Lola (Potente). What makes the film interesting is that there are three versions of the subsequent events depending on small decisions the characters make: in one version Lola dies; in another, Manni; and in the third there is a kind of happy ending. The three parts are connected by Manni and Lola lying in bed and musing on the nature of love and death. The title refers to Lola's frantic race through Berlin trying to find money for Manni. As most Berliners immediately recognized, Lola's route makes absolutely no sense: her apartment is on Albrechtstrasse in Mitte, she crosses the Oberbaumbrücke, runs along Friedrichstrasse, and somehow passes the Gendarmenmarkt along the way (and one scene is filmed in Schöneberg town hall). Nevertheless, the movie was a huge critical and commercial success in Germany and abroad and inspired homage from *The Simpsons*, Bon Jovi, *Buffy*, and others.

In the new millennium Berlin is once again becoming a destination both to set and to film movies. In *Unknown* (2011) Liam Neeson plays an operative who loses his memory in a crash on the Oberbaumbrücke. Of course, Berliners wonder why a knowledgeable taxi driver would take that bridge on the way from Unter den Linden to Tegel airport, but that hardly detracts from the fun of the action movie. In *Hanna* (2011) a teenage assassin escapes to Berlin, where the climactic scene is set, and was filmed in, the abandoned Spreepark amusement park. Several sections of the Bollywood block-buster *Don 2* (2011) with superstar Shah Rukh Khan were shot at locations such as the Brandenburg Gate and the Olympic Stadium, suggesting that Berlin is now definitely on the international map for artists and filmmakers around the world.

7 | Leisure and Pleasure
Popular Culture and Pastimes

The best places to get an aerial view of Berlin (without boarding an airplane) are the TV Tower on Alexanderplatz and the Radio Tower in Charlottenburg. Built in the 1960s, the TV Tower (Fernsehturm) was originally 365 meters (1,200 feet) high, a number supposedly chosen for its memorability. A further ten feet were recently added in renovations, and the tower remains the fourth-highest man-made structure in Europe. It was a prestige project meant to demonstrate East German technological prowess, but ironically it also offered East Berliners one of few remaining views of West Berlin. The first 650 feet comprise a slowly narrowing shaft made of reinforced concrete; the top one hundred take the form of a red and white steel antenna. In between is a 105-foot sphere with seven stories, two of which are accessible to the public. Because of its central location the viewing platform offers amazing urban vistas in all directions. The same views, which almost make Alexanderplatz seem like the beating heart of the city, can be enjoyed with a meal in the revolving restaurant above. This restaurant used to complete a revolution every hour, but recently it was sped up to turn around in thirty minutes, with no spilled drinks so far reported as a consequence. The outside of the sphere is covered with 140 steel panels, which in one blueprint were supposed to be lit in red at night to demonstrate the victory of socialism. Instead, when the sun shines on the panels the reflection creates a cross, which Berliners have dubbed "God's revenge" (against the atheist GDR). For the World Cup in 2006, the sphere was decorated to look like a football.

The TV Tower's counterpart in the West is the Radio Tower (Funkturm). Constructed in the 1920s, this tower is not particularly high by modern standards (c.500 feet), but the height is remarkable considering that the footprint of its base is only 65 x 65 feet. Because

View east from the Radio Tower (Funkturm) towards the TV Tower (Fernsehturm), with the Berliner Dom (cathedral) and the Rotes Rathause (city hall) to the right of the TV Tower and the Tiergarten in front of it. (Rosannaflieder/Wikimedia Commons)

(*top*) Spree with view of Reichstag (Arnoldius/Wikimedia Commons); (*left*) Spree separating at north end of Spreeinsel around Bode-Museum, with view of TV Tower (flickr.com/photos/dalbera); (*right*) *Molecule Man* (1999) by Jonathan Borofsky arising out of the Spree (Avda/Wikimedia Commons)

Hallesche-Tor-Brücke over the Landwehrkanal, with statues of Fishing (left) and River Traffic (right) (cc-by-sa/Wikimedia Commons)

Strandbad Wannsee (lido) with *Strandkörbe* (beach baskets) (t-stern/Wikimedia Commons)

View of the Havel from the Grunewaldturm (A.Savin/Wikimedia Commons)

Unter den Linden with Berliner Dom (cathedral) in the foreground, opera (left), and armory (right) opposite each other at the bend, and Brandenburg Gate and Tiergarten in the background (cc-by-sa-2.0/Wikimedia Commons)

Reconstruction of part of the *Akzisemauer* (Excise Wall) in the Stresemannstrasse in Kreuzberg (Wikimedia Commons)

(*top*) Opera on Unter den Linden, c. 1903 (Library of Congress, Washington DC); (*left*) the two parts of the Jewish Museum: the Kollegienhaus (1734–35) and the Libeskind structure (1992–99) (Wikimedia Commons); (*above*) Kollegienhaus (Josep Renalias/ Wikimedia Commons)

Opposite page:
(*top*) Gendarmenmarkt with (from left to right) Deutscher Dom (church), Schauspielhaus (theater), and Französischer Dom (Jhintzbe/Wikimedia Commons); (*middle*) Rotes Rathaus (city hall) (Kolossos/ Wikimedia Commons); (*bottom*) Martin-Gropius-Bau (Jensens/Wikimedia Commons)

(*above*) Berliner Dom (cathedral)
(Weinandt/Wikimedia Commons)

(*right*) Courtyard in Riehmers
Hofgarten (GraceKelly/
Wikimedia Commons)

(*left*) *Schwerbelastungskörper*
(Assenmacher/Wikimedia Commons)

(*top*) Olympic Stadium (1934–36) (Marcel Schoenhardt/Wikimedia Commons); (*right*) Philharmonie (concert hall, 1960–63) (Manfred Brückels/Wikimedia Commons); (*below*) Potsdamer Platz (1996–2001) with (from left to right) Kohlhoff-Tower (brown building), Sony Center, Beisheim Center (two parts), and replica of Berlin's first traffic light in the middle ground (Mihael Grmek/Wikimedia Commons)

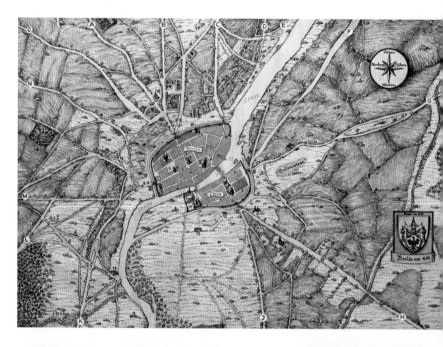

(*top*) Berlin-Cölln around 1600 (h.f. ullmann);
(*above*) Statue of Friedrich Wilhelm I (the Great
Elector) in front of Schloss Charlottenburg (Morn
the Gorn/Wikimedia Commons); (*right*) *Lange
Kerls* (1737) by Georg Lisiewski
(anagoria/Wikimedia Commons)

(*above*) *Napoleon in Berlin* (1810) by Charles Meynier, coming into the city via the Brandenburg Gate (PD-Art/Wikimedia Commons)

(*above*) *Proclamation of the German Empire* (1885) by Anton von Werner, with Emperor Wilhelm I on the dais and politician Otto von Bismarck in white uniform (Museen Nord/Bismarck Museum)

(*right*) *Emperor Wilhelm II* (1890) by Max Koner (Wikimedia Commons)

(*top*) Bill with denomination of one trillion mark (German *Billion* equals American English one trillion) during inflation in 1923; (*above left*) Ruin of old Kaiser-Wilhelm-Gedächtniskirche, aka "Hollow Tooth," with tower of new church (GerardM/Wikimedia Commons); (*above right*) Poster for Olympic Games by Franz Würbel, with stylized athlete and silhouette of Quadriga on Brandenburg Gate (Cambridge University Library)

(*above*) Berlin Wall looking east, with anti-Western slogan (on the Western side!) and view of border fortification (Edward Valachovic/Wikimedia Commons); (*inset right*) Climbing the Berlin Wall in November 1989 (Sue Ream/Wikimedia Commons); (*below*) Reichstag, looking towards the TV Tower (Thomas Wolf/Wikimedia Commons)

(*right*) *Gotthold Ephraim Lessing and Johann Caspar Lavater Visiting Moses Mendelssohn* (1856) by Moritz Daniel Oppenheim, with wife Fromet Mendelssohn in the background;
(*below*) *Heinrich von Kleist* (1801) by Peter Friedel;
(*bottom left*) *Theodor Fontane* (1883) by Carl Breitbach; (*bottom right*) Cover for Rainer Werner Fassbinder's 15-part movie version of *Berlin Alexanderplatz*

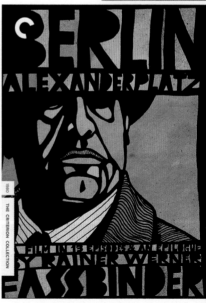

(*above*) *View from the Kreuzberg* (1829) by Johann Heinrich Hintze, with Schinkel's monument in the left foreground (Wolfgang Ribbe/Wikimedia Commons)

(*left*) *The Supper at the Ball* (1878) by Adolph Menzel (Google Art Project/Wikimedia Commons)

(*right*) *Berlin Beach Life* (1901) by Heinrich Zille (Privatbesitz, Berlin/Wikimedia Commons)

(*top*) Pergamon Temple at the Pergamonmuseum (Jan Mehlich/Wikimedia Commons); (*middle*) Fans of Hertha BSC in the Olympic Stadium's east curve (Willy 1961/ Wikimedia Commons); (*above*) Example of guerrilla gardening (Flittergreeze/Wikimedia Commons); (*right*) Polar bear Knut shaking off water (Benjamin Janecke/ Wikimedia Commons)

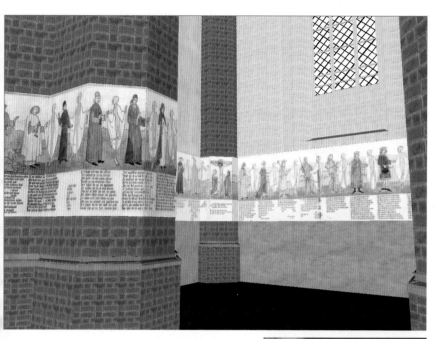

(*top*) Recreation of 15th-century death dance fresco in the Marienkirche (Martin Klitscher/Wikimedia Commons); (*right*) Reconstructed Neue Synagoge (Beek 100/Wikimedia Commons); (*below*) Headquarters of Axel Springer AG (Beek 100/Wikimedia Commons); (*bottom right*) Ampelmännchen (ANKAWÜ/Wikimedia Commons)

(*above*) Oranienburg Castle in Oranienburg north of Berlin (Avda/Wikimedia Commons); (*bottom left*) Steintorturm (tower in medieval wall) in Brandenburg (Avda/Wikimedia Commons); (*bottom right*) Infamous Potsdam windmill c.1900 (Library of Congress, Washington DC)

(*above*) Caryatids (female figures providing architectural support) on Frederick the Great's palace of Sanssouci ("without care") (Suse/ Wikimedia Commons)

of these proportions and because the construction is steel framework with just the elevator and staircase at the center, the tower, like the Eiffel Tower in Paris, seems slender, almost ready to lift off the ground. There is a restaurant at 180 feet and a platform at about 400 feet with excellent views of the Grunewald and the Avus highway to the west and southwest, the Olympic Stadium to the northwest, and towards the Siegessäule (and of course the TV Tower) to the east. From here, it is impossible not to recognize how green a city Berlin remains. The Radio Tower is situated within a huge exhibition center (where the first German radio exhibition was held in 1924) and across the street from the House of Broadcasting (Haus des Rundfunks), where radio shows were produced starting in 1931. Nowadays the tower is primarily a mobile phone relay station.

After an overview of Berlin from one of these structures, it is time to dive into the pleasures of the city. According to Spiegel TV, there are precisely 4,324 sights in Berlin and some 1,500 events every day. Yet what one person enjoys, another may abhor, so you have to choose your own favorites among the unending parade of options to fill your leisure time in Berlin. Leisure is taken and pleasure pursued inside and outside, with high and popular culture, in intimate and crowd settings, among other human beings and among animals, in the built environment and in nature, during the hot as well as cold times of the year, in (stereo-)typically German ways and in new cosmopolitan avenues.

Museumsinsel

The most popular museums in Berlin are at the Kulturforum near Potsdamer Platz and on the Museumsinsel in the Spree. The institutions on the museum island in former East Berlin were started in cooperation between the architect Karl Friedrich Schinkel and the scholar Wilhelm von Humboldt. Describing the island is difficult because on the one hand there are large buildings with their own names, but on the other hand sometimes several museums within one building. The Altes Museum, Berlin's oldest public museum, was built in 1830, followed by the Royal Prussian Museum (today Neues Museum, in comparison with the Altes Museum) in 1859. The

Nationalgalerie (1876, now Alte Nationalgalerie as opposed to the Neue Nationalgalerie at the Kulturforum), Kaiser-Friedrich-Museum (1904, renamed Bode-Museum after a director of the museums, Wilhelm von Bode, in 1956), and the Pergamonmuseum (1930, common name for the Deutsches Museum, Antikenmuseum, Vorderasiatisches Museum, and Islamische Kunst-Abteilung since 1958) completed the ensemble.

All five museums have been continually renovated and re-arranged since reunification. For one thing, the collections that had been separated in the war (either when the Nazis moved them for safekeeping or through looting by the various occupiers) were re-united. Museums in East and West Berlin were already excellent, but with their forces combined the museums on the Museumsinsel are world-class. For another, the buildings had suffered in the war and were not exactly renovated up to international standards during the period of the GDR. For that reason, a master plan was developed that seems to have reached a conclusion for now—until the next renovation.

The Altes Museum and the Pergamonmuseum are the most popular, with over a million visitors per year. This means that it might sometimes be difficult to view a popular object, but the museums are so large that spectacular alternatives are always available. The Altes Museum displays art and material culture from ancient Greece and Rome, including non-dominant cultures in those areas such as the Cycladic civilization and the Etruscans. The Pergamonmuseum is thus named because it was basically designed around a partial re-construction of a second-century temple from the city of Pergamon in Asia Minor. Since this is a reconstruction, visitors can climb the huge structure to experience the architecture and walk along the frieze to inspect every detail. Similarly, the museum has large Roman-style market gate from the Asia Minor city of Miletus (about the same time as the Pergamon temple), excavated in the late nineteenth and early twentieth centuries by German archeologists, and a reconstruction of the massive Ishtar Gate, one of the entrances to the ancient city of Babylon in the sixth century BCE. These three items alone make the Pergamonmuseum a highlight of any visit to

Berlin. Of course, there have been discussions about repatriating these exhibits to Turkey and Iraq, but in contrast to other European powers the Germans usually negotiated the removal of objects to Berlin instead of simply stealing them, so the Pergamon temple, the Miletus market gate, and the Ishtar Gate will probably stay in Berlin in perpetuity.

The other three museums on the Museumsinsel are not quite as well visited, but no less impressive. The Neues Museum is home to the former Ägyptisches (Egyptian) Museum, where the world-famous bust of Queen Nefertiti is on display, and also houses the Museum für Vor- und Frühgeschichte (prehistory and early history) with replicas of the so-called Priam's Treasure from Troy, which disappeared from Berlin in 1945 and turned up in Moscow in 1993. The return of the originals is under negotiation: Russia agreed in principle to send the items back, but some officials consider the treasure compensation for destruction visited on museums and cities in Russia during World War II. The Bode-Museum displays mostly Byzantine art and coins from all over the world, while the Alte Nationalgalerie focuses on nineteenth-century visual arts, especially painting and sculpture.

Kulturforum

The Neue Nationalgalerie, a spectacular modernist structure by Mies van der Rohe built between 1965 and 1968, is located in the Kulturforum off Potsdamer Strasse in former West Berlin. Here, the government tried to build a counterweight to the Museumsinsel, which was inaccessible (or at least very difficult to visit) in East Berlin. The Kulturforum includes the Philharmonie (see p.62) and the smaller Kammermusiksaal and integrates the older St. Matthäuskirche. In addition to five museums (see below), the Staatsbibliothek (national library) across the street completes the Kulturforum. The ensemble is architecturally much less unified than the Museumsinsel, which—depending on your personal taste—is a drawback or a benefit. The Philharmonie and Staatsbibliothek were beautifully designed by the Berlin architects Hans Scharoun and Edgar Wisniewski, but have nothing in common with the museums next door. The Neue Nationalgalerie is an imposing building on its own, but seems to clash with both the nineteenth-century church and Scharoun's buildings.

Today, the Neue Nationalgalerie focuses on twentieth-century art, especially pre-1970. Cubists, expressionists, and surrealists from Picasso to Miró and Magritte to Kandinsky form the collection, only a small part of which can be exhibited at any one time. The Gemäldegalerie next door holds European paintings from Germany, the Netherlands, Italy, Spain, France, and England from the thirteenth to the eighteenth centuries by famous artists such as Dürer, the Breughels, Rembrandt, Velázquez, Gainsborough, and Angelika Kaufmann. A controversy erupted in 2012 when donors of contemporary art more or less demanded that their collections be displayed in the Gemäldegalerie, which meant that the earlier paintings would have to be removed. So far, the Berlin museum services have not found a satisfactory solution to this problem.

The Kupferstichkabinett at the Kulturform is a museum of prints and drawings with over 600,000 items from the Middle Ages to the present, while the Kunstgewerbemuseum (Museum of Decorative Arts) has objects of material culture (and art) such as gold and silver, porcelain and enamel, furniture, textiles, and tapestries. Founded in 1868, the museum was housed in the Martin-Gropius-Bau in the late nineteenth century, divided during the Cold War, and moved to the Kulturforum in 1978—some reunification still needs to happen here. Finally, the Musikinstrumenten-Museum, built in the style of the Philharmonie by Scharoun's student and partner Edgar Wisniewski from 1979, is a museum of musical instruments designed around a giant theater organ, the 1929 Mighty Wurlitzer with 1,228 pipes, over 200 registers, and a four-level keyboard. Visitors can hear the organ with guided tours or accompanying silent films in special events.

Museums for Everything

Outside the Museumsinsel and the Kulturforum, the most famous museums in Berlin are to be found either on Unter den Linden or in the southern district of Dahlem. A group of museums in Dahlem was conceived by the museum director Bode, but not built until 1969. The location of the museums in a mostly residential area far from the center of West Berlin may seem odd, but it made sense in a Cold War context and as an attempt to decentralize the city. The buildings themselves are in the architectural style of New Objectivity and offer a pleasing alternative to the villas (and the Free University) in the vicinity. Two museums are currently open in Dahlem: the Museum für Asiatische Kunst (Asian art) and the Ethnologisches Museum. The latter is highly original: the collection of American Indian artefacts, assembled by Prince Maximilian zu Wied-Neuwied in the 1830s, is one of the earliest and most extensive of such collections in the world, and the full-size reconstructions of South Sea boats are used by children as jungle gyms.

Unfortunately, it seems the museums in Dahlem will not exist much longer. After reunification, a small but influential group of individuals decided it would be a good idea to tear down the East German parliament on Unter den Linden and rebuild the Hohenzollern castle it had replaced. There was no point in simply reconstructing a palace with nothing in it, however, so it was decided to move all museums concerned with non-European cultures into the structure and rename it the Humboldtforum. In other words, Dahlem will lose its exhibitions—but the initiators of the Humboldtforum have offered no convincing plans for Dahlem.

Across from the future Humboldtforum is the Deutsches Historisches Museum, Berlin's main museum for German history. In East German times, this museum was stringently organized around the march towards socialism, so at least there was no doubt over what events meant. Today, the curators have more difficulty balancing the unpleasant (to say the least) aspects of Germany's past with more positive exhibits. Ironically, the museum is in a baroque armory, the oldest building on Unter den Linden. On the other hand, the inner courtyard is decorated by 22 heads of dying warriors by Andreas Schlüter, and the expressions on some of their faces can only be understood as a condemnation of war. Since the armory ultimately proved too small to accommodate the museum's collection, a remarkable extension was built at the back by the Chinese-American architect Ieoh Ming Pei. This structure, accessible from the main building through an underground tunnel, has many glass fronts to make the construction of German history inside the museum as transparent as possible.

In addition to these weighty museums, there are plenty of others that can be more lighthearted (even if their subjects are more or less serious). The Beate Uhse Erotik-Museum recognizes the importance of sex and sexuality in over 5,000 exhibits. The Schwules Museum in Kreuzberg has a permanent exhibition, changing galleries, and an archive on the history of homosexuality since the late eighteenth century. The MACHmit! Museum für Kinder in a former church in Prenzlauer Berg encourages children to "PARTicipate!" in learning and history, while the Jugendmuseum in a former villa in Schöneberg has exhibitions, workshops, internships, and even a printing press for young adults. Adults who have stayed young(-ish) can visit the Ramones Museum, the only museum in the world dedicated to that rock band. Celebrating one of Berlin's contributions to world cuisine, the Currywurst Museum opened in 2009. Financed by private sponsors to the tune of over €5 million, this gem of a museum entertainingly and intelligently explores the ingredients and history of the sausage, *Imbiss* (local food stand), and fast food culture, as well as representations of the *Currywurst* in movies and television. Of course, there is a snack shop.

Sporting Berlin

But for those who would rather enjoy their leisure outside, Berlin has plenty to offer as well. Germany's national sport is soccer, so of course there are many fans in Berlin. Soccer is played on every available green space by amateurs (though now unfortunately it is banned in front of the Reichstag), and of course professionally. The city's most popular team is Hertha BSC (Berliner Sport Club), which was established in 1892. The story goes that the club was founded, or at least that the founders decided to establish the club, on a local pleasure boat called *Hertha*. (The boat's blue and white paint apparently gave the team its colors. Amazingly, the boat is still in business, though no longer in Berlin.) The club's name is, in fact, slightly bizarre: Hertha is considered an old lady's name, and to this day Hertha BSC is known as *die alte Dame*. The club had its biggest successes back in the early 1930s, when it won the German championship twice in a row. At this time, the team played at the Plumpe stadium in the northern working-class district of Wedding.

Daniel Koerfer has analyzed Hertha's behavior during the Nazi period in *Hertha unter dem Hakenkreuz* (*Hertha under the Swastika*) and has come to the conclusion that the club was neither particularly pro-Nazi nor a hotbed of resistance. On the one hand, Hertha did not object when the Jewish team doctor Hermann Horwitz was systematically stripped of his dignity, profession, and possessions and ultimately deported to the Auschwitz concentration camp, where he died. On the other, the club offered a contract to a young Dutch forward who had been brought to Berlin in 1942 as a forced factory worker. By changing his name from the Jewish-sounding Abraham to Bram Appel, the club helped him survive the war—an unlikely outcome for a forced laborer. It could be argued that Hertha put Nazis in leadership positions in the late 1930s and early 1940s—but it is also true that the club was mostly run by Wilhelm Wernicke, a union activist and social democrat and hence opposed to the Nazis. The Nazis certainly used Hertha's games to distract the Berlin population from the war, but Hertha also used its position to support members of the club who were fighting at the front and to create an alternative form of solidarity.

Hertha's fortunes in more recent years have been very much up and down. Since 1963 home games have been played at the (Nazi) Olympic Stadium, which now seats about 75,000 spectators. In the 1980s the club was briefly relegated to the third division and had to play amateur soccer. In the late 1990s and early 2000s, Hertha finished several seasons in a row between third and sixth in the Bundesliga, the German first division—but could never win the championship. Since 2010 Hertha has been yo-yoing between the Bundesliga and the second division.

Hertha is not Berlin's only soccer club. Some Berliners consider Hertha's fans to be racist and anti-Semitic and therefore support Tennis Borussia, who play in purple shirts. TeBe was in the

Bundesliga in the 1970s, but now plays in the sixth division made up of various teams from Berlin. The most successful team from the East is Union Berlin, which enjoyed success in the late 1970s and a fluke participation in the European Cup in 2001, but currently plays in the (respectable) second division. Former East Berlin club BFC Dynamo was supported by the Stasi secret police (and was supposedly Erich Honecker's favorite club), so its ten consecutive championships between 1979 and 1988 are considered somewhat suspect. Now playing in the fifth division, Dynamo has a strong fan base—but these fans are unfortunately best known for their violent behavior. Türkiyemspor Berlin, founded in 1978 and now also playing in the sixth division, has a high number of Turkish-German players, but support from all over Berlin. In 1988, when both Hertha and Türkiyemspor played in the third division, 12,000 Berliners came to watch the match.

As dominant as it is, soccer is not the only sport in Berlin. With globalization, basketball has become more popular. Berlin's basketball team is Alba Berlin, which has an albatross as its mascot but is actually named after its sponsor, the waste disposal and recycling company Alba. Founded only in 1991 (integrating some pre-existing teams), Alba was soon successful and won the German championship six times in a row between 1997 and 2003 (and again in 2008). At the European level, Alba has fared less well, but that has not kept fans away: with an average crowd of over 10,000 per game, this is the most popular basketball team in Germany. Since 2008 Alba has played home ties at O2 World (see below).

Perhaps surprisingly, (ice) hockey seems to be even more popular, and Berlin's main team also plays at O2 World in front of an average of 14,000 spectators (2010–11). Renamed EHC Eisbären Berlin (polar bears) in 1992, the team has its roots in the East German team SC Dynamo Berlin. Today the Eisbären belong to the US-American Anschutz Entertainment Group, who also own the NHL team Los Angeles Kings and the soccer team Los Angeles Galaxy, and run O2 World in Berlin as well as Staples Center and Home Depot Center in Los Angeles. The Eisbären have been extremely successful, winning the German championship in 2005,

2006, 2008, 2009, 2011, and 2012. After being dominated by foreigners (especially Canadians) for a long time, over half of the Eisbären squad is now German.

Events

As the large attendances at soccer, basketball, and hockey matches suggests, major events are popular in Berlin. As a matter of fact, some locals (like my mother) claim that all it takes to make a project successful in Berlin is to declare it an event. Some events take place regularly, others are one-offs.

The *ur*-event in Berlin (after the disgrace of Nazi events, anyway) was probably Ernst Reuter's speech during the Berlin Airlift in 1948, when he made his famous appeal to the outside world not to abandon blockaded Berlin (see pp.81–82) in front of about 300,000 Berliners. John F. Kennedy's "Ich bin ein Berliner" speech to 450,000 on 26 June 1963 belongs in the same category. (Kennedy was not saying, "I am a jelly doughnut," as he would have if he had given the speech elsewhere in Germany; in Berlin a jelly doughnut is a *Pfannkuchen*.) In 2008 Barack Obama had the largest audience of his entire campaign when he spoke to 200,000 at the Siegessäule (Victory Column). In his speech he quoted Reuter and implored Germans and Americans to keep working together.

In less political terms, the seminal event involved fifteen tons of fireworks, accompanied by a sound installation, that the Austrian artist André Heller set off in 1984 on the West side of the Reichstag, apparently with about 500,000 Berliners in attendance. The performance invoked the spectacle of war, alluded to the burning of the Reichstag, quoted an anti-war poem by Bertolt Brecht, and ended with a peace dove ascending to the tune of Handel's *Messiah*. A few years later, Heller put on a similar performance at the (then unused) Tempelhof airport—my own first mega-event. For obvious reasons, Roger Waters' concert "The Wall" in 1990 had a large impact as well. Staged in the no-man's-land between the Brandenburg Gate and Potsdamer Platz, Waters and guest artists played Pink Floyd's twenty-year-old album to an audience of nearly half a million. In the course of the performance, a wall was erected and torn down.

In 1995 the French artists Christo and Jeanne-Claude took advantage of a brief interlude before the Reichstag was renovated and turned back into Germany's parliament: they finally implemented a project they had planned for over twenty years, wrapping the building in over one million square feet of a shimmering aluminum-colored propylene fabric, tied up with some 50,000 feet of blue rope. The wrapping took one week (17–24 June), and the Reichstag remained wrapped for two more (24 June–7 July). During this time, the site turned into a giant meeting place that attracted around five million visitors. Critics (including German chancellor Helmut Kohl) worried that the wrapping would make the building look ridiculous, but most observers instead found the artwork added to the parliament's mystique. Personally, I loved just sitting and watching the fabric change color with the sun. When the wrapping was finally taken down, it was cut into tiny squares that were given away—I still keep a little piece among my treasured mementoes.

Events in recent times have rarely found audiences this large, partly because spaces are harder to find, partly out of security concerns, and partly because events are spread out over longer periods of time. Special exhibitions at museums are sold out months in advance, Berliners enjoy the Lange Nacht der Museen when museums stay open late into the night, and visitors flock to embassies across the city when they open to the public for a day. There are annual exhibitions and festivals—like the Internationale Funkausstellung radio exhibition (since 1924), agricultural show Grüne Woche (since 1926), and the International Film Festival (since 1951)—that attract hundreds of thousands of visitors, but over the week or ten days of the events. Perhaps closest to the earlier mega-events is the Fanmeile (fan mile), which was erected between the Brandenburg Gate and the Siegessäule to allow crowds to watch European and world championship soccer matches on huge screens. Approximately 900,000 fans (presumably not just Berliners) came to watch the German team lose the World Cup semi-final to Italy 0-2 on 4 July 2006 and win the match for third place against Portugal 3-1 four days later. The Fanmeile is revived every two years, but is no longer quite as popular.

Some interesting events were put on to celebrate the twentieth anniversary of the opening of the Wall in 2009. For *Riesen in Berlin*, a French theater troupe marched two marionettes 24 and 49 feet high (with a shoe size of 237) through the city for four days. According to the (somewhat incoherent) story constructed by the French, the two giants were separated by monsters. When the younger giant awakes, she finds and decides to deliver letters between the two halves of separated Berlin. Apparently, some two million Berliners watched the spectacle in Mitte, Tiergarten, and on the Spree. In a similarly spectacular event, 15,000 individuals, including artists from all over the world, created 1,000 eight-foot Styrofoam dominoes that were set up along where the Wall used to stand. During the Festival of Freedom on 9 November 2009, these dominoes were dramatically upset, bringing down the (symbolic) Wall once again. Some critics were unhappy with the often light-hearted decorations of the dominoes, which supposedly failed to reflect the serious nature of the occasion, but the event was a success and is documented in many videos and a coffee-table book. Critics were probably even less pleased on 7 April 2012, when 1,000 Berliners congregated at the Brandenburg Gate for a huge pillow fight.

While the fall of the Wall happened only once (though, of course, it will be commemorated for a long time), other events occur on a regular basis. From 1989 to 2006, the Love Parade was less a celebration of anything in particular than a huge open-air dance party and rave for hedonists, and perhaps not so much for Berliners as for young people who came to Berlin from all over Europe. In 1999 there were supposedly 1.5 million visitors at the parade, and even in 2006 there were still 500,000. By that time, the city government had decided that the event was more trouble than it was worth—what with sex in the streets, rubbish to clean up for days, and transport chaos before and after—and no longer issued permits. More successfully, Berliners have been celebrating lesbian, gay, bisexual, and transgender pride with Christopher Street Day every June since 1979 (500,000 attended in 2011), and cultures from all over the world with the Karneval der Kulturen in Kreuzberg every year around Pentecost since 1995. In 2011 some 750,000 Berliners watched a parade of 100 groups with 4,700 participants from 70 nations. Another popular event since 2004 has been the Festival of Lights. For several weeks in October, landmarks such as the Berlin Dom (cathedral), the Siegessäule, the Brandenburg Gate, the Haus der Kulturen der Welt (see below), and even the KaDeWe department store are illuminated every evening with colored lights and other visual installations.

Concerts

More prosaically, concerts and other performances in Berlin are staged at O2 World, the Waldbühne, Friedrichstadt-Palast, Tempodrom, and Haus der Kulturen der Welt. O2 World was opened right off the Spree in Friedrichshain on the grounds of a former freight terminal in 2008. The construction was controversial because one of the few remaining parts of the Wall had to be moved to make way for a boat landing, and residents in the area were worried that the venue would bring with it traffic and gentrification. It remains unknown how much money the telecommunications company O2 paid for the naming rights and sponsorship. Still, the building itself with a high glass front below a blue wave-shaped top (perhaps meant to evoke a ship on the river), illuminated from within, is spectacular. Recent events have been as diverse as basketball and hockey games, Coldplay, George Michael, Rammstein, Jean-Michel Jarre, Iron Maiden (which I attended), and an "80s night"—in front of up to 17,000 spectators.

The Waldbühne (forest stage) has a much longer history than O2 World. This open-air amphitheater was built in 1936 as part of the Olympic Park in a ravine on the northern edge of the Grunewald forest, so the stage is framed by beautiful trees and scenery. After World War II the stage was used for films, sports, and music. In 1965 the Waldbühne was vandalized after a Rolling Stones concert which the audience felt was too short, only restored seven years later, and even then rarely used for fear of more riots. In 1982 the venue was reopened with a new tent structure over the stage (the audience remains vulnerable to the elements) and soon became a Berlin favorite (personally, I saw Paul Simon and Bruce Springsteen there). For many years, there were regular events such as a showing of the *Rocky Horror Picture Show* to more than 20,000 filmgoers—but then the stage and audience area were left covered in flour, dust, rice, and toast. Events today (usually put on from April through September) are more sedate, like the annual performance of the Berlin Philharmonic Orchestra, which traditionally ends with a rousing rendition of the early twentieth-century local hit, "Das ist die Berliner Luft" ("That's the Berlin Air"). It is difficult to get to the Waldbühne (parking is a nightmare and public transportation requires changing trains and buses), but well worth the effort—many Berliners take picnics and make a day of any concert.

The history of the variety theater Friedrichstadt-Palast goes even further back, though with a different building. Slightly north of the Spree, a covered market was built from 1865, converted into a circus in 1873, and turned into a stage permanently in 1918. In 1980 this building was torn down due to structural flaws, but another Friedrichstadt-Palast was built in 1984 closer to the Friedrichstrasse station. This new venue with about 1,900 seats has its own children's theater group and dance company (who claim to have the longest kickline in the world) and often hosts shows live on television.

The Tempodrom started out in tents in the Tiergarten in 1981. The new Tempodrom, opened west of Potsdamer Platz on the former Anhalter Bahnhof in 2001, combines three venues. The largest structure (with 3,800 seats) is reminiscent of a tent (and Oscar Niemeyer's famous cathedral in Brasilia), but is actually made of stainless steel. For many years, the Tempodrom was Berlin's premier site for world music. In 2010 it went bankrupt, but the new owners seem to be continuing the tradition, while also including more traditional entertainment. The Haus der Kulturen der Welt in the Kongresshalle in the Tiergarten is even more explicitly a venue for performances and workshops from cultures all over the world, though more along artistic than popular lines.

Pools, Zoos, and Bars

Especially in the summer, Berliners enjoy being outside. There are 26 official open-air pools and swimming beaches in Berlin, from the pool at the Olympic Stadium to the shores of the Wannsee and the Badeschiff in the Spree. As a matter of fact, on a beautiful summer weekend day it is sometimes impossible to find a spot to put down a towel unless you arrive quite early. The different sites are often occupied by different and distinct groups, and occasionally fights will break out over conflicting attitudes to behavior, but generally everyone is welcome. As usual in urban swimming places, the idea is not necessarily to exercise, but to get a tan, have an ice cream, or see and be seen.

Other outside venues popular among Berliners are the two zoos—technically two parts of the same zoo. Zoologischer Garten at the western end of the Tiergarten was opened in 1841 as Germany's first zoo, and many of the zoo's buildings from this period are architecturally remarkable in their own right. In 1913 an aquarium was added next door—right across from the Kaiser-Wilhelm-Gedächtniskirche. Almost all of the animals were killed during World War II, but the zoo was subsequently revived by visionary directors. Today, the Zoologischer Garten is Germany's only zoo with a panda bear, and there are some 15,000 animals of almost 1,500 species in appropriate cages or enclosures. Many of the animals receive typically Berliner names or nicknames, like the hippopotamus Bulette and the gorilla Knorke.

One of the zoo's most popular animals, the polar bear Knut, was born in 2006—the first polar bear to be born at the zoo in thirty years. For some reason, Knut caught Berlin's imagination, perhaps because he was raised by zookeeper Thomas Dörflein when Knut's parents rejected him. Numbers of visitors shot up, the press reported regularly, and Knut souvenirs were ubiquitous (including an official stamp). Unfortunately, the story did not have a happy ending: Dörflein (who had been voted most popular Berliner in 2007) had a fatal heart attack in 2008, and Knut died of a brain tumor in 2011.

The other part of the zoo, the Tierpark, was founded in East Berlin in 1954 because the Zoologischer Garten was in the western part of the city. The Tierpark incorporated the Friedrichsfelde stately home, its grounds (which were originally designed by the landscape architect Peter Joseph Lenné), and its cemetery. A 200-foot-high hill made of rubble from the nearby road is also part of the zoo, which has about 7,500 animals in 900 species. Every year, the zoo receives around one million visitors.

Berliners also just like to sit around with a beer (or a *Berliner Weisse*, a weak beer usually mixed with a shot of raspberry or woodruff syrup), which they do in private and public settings, inside and outside. The bar scene changes so rapidly that any attempt to name fashionable haunts would be futile, but some *Kneipen* have demonstrated real staying power: Zur letzten Instanz in Mitte has been around since 1621, the Alte Kolkschenke in Spandau since about 1750, and E. & M. Leydicke in Schöneberg at least since 1877. There are any number of odd establishments, like the toilet-themed and self-styled "adventure pub" Klo, which sports (clean) toilet brushes hanging from the ceiling and urine bottles as glasses. My favorite outside bars (which many Berliners enjoy in temperatures others might consider prohibitive) include Golgatha on the Kreuzberg (mountain) in Kreuzberg (the district), the more staid Café am Neuen See in the Tiergarten, or the Pratergarten in Prenzlauer Berg, Berlin's oldest beer garden founded in 1837. The Bundespressestrand on the Spree near Hauptbahnhof is ironically named Federal Press Beach because members of the press relax here from their onerous jobs across the river. The bar/restaurant has created a fake beach, complete with sand, pools, beach chairs, and beach volleyball, to give Berliners the illusion of being at the seaside in the middle of the city. While the Bundespressestrand is fairly high-class (offering specially designed event-zones for the solvent customer), other bars along the river are more down-to-earth, like the Freischwimmer and the Schleusenkrug (see p.10).

When they are not in bars, Berliners stereotypically also like to barbeque in public places, a tradition possibly introduced by the Turkish population, who were used to a more outside lifestyle. Now, on a sunny summer day, any green space not used by soccer players will be occupied by mobile barbeques. Every few years, the city government decrees a *Grillverbot*, but the prohibition is hardly ever enforced and generally ignored—until the next government tries again. For a while the Tiergarten was commonly dubbed "Europe's largest barbeque."

Schrebergärten

To get away properly, Berliners go to their *Schrebergärten* (plural; singular *Schrebergarten*). Named after a nineteenth-century Leipzig university teacher worried about urbanization, these small garden plots in larger public spaces exist all over Germany (and are functionally equivalent to allotments or community gardens in other parts of the world), but are also quintessentially Berlin. Here, garden areas were developed in the late nineteenth and early twentieth centuries to balance the *Mietskasernen* with their dense population. In their gardens, Berliners (especially from the working class) could breathe fresh air, cultivate a few vegetables, and let their children run free. A typical garden plot had a small shed or house, a few trees, lots of flowers and plants, and the occasional garden gnome (though those are more popular in southern Germany, Austria, and northern Italy, and are usually only employed ironically by Berliners). During and after the two World Wars the *Schrebergärten* were an important source of food for a malnourished city. Today, there are about 70,000 plots in approximately 900 garden *Kolonien*, with a total area of more than 7,500 acres. Many of these allotment complexes are next to train tracks, roads, or power stations, i.e., in territory nobody else wants to use, but others are on land that has not been developed in the middle of the city.

Schrebergärten and their denizens, the *Laubenpieper* (an untranslatable term with connotations of eccentricity), have a mixed reputation in Berlin. On the one hand, the "colonies" are usually organized as clubs with ridiculously strict rules. (It is just as difficult to get into one of these clubs in Berlin as it is to join a co-op in New York.) The city forbids people from actually living in the gardens (not all have electricity and sanitation), but the clubs also regulate the size and color of structures, what plants cannot or must be cultivated, the noise level, and forms of access. It does not help that the average age of a *Laubenpieper* is somewhere in the mid-sixties: stereotypically, these are elderly people with nothing better to do than snoop in their neighbors' gardens.

On the other hand, *Schrebergärten* are still one of the most democratic institutions, with little or no interference from outside. They also still provide a beautiful get-away for people living in high-rise apartment buildings and commuting to and from work underground and in cramped buses. This may change, since developers are trying their best to evict garden colonies where they can—even though any need for more apartment buildings and offices is highly debatable. But until then, the *Schrebergarten* will remain an oasis of leisure in a fast and frantic city.

While *Schrebergärten* have long been institutionalized, Berlin has more recently also witnessed a phenomenon known as guerrilla gardening. In this version of horticultural radicalism, which is partly due to the constant reduction in number and size of the city's green spaces, individuals simply plant grass, flowers, or vegetables in any available area. In some cases, the guerrillas take over abandoned lots or squares, and in at least one place (Prinzessinnengarten in Kreuzberg) there is a café serving food produced on site. Alternatively, Berliners plant the tiny areas around the ubiquitous trees, turning them from brown earth (or other dog-induced browns) to beautiful colors (or at least green). In the extreme, guerrilla gardeners commandeer abandoned shopping carts, fill them with soil, and plant anything from peonies to potatoes. While these "gardens" have the advantage of mobility, they can of course also easily be stolen—but guerrilla gardeners would probably just consider this outcome as spreading the message.

The thirteenth-century Marienkirche (St. Mary's Church)—most remarkable for its c.1484 death dance fresco—in the shadow of the Fernsehturm (TV Tower) on the right. (Dguendel/Wikimedia Commons)

8 | **Faith in the City**
The Religious Landscape

B y most standards Berlin is not a particularly religious place. As in any other German city, Easter and Christmas are celebrated, but probably more because they are associated with bank holidays than because of religious zeal; on Easter Monday and 26 December most Berliners do not have to work. Similarly, the Christmas market around the Kaiser-Wilhelm-Gedächtniskirche is more remarkable for its mulled wine than for its devotion. Church bells can be heard ringing all over Berlin—and the occasional *muezzin* calling faithful Muslims to prayer—but these sounds form little more than a background to other noises of the city. Women in face-covering *burqas* or at least full-length *chadors* can be seen in the streets, but in a city like Berlin they are usually accepted as different expressions of culture rather than of religious faith.

At the same time, these very day-to-day events can be seen as instances of how deeply religion is ingrained in the fabric of the city. There must be hundreds of churches and other sacred Christian buildings in Berlin, not to mention a dozen synagogues, a plethora of mosques and Islamic centers, and a few Hindu, Buddhist, and other temples—and many of them are prominent landmarks. Berliners may not stream to the mosque on Friday, the synagogue on Saturday, or church on Sunday, but that does not mean that they all consider themselves atheists. Perhaps most importantly, it is impossible in Berlin to escape the legacy of religious strife, most prominently the Jewish Holocaust during World War II. For that reason, while there are just about the same number of mosques and synagogues in Berlin, Judaism is more significant in determining the religious landscape and its historical resonance.

Christianity

Christianity is the predominant religion, and religious presence, in the city. A small church apparently stood near today's Spandau as early as 980, and Berlin has been Christian at least since the twelfth century, when local rulers converted from heathen beliefs and built churches and monasteries. Of course, Christians then were all Catholics. The most prominent medieval church in Berlin is the Nikolaikirche (St. Nicholas' Church) in the middle of the eponymous Nikolai Quarter in the center of Berlin. Originally built in the thirteenth century, the church burned down in 1380; the reconstruction was completed in 1470. Architecturally the structure is remarkable for the ambulatory, a series of open chapels extending the side aisles around the altar area. In the seventeenth century the composer Johann Crüger and the poet (and pastor) Paul Gerhardt worked here and created many hymns still sung today in churches across the world. The Nikolaikirche was destroyed by Allied bombing in 1944 and 1945, and finally rebuilt between 1980 and 1983 in anticipation of Berlin's 750th birthday in 1987. Today, it serves as a museum, and the foundations of the original thirteenth-century church have been excavated.

The other medieval church in the center of present-day Berlin is the Marienkirche (St. Mary's Church) right off Alexanderplatz. Today the church is dwarfed by the adjacent TV Tower, but in its time the 300-foot tower was the highest elevation in the densely populated area. Nearby is the Neptunbrunnen (Neptune Fountain) in a large expanse of open land, but until the end of the nineteenth century this was the site of Neuer Markt (new market), where many significant events in Berlin history occurred. Like the Nikolaikirche, the Marienkirche was built in the thirteenth century (c.1270) and burned down in 1380. The structure of the building is unchanged since the subsequent reconstruction, but the interior has continually been updated. Damaged by Allied bombing, the church was reconstructed by the GDR authorities in an empty area cleared of other damaged buildings. Because of deposits of earth and rubble all around, the floor of the church is now significantly lower than the surrounding ground.

Artistically, the most remarkable feature of the Marienkirche is a 72 x 6-foot death dance fresco that snakes around the sides of the entrance hallway. This fresco was painted after 1484, probably covered in the Reformation and rediscovered in the nineteenth century. It portrays members of the two parts of medieval society, secular and clerical, making their way towards the cross in the middle. Each side is hierarchically organized, with members of higher standing closer to Jesus and a figure of death between every two individuals. Supposedly painted by a Franciscan monk, the fresco is a memorial to the transitory nature of earthly life, and to the plague that swept through Berlin in 1484.

Finally, the remains of the Franciscan Graues Kloster (grey monastery) in Mitte (forming a triangle with the Nikolaikirche and the Marienkirche) are reminders of Berlin's medieval Catholic history, at least in the center—there are also various churches in the former villages that are now districts of Berlin. Founded in the thirteenth century, this church and monastery housed a famous school (after the Reformation), which moved to a new location in West Berlin after the monastery was destroyed during World War II. Today, only the haunting ruins of the church survive.

With the Reformation Berlin became a Protestant city, but the forms of Protestantism varied. Until the end of the seventeenth century, Lutheranism dominated (the conversion of Elector Joachim II to Lutheranism was celebrated at the Nikolaikirche in 1539), but then Calvinist or other Protestant rulers stealthily managed to bring the city around to their denomination. Later, plurality of denominations took over, and by the end of the eighteenth century even Catholics were allowed to dedicate new churches. Rulers were often involved in religious disputes; in 1662–63, for instance, the Great Elector Friedrich Wilhelm had the two main denominations sit down for seventeen meetings to discuss possible points of theological agreement—though ultimately without success.

Several significant churches were built in Berlin in the eighteenth century. The Parochialkirche in Klosterstrasse (the street being named after the Franciscan monastery) was designed by Johann Arnold Nering and completed by Martin Grünberg in 1705. While

Nering wanted the church's tower in the center above the nave—which has the shape of a square with semicircular extensions on each side, forming a kind of rounded cross—Grünberg put it above a vestibule. For over two centuries, a carillon played in the tower, but church, tower, and bells were destroyed in 1944. The church was provisionally reconstructed after the war, but used as a furniture depot after 1970. More recently, the church has been reconstructed, and there are plans to rebuild the tower. Another important feature of the Parochialkirche is the crypt, where over 500 Berliners were buried between 1703 and 1878. Because of the unique climatic conditions created by the architecture, the bodies interred here have partly mummified—at least those not stolen by grave robbers during the Cold War. Since the crypt was reopened in the 1990s, archaeologists have been able to make discoveries about sartorial, culinary, and medical conditions in old Berlin.

Located in the Spandauer Vorstadt in Mitte and named after King Friedrich I's (third) wife Sophie Luise, the Sophienkirche was opened in 1713 and completed with a tower in 1734—Berlin's only surviving baroque church tower. Unusually, the Sophienkirche had the altar and pulpit in the middle of the church against the south wall, so that the entire congregation could follow the service. Luckily, the church (which had been outfitted with electric lights in 1892 when the German emperor briefly used this as his main church) survived the war almost entirely intact, and it became a center for dissidents in GDR times. The church is approached through a narrow walkway between two symmetrical sets of buildings, which at least now (2013) serve as a reminder of World War II: one side has been beautifully renovated, while the other shows the scars of bullet holes or bomb damage from the war.

St.-Hedwigs-Kathedrale at the Forum Fridericianum was the first Catholic church in Berlin since the Reformation and had an unusually honorable history during the Nazi period. The day after the anti-Semitic *Reichskristallnacht* (Night of Broken Glass) on 9 November 1938, the provost Bernhard Lichtenberg publicly invited non-Catholics to the cathedral and condemned the pogrom in his homily. Lichtenberg continued his work for a few more years, but was persecuted by the Nazis and died on his way to a concentration camp in 1943. Lichtenberg received the title Righteous among the Nations from the State of Israel and was beatified in 1996. The cathedral was destroyed towards the end of the war, but rebuilt between 1952 and 1963, and it has been the seat of the archbishop since Berlin was elevated to the status of archdiocese in 1994.

In 1817 King Friedrich Wilhelm III decreed a unification of the Reformed and Lutheran churches, creating the theological structure of Protestantism that continues until today—and which explains why Protestantism in Berlin is not quite equivalent to any Anglo-American Christian denomination. This unification was celebrated in the Nikolaikirche. Throughout the nineteenth and early twentieth centuries, church architecture was as much a glorification of the Hohenzollern rulers as it was of God, as can be seen in the Kaiser-Wilhelm-Gedächtniskirche and the Berliner Dom.

For the Kaiser-Wilhelm-Gedächtniskirche, completed in 1895, architect Franz Schwechten used a late Romanesque style reminiscent of the medieval Staufer dynasty, whose members were also emperors of the Holy Roman Empire. Thus, the Hohenzollern established their claim to leading the entire German-speaking areas of Europe, if not all of Europe. Similarly, a mosaic added to the church in 1906 portrays the Hohenzollern rulers of the past centuries next to the German emperors of their day and once again tries to establish continuity between past and present rulers. These political statements in a church were not entirely popular even during their time. The church was destroyed in 1943, and today only the main tower and two smaller towers survive. Since the top of the main tower is missing, the church is popularly known as the *Hohler Zahn*, "hollow tooth." Next to it, Egon Eiermann built the striking Neue Gedächtniskirche and bell tower (1961–63). This octagonal church has honeycomb-like concrete dividers that allow light into the church during the day (coloring the inside blue), and the internal lighting out during the night. Because of a double outside wall that blocks sound the Neue Gedächtniskirche is an oasis of peace and reflection on one of the busiest squares in Berlin.

Even more ostentatious, the vast Berliner Dom (cathedral) was built between 1893 and 1905 on the site of several earlier churches (the last renovated by Schinkel) on the Museumsinsel in the middle of the city. The building was meant to be the Hohenzollern dynasty's home church, and although the line did not last much longer (until 1918), ninety of its members are buried in the crypt. The neo-Renaissance style of the church was taken as a reference to St. Peter's Basilica in Rome and as an assertion that the German unified Protestant Church was equal to its Catholic counterpart. At 375 x 240 feet in area and 380 feet high, it was a massive building that was decorated with ornate towers. (Today's three cupolas are actually understated compared to their taller predecessors.) The central section of the tripartite church could seat a congregation of 2,100. Mosaics portray the beatitudes in unique interpretations: for instance, the peacemakers are protected by a spear-wielding warrior and topped by a figure that seems to be an allusion to Charlemagne, suggesting that only a strong Christian emperor (for instance a Hohenzollern) could guarantee peace in Europe. The cathedral was bombed several times during World War II, and reconstruction did not begin until 1975 since the GDR had no interest in supporting a religious building (or a celebration of the Hohenzollern dynasty) in the middle of a socialist city, particularly one directly opposite parliament. Reconstruction of the outside was mostly finished by 1983 (though no cross indicated the building's purpose) and continued on the inside until 2002, when the last mosaic was restored. Since then the cross at the top of the central dome has been removed due to structural damage. Today the cathedral is used for official functions (such as commemorating German soldiers killed in Afghanistan) and daily services.

Since the reunification of Germany, the Church hierarchy has been somewhat reorganized. On the Protestant side, Berlin is part of the administrative unit of the Protestant Church of Berlin, Brandenburg, and the Silesian Upper Lausitz. Since 2009 the (Protestant) Bishop of Berlin has been Markus Dröge, who sees as his main challenge the integration of Berlin with the other parts of his diocese. On the Catholic side, Rainer Maria Woelki was named Archbishop of the Archdiocese of Berlin in 2011. Catholics received both a boost and strong criticism because of the visit of Pope Benedict XVI to Berlin in 2011, when he read mass in front of 60,000 believers at the Olympic Stadium.

Judaism

It is impossible to write objectively and dispassionately about the history of Jews in Berlin. As if the Holocaust were not bad enough, the Jewish experience has been marked by a series of pogroms, persecutions, and miscarriages of justice. Fortunately, there have been some more positive events, and while they may not redeem Berliners, they at least provide some rays of hope.

Jews lived in Spandau, today part of Berlin, at least from the beginning of the thirteenth century—before Berlin was even officially founded. They had a cemetery in Spandau that survived until 1510, one of several instances when Jews were banished from Brandenburg. Fortunately for posterity, the gravestones were used in the construction of the nearby Spandau Citadel in the following decades, where they were rediscovered during renovations in the late twentieth century. Berlin's oldest gravestone (Jewish or Christian) thus marks the death of one Jona, son of Dan, in 1244.

The thirteenth to sixteenth centuries witnessed a recurring pattern of allowing Jews to settle in Berlin, only to banish them more or less violently shortly thereafter. Documents show that Jews lived in Berlin in 1295 (because clothiers were forbidden from purchasing twine from them). They mostly worked in banking, and it seems that they lived in a ghetto on Jüdenstrasse in today's Mitte district around the Grosser Jüdenhof (Great Jewish Square), which they could lock at night for safety. This provided little protection when the Black Death arrived in 1348: Jews were held responsible for the plague and persecuted, often to death. Remarkably, the Jüdenstrasse survived through the ages, even through the Nazi period, and still runs right next to the Berlin City Hall.

The tide turned again in 1354, when Margrave Ludwig the Roman (from the house of Wittelsbach) allowed six Jewish families to settle in Berlin. Ludwig did not make this concession from the goodness of his heart—he needed to borrow money. Yet he also allowed the Jews to establish a school and a synagogue. The Jews' main profession became their downfall in 1446, when all Jews in Brandenburg were captured, their property was confiscated, and they were expelled from the state—perhaps at the instigation of the German emperor or the pope.

This expulsion did not last long, though, and just a year later Jews were readmitted. This brief episode ended in one of the most ignominious persecutions of Jews before the Holocaust. In 1510 the sacred host and the vessel holding it were stolen from a church in Knoblauch outside Berlin. A (Christian) culprit was soon located, and tortured for good measure. Under torture, this person "admitted" that he had sold part of the host to a Jew, and the hunt was on. Ultimately, between fifty and a hundred Jews were tried and tortured (killing at least ten), and many "confessed" to defiling the host (which they, however, were unable to destroy) and to committing ritual murder of Christian children (even though no children were missing at the time). Thirty-eight Jews were burned at the stake on Neuer Markt next to the Marienkirche on 19 July 1510; two who had converted during the trial were simply beheaded. At this point Jews were once again expelled from Brandenburg, and the cemetery in Spandau was destroyed.

The cycle occurred one more time: Jews were admitted to Berlin (and Brandenburg) in 1539 and expelled in 1573. As finance minister of Elector Joachim II, the Jewish banker Lippold Ben Chluchim had made himself unpopular with the Berlin population. When Joachim died, Lippold was accused of theft and embezzlement—which soon turned into the charge of performing magic and murdering the elector. Lippold was convicted, broken on the wheel, and quartered at Neuer Markt, and all Jews were expelled one last time.

A century later, Jews were readmitted to Berlin by the Great Elector Friedrich Wilhelm (in 1671), and from then until the Nazi period, though anti-Semitism always persisted, the Jewish community grew and thrived. The government extorted money from the Jews—they had to pay for "protection" and to be married—but they also gained the right to hire teachers and employ kosher butchers. A Jewish cemetery was established in 1672 in what is now the center of Berlin (Moses Mendelssohn was buried here), and the first synagogue was opened in Mitte in 1714 in the presence of Queen Sophia Dorothea (wife of King Friedrich Wilhelm I, the Soldier King). This synagogue no longer exists, but its foundation can be seen next to Spandauer Strasse near the Hackesche Höfe. The cemetery and adjacent old people's home were destroyed by the Nazis, but miraculously many of the gravestones survive. Today they have been rearranged as a thoughtful memorial right next to the Sophienkirche, and the foundations of the retirement home have been embedded in the pavement next to a sculpture by Will Lammert.

Berlin in the late eighteenth and early nineteenth centuries would have been a completely different place without the Jewish community, which provided bankers and craftsmen, but perhaps more importantly artists and intellectuals. From a Jewish perspective, this was the time of the *haskala* (Enlightenment), when the community challenged traditional religious rituals, practices, and mysticism under the pressure of modernization. Jews also engaged deeply with the secular culture around them for the first time. Inspired by brilliant intellectuals like Moses Mendelssohn (see pp.90–91), some reformed Jews tried to fit in by engaging in previously forbidden practices like socializing with Christians, following fashions, and attending German universities. Because of these issues, the Jewish community underwent internal strife between more traditional and more progressive elements, and a surprisingly high number of Jews converted to Christianity.

This brief period has garnered much attention from historians such as Steven Lowenstein (*The Berlin Jewish Community*, 1994) and Deborah Hertz (*How Jews Became Germans*, 2007). (Ironically, detailed studies such as these are possible because of the research undertaken for completely different and nefarious reasons by the Nazis.) According to both historians, the conversions were less about religion than about assimilation to an emerging German culture. Lowenstein argues that progressive Jews could not find a home in the traditional Jewish religious community and traded their beliefs (such as they were—many of these converts were cultural rather than religious Jews) for acceptance by German law and society. Rather than embracing Christian religion, they simply became Christians in order to find a new identity and take advantage of social, political, and legal benefits only available to Christians—though residual prejudices remained even after conversion. Focusing on the convert Rahel Varnhagen (see pp.91–92), Hertz is more interested in individual stories and hesitant to generalize about personal motivations for conversion. Again, reasons run the gamut from religious conviction to professional ambition. In retrospect, Hertz insists, it is important neither to praise these Jews as idealists imagining a peaceful coexistence of Jewishness and Germanness, nor to condemn them as sell-outs. Varnhagen supposedly said on her deathbed: "What for a long period of my life has been the source of my greatest shame, my most bitter grief and misfortune—to be born a Jewess—I would not at any price now wish to miss."

In practical terms, Jews or converted Jews influenced Berlin culture through the arts and through literary and intellectual salons. Varnhagen, Henriette Herz, and Dorothea Veit (Moses Mendelssohn's daughter, who later married the philosopher Friedrich Schlegel) hosted gatherings where men and women mingled and discussed literary (and sometimes political) issues of the day. This was the kind of early bourgeois public sphere that Jürgen Habermas imagined as necessary for and conducive to the development of a full civil society and democracy. Most of the salons were located in the Mitte district, on Neue Friedrichstrasse (now Spandauer Strasse—Herz) and (successively) Jägerstrasse, Charlottenstrasse, Französische Strasse, and Mauerstrasse (Varnhagen).

Among the most important Jewish artists of the day were the musicians and composer siblings Felix Mendelssohn and Fanny Hensel, grandchildren of Moses Mendelssohn. Felix (1809–47) was baptized in 1816, but culturally remained a Jew. Today he is known mostly for his symphonies and for his contribution to the rediscovery of the work of Johann Sebastian Bach. Fanny (1805–47), who married the painter Wilhelm Hensel, was a pianist and mostly composed for the piano. The two siblings died within six months of each other and were buried in the Dreifaltigkeitsfriedhof in Kreuzberg, where their graves can still be visited today. Felix is memorialized in Mendelssohn-Bartholdy Park near Postdamer Platz and in an U-Bahn station of the same name; Fanny has a street, a school, and a music conservatory named after her. There is a plaque commemorating both on the Bundesrat building in Leipziger Strasse, the location of the house in which they grew up. In a more quixotic fashion, the square in front of the Jewish Museum was recently named Fromet-und-Moses-Mendelssohn-Platz after Mendelssohn and his wife to satisfy a district requirement that 50 percent of all squares be named after women.

For the rest of the nineteenth and early twentieth centuries, as Germany unified in 1871 and drifted through World War I, Jews remained an important part of Berlin culture and society. During this period there was still some discrimination—they could not be officers or judges—but otherwise Jews may have been more integrated than ever before or after. Bankers, manufacturers, publishers, politicians, authors, and artists were (usually) recognized more for their merit than by their religion. There was even a group of Jews who were close advisors to Emperor Wilhelm II. As an outward sign of this recognition, the Jewish community built several large synagogues in Berlin.

The most famous of these is certainly the Neue Synagoge on Oranienburger Strasse. This temple, built between 1859 and 1866 as the largest synagogue in Germany (with over 3,000 seats), was "new" compared to the first Berlin synagogue in the Heidereutergasse (1712–14). The Neue Synagoge also embraced the more liberal service, which included a choir and an organ, which in turn determined the architecture of the building. The outside has an unusual combination of a central entrance with three arches, two towers, and a bulbous Moorish-inspired cupola. The synagogue escaped complete destruction in the 1938 *Reichskristallnacht* when a courageous (Christian) policeman summoned the fire department, but it was still defiled when the Nazis used it as a depot for uniforms. Heavily damaged at the end of the war, the remains (except for the entrance area) were razed in 1958.

Subsequently, discussions ensued about the future of the space. In 1988 (still under the GDR) the Neue Synagoge Berlin-Centrum

Judaicum Foundation was established to consider courses of action, and ultimately it was decided not to reconstruct the synagogue but to build a Jewish center instead. This was completed and dedicated in 1994 and incorporates elements of the original building. In the courtyard, bricks mark the outline of where the synagogue once stood. The new structure is not technically a synagogue, but does include a prayer room and a ritual bath. The mission of the foundation is to commemorate and discuss the history of Jews in Germany in exhibitions and events and to promote interaction between Jews from Eastern and Western Europe. The building is still heavily guarded because of persistent anti-Semitic threats, but it is also an assertion of Jewish identity. The entrance arch is decorated with a verse (in Hebrew) from Isaiah 26: 2: "Open the gates that the righteous nation may enter, the nation that keeps faith." The golden decoration of the cupola is easily visible from many directions and has become one of the landmarks of the new Berlin.

While the Neue Synagoge is probably the most famous, the largest synagogue still hosting worship in Berlin today is the one in Rykestrasse in Prenzlauer Berg, which seats 1,200. This synagogue was built in the neo-Romanesque style in 1904 when previous facilities proved too small. In typically Berlin fashion, the synagogue was set in the back across a courtyard, while the front house had an elementary school. This architecture proved an unexpected boon under the Nazis, since destroying the synagogue would have meant endangering the surrounding houses. The synagogue was violated by using it as a stable, but at least the building survived. The first Jewish wedding in Berlin after World War II was performed here in July 1945, and the synagogue was even restored under the GDR in 1953. After reunification it was renovated once again starting in its centenary year 2004 (completed in 2007). Today's congregation is mostly made up of immigrants from Russia.

Clearly, this book is not the place to do justice to the horror of the Holocaust, the systematic elimination of over six million Jews throughout Europe, including somewhere around 150,000 from Berlin. The Holocaust started in Berlin in March 1933, when the Nazi paramilitary organization SS tried to "cleanse" the

Scheunenviertel, the working-class quarter mostly populated by Jewish immigrants from Poland, Russia, and the Baltic (see p.34). The same year, the Nazis organized a boycott of Jewish businesses, and in 1935 Jews were stripped of most of their legal rights in an attempt to force them into emigration. Nevertheless, there were still around 80,000 Jews in Berlin around 1940, with more arriving under the impression that it was easier to hide in a big city. In 1941, a large majority of Jews were deported to concentration camps, and the only ones (officially) surviving were about 15,000 "employed" as forced labor in military factories. In February 1943, the Nazi leadership arrested around 8,000 of these workers as well as any other Jews they found in public. Since many of the latter were men in mixed marriages, their wives engaged in a spontaneous protest in Rosenstrasse in early March 1943, and amazingly most of the men were released. With further denunciations and arrests, only about 1,500 Jews survived the war in Berlin.

The Jewish congregation was revived in 1945, and from then until 1992 it was led by the charismatic and controversial Heinz Galinski. Since 2008 the chairperson has been for the first time a woman, Lala Süsskind. Encouraged over the decades by the Jewish congregation (and hopefully motivated by the experience of the past), Berlin has dealt with the legacy of the Holocaust in exemplary ways, and today memorials can be seen everywhere in the city.

There are many highly visible and internationally famous monuments, but perhaps the most moving are the *Stolpersteine* (stumbling blocks) instigated by the artist Gunter Demnig and commemorating not just Jews, but other victims of the Nazi terror such as Sinti and Roma, homosexuals, and Jehovah's Witnesses as well. These *Stolpersteine* are small brass plaques about the size of cobblestones that are sunk into the pavement. They are placed in front of buildings where victims lived and simply give the name, birth date, the date of deportation to concentration camps, and (where known) the date of death. The *Stolpersteine* are very slightly raised from the pavement, so they might indeed lead to stumbling, but more importantly they are supposed to get those who walk past them to remember the Holocaust. Since they are set in the pavement, they are not immediately visible, but once discovered they force the viewer to assume a position with a bowed head. So far, over 30,000 *Stolpersteine* have been placed in over 650 cities in Europe—and, of course, many in Berlin.

In contrast to these subtle reminders, the most prominent monuments to Jewish history in Berlin are the Jewish Museum (see pp.45–47) and the Memorial to the Murdered Jews of Europe near the Brandenburg Gate, commonly known simply as Holocaust Memorial. Designed by the architect Peter Eisenmann and built in 2003–04, it is a field of over 2,700 stelae in orderly rows but of varying heights. According to different interpretations, the stelae are either only important for their visual impression or are supposed to symbolize how a previously orderly bureaucracy became deranged enough to support and carry out the Holocaust. The memorial has been the object of controversy because it commemorates only Jews and not other victims of the Holocaust, and because it turned out that a subsidiary of one of the construction firms involved in building the memorial had produced Zyklon B, the lethal chemical used in the concentration camps' gas chambers. A less serious controversy ensued when young Berliners (and tourists) discovered it was fun to jump from the top of one stela to another, a practice that has now been banned. Under the memorial, an information center lists the names of all known Jewish victims of the Holocaust.

But between the extremes of the *Stolpersteine* on the one hand and the Jewish Museum and Holocaust Memorial on the other, there are some 400 monuments to Jewish history in Berlin. These include such moving memorials as the Spiegelwand (mirror wall) in Steglitz (which forces observers to see themselves reflected over the names of Jewish victims) or the Deportationsmahnmal (deportation memorial) at Putlitzbrücke in Moabit (near the train station where many Jews were deported to concentration camps). This stainless steel construction has an imitation of a Jewish gravestone leaning forward in front of a kind of staircase leading towards heaven; it has been defiled by anti-Semitic vandals several times. Overall, these monuments in their ubiquity show that Berlin as a city is continually trying to come to terms with, and has no intention of ever forgetting, the Holocaust.

Islam

Claims vary as to when the first Muslims came to Berlin. In early modern times, European ideas about Islam mostly came from two sources. For one, an Ottoman army had made a significant incursion in 1683 and was only repelled outside Vienna. While this was actually a power struggle between the Ottoman and Hapsburg empires, it was styled as a fight between Christians and Muslims—an early example of politicians masking expansionist agendas as religious conflict in order to win popular support. A few prisoners of war and their families ended up in Berlin, where some were adopted or employed by the court. The second source of European "knowledge" of Muslims was the collection of stories alternately titled *Arabian Nights* or *One Thousand and One Nights*. These stories were not translated into German until the early nineteenth century, but they were available from 1704 in French, which most members of Berlin's high society and court read and spoke fluently. From the *Arabian Nights* emerged competing stereotypes such as oriental despotism and luxury, the effete ruler, harems, eunuchs, and sexually voracious women, which have bedevilled European ideas about Muslims ever since.

Apart from the prisoners of war, the most Berliners saw of Muslims were probably the occasional delegations from the Ottoman Empire. In 1701 Azmi Said came to congratulate Friedrich I on his elevation to king; Ahmed Resmi visited in 1763 to explore the possibility of a military alliance between the Turks and Prussia; and Ahmed Azmi stopped by in 1791 to convince King Friedrich Wilhelm II to abide by the treaty of mutual assistance (with no success). Most importantly for posterity, Ali Aziz came in 1798 and promptly died. In order to bury him properly, King Friedrich Wilhelm III dedicated an Islamic cemetery in Tempelhof. In the nineteenth century this plot was traded for a different one, which is the location of Berlin's largest mosque today.

After a quiet century and a half, Muslims started coming back to Berlin in larger numbers in the 1960s as Turkish *Gastarbeiter* (guest workers) and immigrants. (There had been some Muslim prisoners of war during World War I who subsequently founded Berlin's first mosque, the Ahmadiyya Mosque, in Wilmersdorf in 1928.) Today there are about 150–200,000 Muslims in Berlin, about three-quarters from Turkey and mostly Sunni, though there are also Shia, Sufi, and Alevi Muslims. Since 11 September 2001 they have struggled with the same stereotypes as Muslims everywhere, a problem exacerbated by the fact that Islam has no unified religious or administrative structure to counter bias—though there are several governing bodies in Berlin that valiantly continue to combat prejudice.

Because of settlement patterns, Muslims are most visible in Kreuzberg, Neukölln, and Wedding. Over the years Islam has gained a greater degree of acceptance, and a form of instruction in Islam can be offered when Christian and Jewish schoolchildren go to their own respective religious lessons in school. There are occasionally disagreements over Turkish women's headdresses or participation in physical education, but these are now fairly infrequent. For a while so-called honor killings were in the news, but by now even the most backwards Berliners recognize that this (very rare) phenomenon is less about Islam than about extremely old-fashioned cultural norms, often compounded by clashes between rural and metropolitan ideas.

The largest and most visible mosque in Berlin is the Şehitlik Mosque, which is situated on the northern edge of Tempelhof airport. This mosque takes its name and location from the site where the cemetery for Ali Aziz was moved in 1863, but was actually built from 1999. Designed in imitation of classical Ottoman architecture, the mosque accommodates 1,500 faithful for Friday prayers in a prayer hall of almost 4,000 square feet between graceful 110-foot minarets. But just as importantly, the Şehitlik Mosque is a place for community engagement: there are facilities for language classes, club meetings, and exhibitions, and non-Muslim guests are welcome to wander around or go on guided tours.

Berlin Temples

In addition to mosques, synagogues, and churches, many other places of worship are available in Berlin. There is a Buddhist House (1922–24) in Frohnau for Taiwanese Buddhists, a Fo-Guang-Shang (Mountain of Buddha) Temple (1998) in Wedding for Humanist

Buddhists, and a Shaolin Temple (2004) for Chinese Buddhists in Charlottenburg—the largest Shaolin temple and monastery outside of China. There has been a *gurdwara* for Sikhs in Reinickendorf since 2002, and a Sri Ganesha Hindu Temple is planned near the Hasenheide Park in Neukölln. Interestingly, except for the Shaolin Temple, these places of worship are all in outlying districts, suggesting that Berlin remains predominantly a Christian, Jewish, and Muslim city—even if many would not consider it an overly religious city in the first place.

Berlin's first mosque (and Germany's oldest), the Ahmadiyya Mosque in Wilmersdorf, built in 1928 with two 100-foot minarets and a prayer hall for about 400 worshippers. (Ceddyfresse/Wikimedia Commons)

9 | Changing Faces
Migration and Social Change

Like many other modern metropolitan cities, Berlin has been a destination for migrants throughout its history. Indeed, it is almost impossible to speak of an "indigenous" Berlin population—though that does not stop conservative politicians and commentators from invoking the good old days before one or another group of immigrants supposedly destroyed the fabric of the city. In fact, it could be argued that Berlin was founded by immigrants: in the late twelfth century, Albrecht the Bear, the new Margrave of Brandenburg, invited people from other parts of Germany as well as surrounding countries to settle in his state. Since Berlin was founded some time in the following fifty years and since there is little archaeological evidence of early occupation, it is quite likely that these immigrants formed the original settlement.

According to the last available data (June 2012), there are some 487,000 foreigners officially living in Berlin among a population of about three and a half million. Fourteen nationalities are represented with over 10,000 members and give a rough sense of the main groups of non-Germans in Berlin. With 102,000, Turks are far and away the largest group. People from Poland come next (45,000), followed by 17–18,000 each from Serbia, Italy, and the Russian Federation. Vietnam, Bulgaria, France, and the US all have around 14,000, while there are about 11,000 from the UK. Finally, Greece, Spain, Bosnia and Herzegovina, and Croatia have just over 10,000 migrants each.

Yet these figures are also misleading in the sense that foreigners officially living in Berlin are only the tip of the iceberg. As in other cities, already settled populations and new Berliners have struggled for centuries between accepting the language and culture unfamiliar to them and holding on to their own traditions. Thus, immigrant groups have become Berliners, so while they are part of the fabric of the city they are not captured in these statistics. In Berlin this kind of immigration can (in very general terms) be divided into four periods: the Enlightenment, when Bohemians and Huguenots put down roots; the nineteenth century, which witnessed the arrival of new citizens from other German-speaking parts of Europe; the post-war period, when Italians, Yugoslavs, and Turks were invited to West Berlin, while Vietnamese came to East Berlin; and the post-reunification period, when Russians formed the largest portion of immigrants. Each of these groups added new and distinctive facets to Berlin, including the form of the local dialect, the look of the cityscape, and the multiethnic make-up of the city.

French Huguenots

The first significant "new" immigration occurred at the end of the seventeenth century, with some 5–6,000 French Huguenots settling among 25–30,000 Berliners. Though it may seem a long time ago and the numbers relatively small, the results can still be seen and heard in Berlin today. This wave of immigration is also symptomatic of a more general phenomenon in that it is often taken to demonstrate how tolerant Berlin is—but was really mostly politically and economically expedient.

At least two religious developments coalesced to facilitate Huguenot immigration. In 1598 the Edict of Nantes had given French Protestants—called Huguenots for not entirely clear etymological reasons—some freedom of religion in Catholic France. In the 1660s and 1670s, though, that freedom was slowly eroding, and in 1685 the Edict was revoked. This meant that many Huguenots fled France and needed a new home. At the same time, the Great Elector Friedrich Wilhelm, a Calvinist Protestant, was trying to establish his religion in mostly Lutheran Berlin. Obvious attempts to change the religious landscape, however, had been monumental failures: one Calvinist pastor was robbed down to his green underwear, in which he proceeded to preach. Sensing an opportunity to transform the religious make-up of the city—and to repopulate the city after the ravages of the Thirty Years' War—Friedrich Wilhelm published an edict of his own inviting the Calvinist Huguenots to come to Berlin and Brandenburg. The tax incentives and freedom from guild laws he promised certainly helped as well.

The refugees who arrived in Berlin were unusual in being mostly fairly well educated and skilled. They introduced or revolutionized large parts of the textile industry, especially wool and cotton manufacturing, and brought or refined other trades including enamel production and clock-making. Though in retrospect the French quickly became an integral part of Berlin, they were not always welcomed at the time. Not for the last time, the already settled population claimed that the newcomers were taking their jobs and harassed them where they could. Though the numbers of French were not large by present-day standards, they constituted up to a quarter of the Berlin population by the end of the 1680s. In that sense, the Great Elector succeeded in at least one of his goals: by the 1690s, Berlin had a strong Calvinist presence.

In addition to their religious and economic influence, the Huguenots had a profound cultural and institutional impact. They worshipped in five churches across the city, most prominently in the French Friedrichstadtkirche of 1701, which was connected almost a century later to the Französischer Dom on the Gendarmenmarkt. Today, this structure is home to the Huguenot Museum. Intellectually, the Huguenots had an advantage since in the Enlightenment French was considered the *lingua franca* of Europe, and the clubs and associations they founded contributed to the cultural development of the city. The French High School (Französisches Gymnasium or Lycée Français) was established in 1689 and remains an excellent bilingual school over three hundred years later. Finally, a number of expressions in the Berlin dialect (of German) can be traced to the French influence (though some linguists believe this was as much due to the occupation of Berlin by French soldiers in the Napoleonic Wars). A meat patty is a *Bulette* (*boulette* in French), to cry in Berlin is *plärren* (*pleurer*), and *Muckefuck*, a coffee imitation made from chicory, comes from *mocca faux* (false coffee). The curious Berlin dialect expression *etepetete* (conceited, affected) supposedly derives from the French *être, peut-être* (approximately: maybe, maybe not).

Industrialization and Immigration

The next wave of immigration started with the unification of Germany in 1871 and never really stopped until World War I. This immigration was mostly economically motivated, though not so much directed by the government. Instead, the immigrants responded to two developments: the loss of land and employment in their areas of origin (especially east of Berlin), and the destruction of the guild system by modern industrialization. The scale of this immigration is hard to imagine: hardly forty percent of Berlin's 1875 population had actually been born in the city, and in 1900 sixty percent were first- or second-generation immigrants. These immigrants mainly came from two areas: the closer eastern parts of Germany and the eastern European countries and areas beyond.

In the nineteenth century new agricultural developments such as synthetic fertilizer allowed for the cultivation of Brandenburg, the adjoining regions of Mecklenburg, and East and West Prussia to an unprecedented degree. Farms started growing ever larger, pushing individuals and families off the lands they had tilled for centuries. In a parallel development, small industries such as weaving, which had traditionally supplied Berlin and supported the regions of Bohemia and Silesia and parts of Poland, became obsolete due to industrialization. The famine and rebellion of the weavers struck a chord in the German imagination; most German children even today know Gerhart Hauptmann's play *The Weavers* as well as the poem "The Silesian Weavers" by Heinrich Heine. Heine's poem was first published in the journal *Vorwärts!*, edited by Karl Marx, who used the weavers' plight to "prove" the horrors of capitalism.

In any case, these displaced workers and farmers streamed to Berlin, where they barely held on in tent cities on the outskirts of the metropolis. In the short term, they contributed to an exponential growth in the population: from 826,000 in 1871 the city grew to 1,889,000 in 1900. Ultimately, the Berlin government was forced to deal with the situation, and its solution has shaped the face of Berlin until today. In order to create housing, the government supported the construction of thousands upon thousands of four-story tenement buildings. These were the cramped, damp, dirty, and dangerous

Mietskasernen, which remained atrocious housing when occupied by the next wave of immigrants, the Turks—but which today, after extensive renovation across the city, are desired and beloved as the Berlin tenement apartments known as *Altbauten* (see pp.54–57).

Turks in Berlin: the Beginnings

The third large wave of immigration to Berlin, and the one that most shaped the city as it exists today, came from Turkey. The history of Turks in Berlin is often divided into three generations, and technically only the first of these were immigrants, the next two being their children and grandchildren. Turks had long been present in Berlin (see p.165), but large-scale Turkish immigration began in 1961. This story is told in compelling detail by Hilke Gerdes in *Türken in Berlin* (Turks in Berlin).

In the late 1950s economists had projected that there would not be enough workers to fill all job openings in a booming economy, so Germany signed treaties with a number of states allowing qualified individuals to come to their country. Turkey was one of these states. (Thus, the arrival of Turks in Berlin was not related to the building of the Wall, as some critics have asserted. Other states that signed similar treaties and sent smaller numbers of immigrants to Berlin included Spain, Greece, Morocco, Portugal, and Yugoslavia.) On the other side, Turkey was in the midst of an economic depression and worried about illegal emigration, so the government requested permission to send workers to Germany. Both countries expected the workers' stay in Germany to be temporary; Germany assumed that the economy would eventually adjust to rely on German workers, and Turkey hoped that the emigrants would send money home and return with new skills to revive the Turkish economy. For that reason, both countries originally called these individuals *Gastarbeiter* (guest workers). From today's perspective, they constitute the first generation of Turkish immigrants.

After the treaty, a government office in Istanbul screened applicants and sent successful candidates to Germany by railway. The trains arrived in Munich, from where the immigrants were distributed all over the country. Many applicants experienced this process as exploitative and inhumane. The most demeaning part was the medical examination, where groups of ten to fifteen men (mostly) had to strip in front of a doctor and were inspected like farm animals. Back at home, Turks were instructed in German culture and customs and were made to feel they were their country's ambassadors, but their experiences in Germany were often quite different. Once in Berlin, they were housed in guesthouses with limited interaction with the local population. After 1964, German law required that these dormitories had at least forty square feet for each person and no more than six people to a room; in 1973, eighty square feet in rooms of four. These laws, meant to improve the workers' living conditions, were not always followed or enforced, and workers sometimes felt as if they were in prison. In addition, the small rooms meant that Turks had no space to congregate except on the street, where they were perceived by some Berliners as threatening.

Most *Gastarbeiter* had little or no knowledge of the German language, making it extremely difficult to function beyond their Turkish enclaves. This situation was exacerbated by the fact that both Turks and Germans expected the workers' time in Germany to be limited and thus both saw no need for integration. Mostly from a rural background, the immigrants found Berlin daunting. When they went shopping, they did not recognize many of the foods in German stores, and simple things such as toilet etiquette were different enough to cause difficulties. For the male immigrants, gender relations presented a particular problem: German society in the early 1960s was more open and progressive than Turkey with regard to gender roles, and some guest workers misinterpreted German women's behavior as suggestive or even promiscuous. All in all, then, the immigrant experience was far from unproblematic and isolated the guest workers, especially in the early years.

The situation for (female) *Gastarbeiterinnen* was similar in many respects, but there was also a sense in which their experience was quite different. In Berlin the companies recruiting guest workers included several in the technology sector: Siemens, Telefunken, and DeTeWe (Deutsche Telephonwerke, German Telephone Company).

Since the work involved carefully handling small components, these companies hired more female than male employees. The *Gastarbeiterinnen* were certainly motivated by the same reasons as their male counterparts to apply for immigration, such as the economic crisis in Turkey and the wish simply to experience different places (supported by the idea circulating in Turkey at the time that Germany was some kind of paradise). But women also often used the opportunity to come to Germany specifically to escape bad marriages and family situations, and more generally to get away from the restrictive culture prevalent in Turkey.

In 1962 only 511 Turks were officially registered in West Berlin among a population of a little over two million. By 1965 there were about 2,800, a number that rose to 10,000 in 1967 and some 20,000 in 1968. In 1973 there were approximately 79,500 Turks in Berlin, while the population of Berlin as a whole had dropped slightly. Immigrants particularly settled in certain districts: 24 percent of the Kreuzberg population were non-Germans (in 1974), 17 percent in Wedding, and 15 percent in Tiergarten. Worse (since the Berlin government was woefully unprepared), almost half of the children in Kreuzberg's primary schools were not of German origin at the end of the 1970s—37.7 percent in Wedding and 29.7 percent in Tiergarten.

Turks in Berlin: the 1970s

Throughout the 1970s the city government and Berliners tried to cope with the influx of this first generation of Turkish immigrants in various ways, while for their part the immigrants started interacting more assertively with Berlin society. On one level, the situation was addressed with bureaucratic solutions formulated in comically and stereotypically long German words. There was an ongoing debate about whether Germany was an *Einwanderungsland*, i.e., a country of immigration. In other words, it now became clear that many *Gastarbeiter* were here to stay, and the question arose whether and to what extent they should be expected to adopt German culture (or which version of German culture). Writing about immigrants in Switzerland, the German-language writer Max Frisch formulated concisely what had happened: "We called for employees, and human beings arrived."

In the early 1970s many Germans and Berliners considered the growing number of Turks in Germany a threat and discussed ways to minimize their presence. In terms of education policy, the watchword was *Rückkehrfähigkeit*, i.e., the ability to return. In other words, the education of Turkish students at Berlin schools focused on getting rid of them rather than helping them acquire and develop skills to thrive in Berlin. In the then three-tier school system (the top tier leading to university, the middle to office jobs, and the lowest to manual labor and often unemployment), most Turkish students got stuck in the lowest level.

Even more radically, in 1973 the German government imposed an *Anwerbestopp*, a stop to recruitment of foreign workers (from outside the European Union, then still the European Community). While this policy had some short-term "success" in terms of reducing the number of guest workers in Germany, it also had the opposite effect. Since now reuniting families (*Familienzusammenführung*) was the easiest way to bring in a new workforce, many Turkish men brought their wives and children to Berlin. This in turn cemented their status as actual immigrants rather than temporary guest workers.

For their part, Turks in Berlin became a much more heterogeneous, but also more organized group in the 1970s. Moving out of company housing, they ended up in certain districts for reasons beyond their control. Berlin housing, mostly *Altbauten* from the turn of the century, was deteriorating, but landlords were more interested in tearing down buildings than renovating them since redevelopment paid more than rent. As landlords waited for permits and the right economic climate, they rented their properties to those segments of the population who could not find housing elsewhere and would not protest about the dilapidated conditions. Prominent in this portion of the population were Turkish guest workers.

Since many of the *Altbauten* were near the Wall in Kreuzberg, Wedding, Tiergarten, and Neukölln, strong Turkish communities developed in those districts. Up this day, there is a functioning economic and cultural Turkish network in these areas: Berliners with a Turkish background can learn Turkish in school, shop at Turkish corner shops, get their *döner* from their favorite *Imbiss* (local fast food stand), go to the mosque, listen to Turkish rap and hip-hop, and read Turkish newspapers here. The Turkish market at Maybachufer in Neukölln is a destination for Berliners (of Turkish or German background) and tourists alike. A new Turkish-influenced dialect of German was heard here—and later captured in books like Feridun Zaimoglu's collection of short stories or interviews *Kanak Sprak* (1995). This title reclaims a derogatory and racist term for foreigners, *Kanake*, and combines it with the German word for language to coin a name for this dialect. (More recently, linguist Heike Wiese has identified what she calls a multiethnolect, a form of German influenced by the languages of various immigrant communities, and named it *Kiezdeutsch*, which approximately translates to "'hood German.")

Yet living near the Wall came with dangers of its own: on 11 May 1975, his fifth birthday, young Cetin Mert accidently dropped a ball into the Spree, which marked the boundary between West and East Berlin. Trying to retrieve the ball, Cetin—who did not know how to swim—fell into the water himself. West Berlin police and firemen arrived quickly, but were not legally allowed to enter Spree waters; their East Berlin equivalents were not as fast, so Cetin drowned. Adding insult to injury, East German authorities did not release the boy's body for several days. The funeral turned into a protest against the way the GDR handled the border.

At the same time, the situation in Turkey was changing, as the country moved from economic difficulties into political crisis. A military coup d'état in 1971 was followed by the invasion of Cyprus in 1974. The oil crisis of 1973 compounded the situation, and the economy remained depressed until the early 1980s. The military government curtailed human rights and persecuted political activists. For that reason, a new group came to Germany, namely political refugees or asylum seekers. In the minds of the Berlin population, these two different groups—Turks voluntarily leaving their country and coming to Berlin to improve their lives, as opposed to those who had to flee their country to save their lives—were often confused. The former were sometimes resented for supposedly taking work from Berliners (though that was rarely the case), while the latter were accused of inflating the threats to them in Turkey and designated *Scheinasylanten* (false asylum seekers). The situation came to a symbolic head in 1983 when a Kurdish Turk committed suicide by jumping out of the sixth-floor window of a Berlin court building where the judges had denied him asylum.

By then, Turks were well organized in cultural and political groups. The first Turkish-language journal had been founded in 1963, and radio programs were broadcast in Turkish from about the same time. Students founded political organizations like the Progressive People's Union of Turkey (1973), women established groups such as the Turkish Women's Club (1975), and the military-backed government party in Turkey set up a branch in Berlin, the deceptively named Federation of Turkish Democratic Idealists' Clubs in Germany (1978). Altercations between left-wing critics and right-wing supporters of the military junta in Turkey in Berlin obviously did not promote integration. The most devastating confrontation between the groups happened on 5 January 1980, when teacher and union representative Celalettin Kesim, who had been in Berlin since 1973, bled to death at Kottbusser Tor after being stabbed—even though plainclothes police were monitoring the clash. Three thousand Berliners attended Kesim's funeral. The German-Turkish artist Hanefi Yeter, also in Berlin since 1973 (and in Istanbul since 2000 as well), created a memorial for Kesim near Kottbusser Tor in the 1990s.

Berlin in the 1980s was characterized by two related developments: a downturn in the economy and an ongoing conflict between established politicians and the alternative political culture. Members of the radical counterculture established strongholds in the buildings and districts where the Turkish population lived, but they hardly had similar goals, and the leftists often treated Turks as an exotic backdrop to their projects. Turkish Berliners mostly wanted to live in peace and quiet, while radical Berliners wanted to change society. Certainly, the Turkish citizens might have been sympathetic: of the

118,000 in Berlin in 1983, 89 percent had no running hot water, and a stunning 73 percent had no inside toilet—a relic of turn-of-the-century tenement construction. Even so, they were not as politically engaged, and the two groups rarely came together in joint action. By this time, many Turks had established their families in the city, and many of their children had been born there, constituting a second generation of Turks in Berlin.

At the same time, Germany and Berlin were becoming more conservative in their approach to immigration. Starting in 1980, Turks were required to have visas to enter Germany, and in 1981 reuniting families became much more difficult. In 1981 a conservative city government came to power in Berlin with a schizophrenic attitude to migrants. While progressive in being the first in Germany to create the position of Envoy for Foreigners' Affairs (*Ausländerbeauftragter*), one of its most vocal members was the Secretary of the Interior Heinrich Lummer, whose pronouncements at times sounded racist. Legislation that became known as the Lummer-Edict decreed that any Turk who turned eighteen, had lived in Berlin for less than five years, and did not have a job was to be deported.

Still, the number of Turks in Berlin continued to grow, and by 1990 there were about 134,000. Throughout the 1980s the rumor circulated that Berlin was the world's second-largest Turkish city, which of course was untrue, but expressed many Berliners' anxiety about immigration. In this period Turks became disenchanted even with well-meaning Berlin supporters, whom they came to see as patronizing. For instance, the journalist Günter Wallraff had gone undercover as a Turkish guest worker under the alias Ali Sigirlioglu and reported his experiences in the bestseller *Ganz unten* (translated as *Lowest of the Low*)—but Turks wondered why they needed a German to "expose" a situation they knew all too well. Instead, they demanded equality and started building the necessary infrastructure in support groups for students, self-help organizations, and advice offices. In the 1980s a delegate of Turkish descent was elected to the Berlin parliament for the first time, while the first Turkish-language cinema was opened in 1983.

Turks in Berlin: the Third Generation

Since the fall of the Wall and the reunification of Berlin (and Germany), Turks in Berlin can be characterized as the third generation of immigrants. Since the early 1990s these immigrants have been struggling to shed that label and to be seen simply as Germans (who happen to have ancestry outside Germany). Officially, they are now designated as having *Migrationshintergrund*, a migratory background, rather than as immigrants. The process of their integration can be traced in various economic and cultural developments. The number of small companies run by Germans of Turkish descent, for instance, has increased dramatically since 1989—on both sides of the former Wall. This growth of Turkish businesses is in part due to unemployment and discrimination, since after reunification Berlin experienced an economic slump, which as always hit immigrants particularly hard—and forced them into creative ways of making a living such as founding companies. At the same time, banks seem to have been particularly cautious in providing these entrepreneurs with loans (which some might call discrimination), forcing them to work even harder to get by. Today, Turks are still disproportionately represented in the food industry (where they make up forty percent of businesses), but these companies exist side by side with various business associations, banks, and support networks that cater to the Turkish community. Arguably, these enterprises are now simply part of an international business landscape in Berlin.

Politically, the struggle can be seen in the development of citizenship laws. Since 2000 anyone with one parent living in Germany for at least eight years has been entitled to dual citizenship. Yet young people have to choose only one citizenship at the age of 23—and can only choose German citizenship if they hold gainful employment, a difficult proposition in the current economic climate. In terms of educational policy, Berlin has had the Turkish-German bilingual Aziz Nesin Primary School since 1996. In contrast to English-German, French-German, and other language combinations, Turkish-German initially met some resistance, but by now the school is well established—of course in Kreuzberg. There are now various city parliamentarians with a Turkish background, especially to the left of the political spectrum in the SPD, the Green Party, and Die Linke (Left Party). More unusually, Emine Demirbüken-Wegner, in the Berlin parliament from 2006 to 2011, is a member of the conservative CDU. She often found herself in a difficult position, criticizing (and attacked by) members of her own party while mocked as a sell-out from the left.

Culturally, the debate has centered around terms like multiculturalism, assimilation, integration, and participation. For much of the 1980s and 1990s, well-meaning Berliners of German or Turkish descent argued for a peaceful coexistence of Turkish and German cultures, insisting that differing cultures cannot judge, but must simply accept each other. Of course, this led to difficult situations concerning German racism or Turkish honor killings (see p.166), both fortunately rare by the new century. In contrast, conservatives demanded full assimilation, a complete rejection of Turkish culture by Turks who wanted to remain in Germany. Ironically, this coincided to some extent with the generational divide among Turks in Berlin: while first-generation immigrants often saw themselves mostly as Turkish, members of the second generation (who had often grown up in Berlin and rarely or never been to Turkey) often wanted to define themselves as German. Unhelpfully, Turkish Prime Minister Recep Erdogan called assimilation a human rights violation in 2008. The idea of integration was a kind of compromise—as long as it was not a code word for assimilation. Instead, integration meant that individuals embraced multiple identities or various cultural affiliations and practices. However, this could only work with participation in a community, through a conscious effort to work through similarities and differences. This seems to be happening in the third generation.

Most of all, contemporary Turks in Berlin are keen to avoid being defined primarily as Turkish. On the one hand, filmmakers, musicians, writers, painters, sculptors, and comedians (like the brilliant and hilarious police-officer-turned-stand-up-comedian Murat Topal) continue to address the theme of immigration or foreigners (*Ausländerthematik*); yet on the other, they simply want to be recognized as artists in their metier. They are succeeding in that quest, and as they can often no longer be identified by their names (real or assumed), they are judged only by their work. Turks are trying to help Germans see that they are not a homogeneous group in any sense, but include different ethnicities (Turks, Kurds, Zaza), religions and denominations (Sunni, Shia, Sufi, and Alevi Muslims, as well as Christians), backgrounds (rural, metropolitan), social groups, sexual orientations, etc. This approach works because Berliners of all stripes are rejecting nationalism as their main category of identification and are embracing multiple identities instead. Perhaps the best symbol of the new coexistence was a sports event. On 25 June 2008 the semi-final of the European championship in soccer—a semi-religious experience for many fans—was between Germany and Turkey. In Berlin in the past, this match might have led to confrontations in the streets. In 2008, however, many cars flew a Turkish flag on one side and a German flag on the other, there were no riots, and the result (Germany won 3-2) was almost irrelevant.

Vietnamese in East and West

While large numbers of Turks were coming to West Berlin, immigrants were also coming to East Berlin, but this development gathered pace a decade or two later. There were only about 12,000 foreigners in East Berlin in 1970, but approximately 94,000 in 1989. With 59,000 arrivals, Vietnam supplied the largest group. The GDR made a point of distinguishing between *Gastarbeiter*, who in communist rhetoric were proletarians exploited by the capitalist West, and their own *Vertragsarbeiter* (contract workers), who were comrades from brother countries visiting Germany to learn skills and share them in their home countries in order to strengthen socialist economies worldwide. Unfortunately, the rhetoric did not always match the reality. The Vietnamese lived in dormitories reminiscent of the early accommodation offered to Turkish guest workers in the West, were forbidden from traveling within East Germany (and barely allowed to move about in Berlin), and experienced racism when they did mingle. Married couples were not allowed to live together, and women who became pregnant had to have abortions or were deported.

At the same time, a (smaller) Vietnamese community was developing in West Berlin. In contrast to the East, these were political refugees known as "boat people." By 1989 there were about 2,000 such refugees in West Berlin. Since the fall of the Wall, these two groups have not entirely come together. For one thing, the contract workers from the former East were often staunch communists, while the refugees from the former West had fled that very political system. The latter group may have gloated over the "victory" of capitalism, but they were outnumbered by the former. In addition, most *Vertragsarbeiter* apparently come from northern and central Vietnam, while most refugees come from the south. It remains to be seen if these groups will integrate with each other first or simply dissolve into their identities as Berliners.

Immigration since Reunification

With the fall of the Wall, Berlin was opened to the East. Of course, people from Eastern Europe could always visit East Germany, but in reality their mobility was heavily limited by the various governments. Now, the largest groups of foreigners to come to Berlin were Russians and Poles.

Officially, around 45,000 Poles live in Berlin, but some demographers claim that as many as 130,000 Berliners have Polish as their native language. This group is different from Turks and Vietnamese in that they cannot be identified on sight (at least stereotypically), and for that reason they are sometimes considered "invisible immigrants." Still, they have been associated with at least two stereotypes: shoppers and car thieves. Especially in the early 1990s, when Germany was economically ahead of Poland, Polish people took day trips to Berlin—a mere one or two hours from the border—to acquire food and electronic goods unavailable in their home country. They arrived in buses at Kantstrasse in Charlottenburg, went to shops that had sprung up around Stuttgarter Platz specifically catering to them, and returned home laden with large woven plastic bags known as *Polenkoffer* (Polish suitcases). The origin of the car thief stereotype is a mystery, but perhaps it was connected with Poland joining the European Union in 2004, which made it easier to move cars—both those stolen and others used for perfectly innocent travel.

Russians are, according to official figures, not as numerous as Poles, but unofficially there may be as many as 300,000 Russian-speakers in and around Berlin. Russians have also been associated with particular stereotypes—especially the myth of the *Russenmafia*—but more importantly have to deal with their own very real history. During the Cold War the GDR and USSR were official friends and brothers; Russian soldiers were stationed as "protection" against the West, and Russian was widely taught in East German schools. In reality, many East Germans saw the Russians as a less-than-popular former occupation force determining their destiny against their will. The occupation is obviously over, but the relationship between Germany and Russia is still complicated (and not simplified by the fact that Russia seems to be moving back in the direction of authoritarianism).

One reason stereotypes about Russians make absolutely no sense is their many distinct backgrounds. Of course, there are those who are in Berlin to take advantage of economic and educational opportunities. In the 1980s Jews were allowed to leave Russia in large numbers, and many came to Berlin. Another group are the Russian Germans known as *Aussiedler* (re-settlers). These *Aussiedler* moved to Russia at various czars' invitations several centuries ago and lived all over the country since then, but held on to (what they considered) their German language and heritage. During the World Wars the Russian Germans, who had often been economically quite successful, were perceived as threats and dispersed over the country (if not simply killed). Under West German law from 1945 (until 2000), German heritage qualified people to become German citizens, so once the Iron Curtain fell many Russian Germans applied to move there. The Germany they came to was not the Germany of their heritage and imagination, but most integrated quickly. In writer, talk-show host, and journalist Wladimir Kaminer, Russian Germans of all stripes now have their own chronicler and champion (see pp.107–08).

The New Berlin

Two groups of newcomers to Berlin since reunification most predictably raise the hackles of the (supposedly) indigenous population. First, fashionable bohemians in their twenties and thirties come to the city in droves—either as so-called "party tourists" or as artists. This group is reviled for apparently driving up the rent in districts such as Neukölln and Kreuzberg and contributing to gentrification. Rents are indeed rising, but probably because the city government sold off cheap flats and eased rent control rather than because of the influx of young people from the US and Europe.

According to some wits, however, the most "dangerous" immigration has been that of Swabians. In this narrative, districts like Prenzlauer Berg, the coolest part of Berlin in the 1990s, have been taken over by this group, bringing with them a strange language (the Swabian dialect, which can be virtually incomprehensible to Berliners) and bizarre foods (like the now ubiquitous *Spätzle*, a soft egg noodle). Wolfgang Thierse, the vice president of the German parliament and a long-time resident of Prenzlauer Berg, recently complained that he could no longer get *Schrippen* (Berlin dialect for the famous German bread rolls) at his local bakery, but had to ask for *Wecken* (Swabian dialect for the same). In response, a group of "radicals" attacked a statue of the artist Käthe Kollwitz with *Spätzle* and demanded that the area around Kollwitzplatz in Prenzlauer Berg become an autonomous Swabian quarter, "Free Schwabylon." The fact that Berlin now turns debates about immigration into food fights is a positive sign that newcomers are no longer seen as a threat, but that Berliners embrace the linguistic, cultural, religious, and culinary diversity of their multi-faceted metropolis.

Kaufhaus des Westens, named after its position in relation to the old center of Berlin rather than its location in West Berlin (during the Cold War), continental Europe's largest department store with 380,000 items on 650,000 square feet. (Gellerj/Wikimedia Commons)

10 | **Spending Power**
Trade and Consumerism

After the fall of the Wall and reunification, Berlin's economy experienced a major slump. For the duration of the Cold War the city's budget had been propped up by subsidies from West Germany and from the Western Allies (the US, Britain, and France). Now, any subsidies went to support the economy of former East Germany, while the Allies reduced their presence in Berlin. Throughout the 1990s unemployment rose, companies closed down, and entire industrial areas became derelict—especially in the East, which hardly boasted up-to-date facilities. It took the Berlin government a few years to face the reality of narrowing resources, and the first response was to take out loans, which made the situation even worse. In 2001 the Berlin government led by Mayor Eberhard Diepgen collapsed under a banking scandal when it was exposed that a government-owned company had speculated (badly) in the housing market. This scandal added about €20 billion (£16.5/$26.5 billion) to the city's debt, and today every Berliner owes (statistically speaking) somewhere around €18,400 (£15,700/$24,900) in loans. There is a debt clock that tabulates Berlin's debt every second at the Bund der Steuerzahler Berlin in Lepsiusstrasse, and another that shows Germany's debt at Französische Strasse.

Fortunately, the economy improved in the first decade of the new century. Reunification turned out to be a boon since large swathes of East Berlin were renovated to exacting standards. West Germany had benefited after the end of World War II because industry, largely destroyed in the war, was rebuilt with the latest innovations and technology with the assistance of the US Marshall Plan; similarly, parts of post-Cold War East Berlin were so derelict that they could be renovated to levels that surpassed the West. In 2011 there were over 1.7 million employed individuals in Berlin, while almost 230,000 remained unemployed (twelve percent). This was worse than in other parts of Germany, but an improvement from Berlin's previous decade (1997–2007), when the unemployment rate fluctuated between fifteen and nineteen percent. In 2011 Berlin's economy grew by 2.3 percent, which was acceptable at the tail end of a world-wide recession, but not as good as Germany overall, which grew by three percent.

Perhaps the most troubling aspect of Berlin's unemployment is the fact that over eighty percent of the unemployed receive the benefit known as Hartz IV. These are long-term unemployed who receive less than €400 (£320/$458) per month (as well as housing and health insurance) from the state. Hartz IV recipients are required to pursue jobs and cannot legally refuse work, but in practice few of them ever find gainful employment. In other words, this is the making of a new underclass with few economic prospects and little motivation to abide by the written and unspoken laws of society. Conversely, Hartz IV takes better care of the unemployed than many other countries' welfare systems, and in Berlin it is possible to lead a frugal but not uncomfortable life on this small amount of money. As a matter of fact, some Hartz IV recipients have turned their situation into an art form and are happy and productive members of society on what little money they have. Maybe for that reason, Berlin's mayor Klaus Wowereit called the city "poor, but sexy" in 2004.

Today, Berlin's economy is dominated by the service sector, which is responsible for 87 percent of all jobs. This figure includes 23 percent in trade, hospitality, and transport; 23 percent in finance and housing; and over 40 percent in public and private services. In practice, service sector employment might mean facilitating business and scientific meetings (Berlin is one of the most popular cities on the European conference circuit, and its spaceship-like International Congress Center is one of the largest such facilities in the world) or working in government, at the universities, or in tourism. In 2010, twenty million visitors came to Berlin. Oddly, Berlin has also established itself as a location for call centers: there are 240 such centers with 25,000 employees. Berlin tries to be at cutting edge of industries such as fashion and architecture—with mixed success.

In contrast, fewer than eight percent of Berlin jobs are in manufacturing and just over four percent in construction. Berlin claims to be a center of innovation: over 44,000 companies were founded in 2011 (though some 29,000 closed as well). Certainly, the city is an attractive business location because of low rents, the presence of the federal government, manifold cultural and economic opportunities, and the closeness to markets in, and workers from, Eastern Europe. Many new start-ups settle in "technology parks" like Adlershof (former site of the GDR Academy of Sciences) and the Siemens Technopark Berlin.

Of course, the main employers in Berlin are not start-ups, but established companies in transport, health, technology, communications, and services. Deutsche Bahn, the German railway company, is Berlin's top employer with 18,600 workers, and the local BVG, which runs buses, the underground network, and the tram system, comes in fifth with 10,700. Vivantes Netzwerk für Gesundheit, in charge of eight hospitals and a dozen residential care facilities, employs 14,200, and the Charité—the hospital that was founded in 1710, produced at least ten Nobel Prize winners in medicine, and still trains thousands of medical students—12,900. The international technology giant Siemens employs 13,400 people, and Daimler 6,000. Deutsche Telekom has 7,600 workers, and the mail and transport service Deutsche Post (which includes DHL) 6,500. The top ten employers in Berlin are rounded out by Kaiser's Tengelmann, a supermarket chain with 6,500 employees in Berlin, and the Landesbank Berlin with 6,500 as well.

Many companies also have their national or international headquarters in Berlin. Not surprisingly, local companies like the BVG, the Landesbank, and Rundfunk Berlin-Brandenburg (radio) are located here. Axel Springer AG, a media giant, was founded by the eponymous Springer (1912–85), a staunch anti-communist who made a point of constructing his multi-story corporate headquarters directly overlooking the Wall, where the East German regime (he hoped) could not but concede the victory of capitalism and East Berliners would be inspired to change their system. When the London *Times* moved in 1986, Springer bought the oak paneling of the newspaper's original eighteenth-century offices and had it installed in the top floor of his own building. Yet even this did not buy him respectability, especially considering that his company's flagship newspapers were the tabloids *Bild* and *BZ*. (Berlin still has four decent daily newspapers today: *Tagesspiegel*, *Berliner Zeitung*, *Berliner Morgenpost*, and *Taz: Die Tageszeitung*.)

Other historical companies with headquarters in Berlin include Bechstein, the producer of pianos, and Königliche Porzellan-Manufaktur, who have been producing china since 1763. Perhaps Coca-Cola's presence in Berlin is nostalgically connected to Billy Wilder's 1961 comedy *One, Two, Three*, which featured the head of West Berlin's Coca-Cola operations as the main character (see p.126). There also seems to be a concentration of the pharmaceutical industry (Bayer Schering Pharma, Berlin-Chemie, and Pfizer Germany) as well as media companies (Sony Germany and Sony Europe, Universal Music, and Viacom Germany).

Shopping in (East) Berlin: Alexanderplatz

Of course, consumers in Berlin rarely encounter these companies in their corporate incarnations, but see their public faces in shopping areas, malls, and particular shops. Traditionally, Berlin has been a city of department stores, and some of these enterprises survive. More recently, though, malls (defined as conglomerations of separate stores with entrances from a shared inside space) have become more popular, and there are now some sixty in Berlin. While department stores combined what scholars distinguish as shopping for necessities (at cheap prices) with shopping around for pleasure—or buying as opposed to shopping—malls tend to encourage the latter, i.e., consumerism for its own sake. The history of Berlin's addiction to consumerism is explored in detail in *Kaufrausch Berlin* by Katja Roeckner and Jan Sternberg. According to these authors, the biggest concentration of shops and malls is between the Brandenburg Gate and Alexanderplatz.

Alexanderplatz has been around since about the thirteenth century and was given its current name after the visit of the Russian Czar Alexander I in 1805. During the Cold War the GDR decided to turn the plaza into a "socialist square" for large rallies in imitation of Red Square in Moscow. To that end, most of the buildings that had survived the war were demolished and replaced with new socialist architecture. The square itself ended up four times its pre-war size at over 860,000 square feet—the equivalent of eleven football pitches or 64 Olympic pools, a truly gargantuan size that in practice resulted in a mostly empty, windswept wasteland.

East Berliners continued to come to Alexanderplatz for the shopping, however. On the northwest side of the square, the Centrum Warenhaus had been built in 1967–70—on the site of the destroyed department store of Hermann Tietz, who had been one of Berlin's four foremost retail entrepreneurs during the late nineteenth and early twentieth centuries (see below). The Centrum Warenhaus was the largest department store in East Germany, with a sales area of over 60,000 square feet. It was remarkable for its architecture (especially the honeycombed aluminum façade) and logistics (supplies coming in underground), and supposedly up to 60,000 customers per day visited the store. Many of those came to look more than to buy anything as the offerings were much more varied than anywhere else in the GDR. This was possible in part simply because the regime wanted to impress Western visitors, and the charade could be kept up because stores all over East Germany simply had to cede their supplies to Berlin.

In the twenty-first century, the store was taken over by Metro AG and renovated several times. With the latest changes in 2004, the façade was changed to a more conservative (or boring) travertine marble and glass. At the same time, the sales area was more than doubled to 375,000 square feet, mostly by changing the fourth and fifth stories from restaurant and administration into shopping space. A glass dome over the middle of the building is set on top of an open area that allows natural light down all five floors of the building. Around the edges of this area, twenty escalators take customers up and down. Now, the store is called Galeria Kaufhof and is organized more like a mall, with distinct areas for different kinds of shopping.

On the northeast side of Alexanderplatz, another shopping center was built in 2007. The official name of this rather ugly steel-and-glass square block is die mitte (with the German word for "middle" in trendy lower case), but it is more commonly known simply as Saturn, the name of the main occupant, a large electronics and entertainment chain. There are nine more floors in the building, but die mitte does not count as a shopping mall since the stores do not have entrances to an interior space, but rather to the square outside. Here, there are now almost always smaller vendors offering everything from socks to sausages, and Alexanderplatz is much livelier (if not necessarily more beautiful) than it was in GDR times.

In contrast to die mitte, Alexa southeast of Alexanderplatz is a pure shopping mall, with 180 shops and over a dozen food outlets under one roof. There is even a kindergarten, where parents can leave their children (for a fee) as they shop, and a gigantic model train landscape. This is a true temple to consumerism, with little consideration for nature, diversity, or even comfort: there are no outside views from inside the mall, the stores are generally branches of national and international chains, and the architecture has been compared to a prison. (Ironically, the mall is on the site of the former police and Gestapo headquarters.) Apparently, the concrete façade painted like red sandstone (especially the round arches around the entrances) is supposed to be reminiscent of Art Deco, but Mayor Wowereit probably summarized most Berliners' feelings when he was caught murmuring, "Wow, that's ugly." Various nicknames are circulating—"pharaoh's grave" because of the lack of windows, "pink bunker" because of the color, and "banana" because of the overall shape of the mall—none of them very complimentary. Still, 80,000 customers stormed the flagship store Media Markt the day Alexa opened, and in financial terms it still seems to be a success.

Shopping in (East) Berlin: Unter den Linden and Friedrichstrasse

Going down Unter den Linden from Alexanderplatz towards the Brandenburg Gate, the shopping becomes more exclusive. There are a number of car dealerships that look so forbidding that they probably survive more on prestige than sales. The Automobil Forum displays Volkswagen and Audi, but also Bentley, Bugati, and

Lamborghini—clearly more for window shopping than actual purchases. In contrast, an increasing number of souvenir shops sell an amazing amount of cheap and not-so-cheap trinkets, probably mostly from low-cost countries. Twenty years after the fall of the Wall, these stores still sell mounted little pieces of concrete rubble supposedly from that edifice. (If these are all genuine, the Wall must have covered rather than surrounded Berlin.)

Berlin Story Salon on Unter den Linden is a shop no visitor should miss. For the historically inclined, the publishing arm of the store produces its own excellently designed and extremely well-researched books on various aspects of Berlin history and culture. (The book you are reading would have been very different without Berlin Story publications.) The bookshop itself is the best place in the city (with the possible exception of Dussmann, see below) to find books on Berlin in any language, organized in tables and shelves around topics, periods, and areas of the city.

To the north and south of Unter den Linden, Friedrichstrasse is its own center of retail activity. The most impressive structure here is Quartier 207, better known by the name of its main occupant, the French department store Galeries Lafayette. Jean Nouvel, the architect of Quartier 207, calls his building futuristic and reductionist, and at least from the inside this claim holds true. The five stories of Lafayette are organized around a core of two reflecting glass cones in the middle of the building, which let in natural light and mirror it all over the store. (Actually, this core feels more spherical once inside the building, but the architect calls the upper and lower halves cones.) According to Nouvel, this building symbolizes "the incorporeal, the virtual, and the abstract, with buoyancy, transparency, and openness in all directions."

Between Unter den Linden and the train station on the northern part of Friedrichstrasse is the middle-brow Kulturkaufhaus Dussmann (culture department store), one of Berlin's largest employers with 5,600 employees. It is unfortunate that this privately owned multinational media mall—which benefits from its vicinity to the train station with long opening hours—may be supplanting smaller book and music stores, but simply because of its size it can stock an impressive range of items. The basement boasts the world's largest collection of classical music, all of which can be sampled on CD players in the store—I have spent many an hour (and lots of money) here. On the other four stories, music (including sheet music), books, films, concert tickets, and stationery are available as well. Of course, there is a café, and the English bookshop has recently opened in its own (connected) space on a side street.

My personal favorite, though, is on Französische Strasse right off Friedrichstrasse: the Ritter Sport Shop. Ritter Sport, for the uninitiated, is the unparalleled German chocolate (now available in many places in the US and UK) that since 1970 has carried the catchy slogan, "Quadratisch, praktisch, gut" (square—the shape of the bars; practical—the unique opening mechanism; good—excellent, as a matter of fact). A regular Berlin grocery store has probably at least ten types of Ritter Sport; the shop has all thirty-plus. First, there are the 25 standard-size flavors from milk and dark chocolate to mousse au chocolate and strawberry yogurt, from Neapolitan waffle to *Knusperkeks* (milk chocolate on a biscuit), from white whole nuts to peppermint. Many of these come in tiny bars in boxes of ten as well as in large sizes. Ritter Sport also produces organic chocolate bars in five flavors, four different kinds of diet chocolate, and two lactose-free varieties. There are several seasonal chocolates (like roasted almond for Christmas and yogurt-based flavors in the summer), and every year a flavor of the year is (s)elected.

But the shop offers much more than just chocolate. There is merchandizing in embroidered polo shirts, presentation chocolates, footballs with the company emblem, and carrier bags sewn together from the square wrappers. Yet the most popular feature, which doubtless reminds many visitors of *Charlie and the Chocolate Factory*, is the front of the store, where customers can create their own chocolate. There are two fountains, milk and dark chocolate, and about thirty ingredients to be added: everything from anise seed to wine gums, cornflakes to chilli, dried bananas to sweet and sour roasted almonds. Customers select their chocolate and ingredients, and a chocolatier behind the counter mixes everything, pours it into the typical square form, and puts it into a deep freezer. Half an hour later, the chocolate is solidified and ready for you to collect.

Ritter Sport is not even the only such enterprise in the area: Fassbender & Rausch on the Gendarmenmarkt two blocks away claim to be the biggest chocolate store in the world. The two families who own it have been offering an extraordinary variety of exquisite chocolates, pralines, truffles, and other sweets since 1863, and united in 1999. Their shop's ambitions are more historical and aesthetic, and their Reichstag, Brandenburg Gate, or Berlin bear made from chocolate—each over six feet wide or high—are worth a visit whether or not one can afford the chocolate.

Beyond Friedrichstrasse, the next big shopping area is Potsdamer Platz with its Sony Center. A few bits of warmth survive in this cold, artificial space in the shape of the Legoland Museum and store and a section of Wall left outside. Across from the Sony Center, a little behind Potsdamer Strasse, is the Potsdamer Platz Arkaden, an only slightly less sterile shopping mall. Across from Potsdamer Platz is the former location of the 1897 Wertheim department store on Leipziger Strasse, the flagship of one of the four department store empires of the previous centuries with a gigantic sales area of over 750,000 square feet. At one point, Georg Wertheim was considered one of the not-so-secret "rulers of Berlin." Like Hermann Tietz, Wertheim had a Jewish background and was forced to give up his company under the Nazis. The building was bombed in World War II and finally demolished in 1955. The basement survived longer, and after the fall of the Wall the popular nightclub Tresor opened in the former vault room. Today, a consortium of investors is developing the site into a huge mall, office and residential structure under the inane slogan, "Shopping Is Coming Home."

Shopping in (West) Berlin: Kurfürstendamm

Even before all of these shopping areas became inaccessible to West Berliners with the construction of the Wall, alternative retail districts started developing in other parts of the city. During the Cold War the most important of these in West Berlin was the shopping mile along Kurfürstendamm and Tauentzien.

The eastern end of this area at Wittenbergplatz is anchored by the KaDeWe (Kaufhaus des Westens), which claims to be the largest department store (*Kaufhaus*) in continental Europe with floor space of almost 650,000 square feet and a stock range of some 380,000 different items. (Only Harrods in London is larger.) Opened in 1907, the store was named after its location west of Berlin's old (and new) center around Unter den Linden and Potsdamer Platz. It was the creation of Adolf Jandorf, the third of the great Berlin department store entrepreneurs (after Tietz and Wertheim), who wanted a store to cater to Berlin's *nouveau riche* clientele, who tended to live in the new western districts. In the early twentieth century there were many prominent customers (or at least visitors) such as the Russian-American author Vladimir Nabokov, who modeled a department store in one of his novels on the KaDeWe, and the British Marxist historian Eric Hobsbawm, who perused the excellent book selection for his research in order to avoid having to spend money on books. Jandorf sold his store to the Tietz family in 1926, so it was also taken over by the Nazis. On 23 November 1943 a fighter jet crashed into the building, and the ensuing fire almost entirely destroyed the structure. The KaDeWe opened again in 1950 and has been expanding ever since. The original iron gate at the main entrance is still raised and lowered every day, and until recently visitors were still greeted by a concierge in suit and top hat.

Like many other department stores, the KaDeWe has a middle section open across all seven stories of the building. (The seventh floor was renovated as a conservatory and opened as a restaurant in 2006.) There are 64 escalators and 26 elevators in the store, which is visited by around 50,000 customers every day, who are served by 2,000 employees. The average visitor apparently spends an astounding three hours in the store, which has its own spa and wellness area, and there are even tours of the building. By common consensus, the most impressive shopping area is the sixth floor, the *Feinschmeckeretage* (gourmet floor)—there are elevators that go only to the sixth floor. Any sort of food or drink from anywhere in the world can be purchased here, and the range is truly staggering: 3,400 different wines; 1,300 cheeses; 1,200 varieties of sausage, ham, and prosciutto; 400 different kinds of bread; and about 100 kinds of fish. Food is produced here as well: there are 110 bakers and 40 pastry chefs on the payroll. There are thirty cooking stations where food from all over the world is prepared and can be eaten sitting at a bar watching the chef. Surprisingly, most of this is quite affordable.

With the advent of the KaDeWe, Tauentzien turned into an up-market shopping street in the early twentieth century, though today it is no longer exclusively for rich Berliners. The stores now tend to be national and international chains, so the selection is not very different from London, New York, or Sydney. There is, however, a unique building at Breitscheidplatz where Tauentzien turns into Kurfürstendamm (known simply as Ku'damm): the Europa-Center. The Romanisches Café, an internationally famous haunt of writers and artists in the 1920s and early 1930s on the same site, had been destroyed in the war, and in the 1960s the Berlin government decided to build a new landmark here. The Europa-Center (1963–65) was designed as a multifunctional building with an office high-rise of 22 stories, two inner courtyards, a hotel, apartments, a cinema, and even an ice rink. Unfortunately, the last two have since been discontinued.

The commercial part of the Europa-Center, though, was a shopping mall before that term was coined in 1967. Today, there are about a hundred stores and restaurants, and some 30,000 visitors enter the structure every day. They are attracted by the shopping and culinary experiences, but also by one strange yet mesmerizing artwork (if that is what it is): the Clock of Flowing Time. Designed by the Frenchman Bernard Gitton and set up in 1982, this is essentially a clock where time is told through colored water in stacked round glass containers. When the sixty containers indicating the minutes are full, they empty, filling up an hour container. Every twelve hours, the hour containers empty as well. In contrast, the Set Theory Clock on Budapester Strasse outside the Europa-Center, which shows the time with a complicated combination of lights and was specifically invented for this purpose in 1975, is rather difficult to comprehend. But the most visible part of the Europa-Center is probably the thirty-foot, three-ton revolving Mercedes star on top of the building.

Rumor has it that it was put there to remind East Berliners of the (impending?) victory of capitalism, but actually it was probably just good advertising.

Berliners love to buy ice cream in the Europa-Center, peruse the stalls (especially when the Christmas market is set up), stop for a quick look at the ruin of the Kaiser-Wilhelm-Gedächtniskirche, or watch the ubiquitous breakdancers on Breitscheidplatz before doing more shopping. The area here used to be full of cinemas: the Royal Palast in the Europa-Center, the Gloria Palast on Ku'damm (originally from 1923 and rebuilt after the war—now a jeans store, though the restored foyer with cashier's kiosk and spiral staircase is preserved and protected), and the Marmorhaus (with its beautiful marble façade of 1913 which still advertises the cinema's name even though it is now a clothing store). Today, only the Zoo Palast still exists (a 1956 building on the site of a theater going back to 1915), which served as the main site of the Berlin Film Festival between 1957 and 1999.

The rest of Ku'damm is also full of tall buildings, and the shops become increasingly local in character the further one gets away from Wittenbergplatz and Breitscheidplatz. Café Kranzler, for instance, was founded in 1825 and still serves traditional *Kaffee und Kuchen* (coffee and cake), albeit in a newer building. In addition, Ku'damm long served as a kind of parade route: there were demonstrations here during the student revolution of the late 1960s, East Berliners made it their first destination when the Wall fell, and cars drove up and down celebrating with flags when Germany won the soccer world championship in 1990. Since then Ku'damm has lost some of its status to the shops, malls, and areas to the east, but it is still a thriving part of the Berlin shopping environment.

Off the Beaten Track

In spite of a few interesting shops described above, most of the stores around Alexanderplatz, Friedrichstrasse, and Kurfürstendamm are run-of-the-mill international chains—for quirkier experiences visitors need to explore other areas of the city. Bergmannstrasse in Kreuzberg, for example, is home to a number of unique institutions such as a shop devoted to presents for men, the wittily named Herrlich (a pun on "excellent" and "manly"), the garlic-themed store and restaurant Knofi, and Coy Art to Wear, a shop full of beautiful hats and scarves. You can also find Barcomi's, a café that was one of the first in Berlin to offer decent bagels (plus excellent baked goods and coffee roasted in-house), and Biocompany, a natural foods store that now has some thirty branches.

A vibrant market for Ostalgie-products, i.e., things that celebrate nostalgia for East Germany, flourishes all over Berlin. The most celebrated Ostalgie outlets are the *Ampelmännchen* shops. East German pedestrian traffic lights had different little green or red figures, *Ampelmännchen*, from the Western ones, and after reunification the German government briefly contemplated standardizing all traffic lights according to the Western image. A protest movement to save the Eastern *Ampelmännchen* immediately started (and was successful), and in the process the figure itself became iconic. Now the shops in various locations all over the city sell everything from laptop covers to teddy bears in the shape of *Ampelmännchen*. While the *Ampelmännchen* is now mainstream, Dederon in Kreuzberg sells items made from a particular synthetic fabric called Dederon invented in the GDR as well as many other (n)ostalgic items.

Bookshops seem to be disappearing entirely across much of the Western world, but in Berlin some are holding on, partly by catering to specific tastes and audiences. Schropp, which has been in existence since 1742 and is now situated in Hardenbergstrasse, specializes in travel literature and maps—like Stanfords in London. Bücherbogen at Savignyplatz has one of the largest collections of books on the visual arts (especially painting and dance) in the world. Both of these bookshops have many books in English, but Bücherstube Marga Schöller in Knesebeckstrasse has been focusing on books in English for eighty years. Goal near Kottbusser Tor had a wide selection of books, but also any other imaginable item related to soccer—but has recently moved entirely online.

Rather less pleasant than these quirky stores are shopping streets and malls all around the city. The malls are sometimes hard to tell apart, with about a hundred stores each, a combination of shopping and gastronomy and attached parking. Starting in the west, north of Ku'damm, here are some of the areas, malls, or stores where Berliners shop, in clockwise order:

The **Wilmersdorfer Strasse** in Charlottenburg is special in being one of the few shopping streets that is almost entirely pedestrian. South of the S-Bahn, where traffic still flows, are smaller shops and cafés, several around the beautiful square called Hindemithplatz (after the composer) since 1995 with the St.-Georg-Brunnen (fountain) of 1904. Stuttgarter Platz—which was traditionally a red-light-district, was taken over by East European import-export shops in the 1990s and is now being gentrified—separates the southern and northern parts. The northern, pedestrian part of Wilmersdorfer Strasse has fewer local stores and has succumbed to the craze for malls with the Wilmersdorfer Arkaden of 2007.

The industrialist August Borsig built a factory in Tegel in the north of Berlin in the nineteenth century with the later landmark Borsigturm (tower) of 1924, one of Berlin's earliest skyscrapers, by Eugen Schmohl (who also designed the Ullsteinhaus in Tempelhof, see p.12). After the Borsig engineering firm went bankrupt in the 1980s, the French architect Claude Vasconi renovated the steam engine factory in the 1990s into the **Hallen am Borsigturm** mall. The Hallen complex contains a bowling alley and a cinema that hosted Germany's first 5-D movie experience.

South and slightly east of Tegel, the **Gesundbrunnen-Center** is in the eponymous quarter, between the districts of Wedding (former West Berlin) and Mitte (East Berlin). At least in part, this mall was situated here (near the S-Bahn tracks) to bring Berliners together through shopping. Oddly, the building was designed with long horizontal lines to resemble a cruise ship, complete with a glass tower at the main entrance that symbolizes the ship's bridge. Fortunately, the Humboldthain park across the street is an easy enough escape from rampant consumerism.

Further to the east, **Schönhauser Allee** is a more proletarian shopping street in the district of Prenzlauer Berg—though it does not belong to the hip part of that district renovated in the 1990s. Schönhauser Allee, memorialized in Wladimir Kaminer's eponymous short story collection, is dominated by the U-Bahn tracks that run above ground here, bisecting the street. There are several landmarks along or close to the road, including the Gethsemanekirche, a center of the protests that led to the end of the GDR, and the Kulturbrauerei, where culture is now produced in the place where one of Berlin's most popular beers, Schultheiss, was brewed until 1967. At the Eberswalder Strasse U-Bahn station, Konnopke Imbiss has been selling sausages since 1930 and *Currywurst* (among Berlin's best) since 1960. Schönhauser Allee went into a slump in the 1990s, but has recently made a come-back. This may partly be due to the Schönhauser Arcaden mall, opened in 1999.

Northeast of Prenzlauer Berg is the **Linden-Center** in the Hohenschönhausen quarter of the Lichtenberg district. The GDR had opened a mall, the Handelshaus, on this site in 1985. The Handelshaus lasted less than a decade before it was demolished and replaced with the Linden-Center, which opened in 1995. This mall tries to gain legitimacy by sponsoring the Anna Seghers Library in the building (named after a famous East German author) and hosts events and exhibitions such as beach volleyball tournaments and a frog zoo.

Some other new malls (moving east and south from Hohenschönhausen) have at least a few redeeming features. The **Eastgate** in Marzahn (2005) offers interesting exterior and interior architecture and claims to be an "adventure center" as well as a shopping center. The less said about the **Spree-Center** in Hellersdorf and **Forum Köpenick** (1997) in Köpenick, the better. The **Ring-Center** on the border of Friedrichshain and Lichtenberg has three parts: Ring-Center I (1995) and Ring-Center II (1997) are fairly nondescript, while Ring-Center III (2007) is a rounded structure imitating the market halls the mall replaced.

Back over the southern border in (former) West Berlin, the **Karl-Marx-Strasse** in Neukölln has plenty of history and some interesting shops. At Hermannplatz on the northwestern end of the street (technically in Kreuzberg), the architect Philipp Schaefer built a huge department store in the 1920s for Karstadt—the fourth of the big department store families and companies in the late nineteenth and early twentieth centuries. This building was meant to imitate similar stores in New York and Chicago and took a mostly vertical architectural form crowned by two towers that were extended even more by light columns at their tops. With nine floors (two of those subterranean), direct access to the underground, 24 escalators, 24 elevators, and a roof terrace restaurant with an orchestra to entertain customers, this was considered the world's most modern department store. Unfortunately, it was destroyed at the end of World War II—whether by arson or intentionally blown up to deny Russian snipers a vantage point is still undetermined. The old Karstadt, of which only a small corner remains, was replaced with an architecturally much less inspired department store.

Karl-Marx-Strasse, which goes from Hermannplatz to the southeast, was actually only given that name in 1947 in a gesture either of conciliation or of defiance towards the communist east of Berlin. There are beautiful old buildings along the street, including the Neukölln town hall of 1909, the Passage cinema with an original building from the same year, and the 1876 Café Rix in the Saalbau Neukölln, a performance venue for concerts and balls as well as a coffeehouse. Much of the shopping here takes place in the predictable chain stores, but some local shops have survived as well, especially when run by Turkish immigrants.

South of the Karl-Marx-Strasse in the Buckow quarter of Neukölln are the **Gropius-Passagen**, actually Berlin's largest shopping mall at 915,000 square feet. There are 2,100 spaces in three car parks for shoppers, and about 180 shops to visit. Maybe the fitness center in the mall helps build up the stamina to survive the experience, and free wireless internet access allows shoppers to send distress signal to the outside. Since the Gropius-Passagen are so far from the center, they are frequented mostly by people who live in the adjoining districts or south of Berlin.

Further to the west in the district of Steglitz is the **Schlossstrasse**, probably West Berlin's third most important shopping street (next to Wilmersdorfer Strasse and Ku'damm). In architectural terms, one of the most interesting shopping structures here is the VW Pavilion of 1951, where cars were displayed in a semi-circular building with an all-glass façade. One of the more recent shopping meccas is Das Schloss (the castle), which wraps in an L-shape around the neo-Gothic former town hall. The entire ceiling of Das Schloss is a projection screen, so that the day (and the shopping experience) can be extended indefinitely. Most recently, the Boulevard Berlin mall (which integrates parts of the architecture of the older, protected Wertheim department store it replaced here) opened in April 2012. This addition supposedly made the Schlossstrasse the largest shopping area in all of Berlin.

From the northern end of Schlossstrasse at Walter-Schreiber-Platz, it is almost a straight shot north to Breitscheidplatz between Ku'damm and Tauentzien, completing the circle of shopping. That way, no Berliner (or tourist) is ever without the opportunity to indulge in some consumerism.

Sections of the Berlin Wall (12 feet high, about three tons each), apparently graffitied by a graphic artist going by the name of Indiano, now reassembled at the Newseum in Washington, DC.
(Queerbubbles/Wikimedia Commons)

11 | The Dark Side
Vice and Criminality

Previous chapters have highlighted Berlin's glories and achievements in such areas as art, architecture, literature, and even the economy. Yet each of these areas comes with a dark side in the shape of failure, disappointment, or challenge. The newspaper *Die Welt* recently called the city Germany's "Capital of Problems," and it was not just referring to the population's notoriously foul language and bad temper. Berlin's beautiful nature, for instance, is under threat from man-made hazards such as pollution and excessive development. Because of global climate change, summers in Berlin are becoming hotter and hotter—average temperatures are predicted to rise by 4.5°F (2.5°C) over the next decades. This creates a domino effect of difficulties: elderly people especially will experience health problems, some even dying from heat; there will be less rain, and rivers and lakes will become shallower; air-conditioning, currently quite rare in Berlin, will become ever more necessary and widespread; resources such as water and oil (to power air-conditioning) will be stretched; rents (which in Germany often include fuel costs) will rise.

Similarly, the dark side of a slowly growing economy is that poverty in Berlin remains rampant. Mayor Wowereit's claim that Berlin is poor but sexy is a good line, but it obscures real social problems. According to recent studies, over a fifth of Berliners live in danger of poverty (earning less than sixty percent of the average income in the city). Worse, that number rose by 24 percent between 2006 and 2011. Around 10,000 Berliners are homeless. In 2011 the German government was accused of deliberately hiding these facts when an official study minimized poverty at the same time that a report from an impartial non-governmental organization documented its rise. Again, poverty in Berlin is more than a theoretical problem: it is virtually impossible to travel on the U-Bahn without encountering a homeless person begging for money (in the guise of selling one of two or three competing newspapers written by the homeless).

Other social problems may or may not be connected to poverty. Underground transport networks across Germany have witnessed apparently unmotivated attacks on innocent passengers in the last few years. Usually, the perpetrators are small groups of young men, frequently intoxicated, who often remain unidentified. In some cases, victims seemed to be selected because they are perceived as weak: the elderly, drunks, and even a pregnant woman. But when a six-foot-two-inch Olympic athlete was attacked in December 2012 it became clear that anyone could become a target. There has also been a rise in anti-Semitic and anti-foreigner violence—a dark reminder of Berlin's Nazi past and its difficulty in dealing with immigration. Berlin is famous in Germany for regular riots on Workers' Day, 1 May, when extremists from all across the country gather in Berlin spoiling for a fight with the police. The confrontation is now so ritualized that damage can be kept to a minimum. Another form of damage that is immediately visible all over Berlin is graffiti. While some of this is clearly art, most of the ubiquitous tags on apartment buildings and buses and trains hardly contribute to the beauty of the city.

State Violence

Berlin showed its darkest side during the Nazi period, when crimes of unspeakable magnitude were committed in the name of Germans, and often with the collaboration or even active participation of the population. For instance, nine of twelve Berlin synagogues were destroyed during the *Reichskristallnacht* (Night of Broken Glass) on 9 November 1938. The action was initiated by the SA and SS, Nazi paramilitary organizations, but Berliners (with a few exceptions) were happy to join the destruction and looting. In 1933 some 160,000 Jews lived in Berlin; by 1940 that number had been reduced to 80,000; and only about 1,500 remained throughout the entire war. About 90,000 Berlin Jews had managed to escape and emigrate, but somewhere around 150,000 were deported and murdered in concentration camps all over Germany and Eastern Europe.

The Holocaust committed against the Jews was accompanied by similar extermination campaigns against the handicapped, homosexuals, Roma and Sinti, and, of course, political opponents. The question of how Germany (and Berlin) could allow these crimes against humanity to occur will probably never find a satisfactory answer. Some historians believe there is a particular strain in the German character that made the country submit to the insane theories and practices of the Nazis, but even these scholars disagree as to whether that character is somehow timeless or whether it was a particular historical incarnation. More likely, the Holocaust happened because of a mixture of various factors: a hierarchical society used to obedience, certainly, as well as influenced by a history of anti-Semitism, but also the experience of economic crisis and hyperinflation, the trauma of a lost world war and a subsequent peace treaty perceived as unjust, a group of rhetorically and strategically gifted and extremely motivated individuals, and most people's tendency to see only what they wanted to see around them. This explanation is obviously not meant in any way to excuse the Holocaust, but perhaps to help understand how such horrors could occur. Unfortunately, the break with the Nazi past was not as clean as many Berliners would have liked. In the East, some concentration camps—like Buchenwald and Sachsenhausen—were shockingly kept open as camps for prisoners of war, collaborators, and political prisoners after World War II. The former jail in the Berlin district of Hohenschönhausen was used for the same purpose. At the same time, the Soviet administration had a vested interest in cleansing East Germany of Nazis, which it did more or less successfully. In the West, the US military used the Dachau concentration camp as a prison for war criminals and held various trials there. Every so often in the following decades, though, high-placed politicians, businessmen, and artists were exposed as Nazi collaborators or even active members of the Nazi party. This generation is dying out, but German society continues asking how far collaboration with the Nazis might have been simply necessary for survival, and to what extent individuals are morally and/or legally responsible for the crimes committed in their names.

THE DARK SIDE

The biggest crime committed against the citizens of the GDR was perhaps not so much keeping them in the country against their will (or at least in the communist bloc) as spying on them through the infamous Ministerium für Staatssicherheit, abbreviated to Stasi. This ministry used every method from observation, manipulation, intimidation, and blackmail to outright assassination to ensure what it perceived as the state's safety and security. While some of the Stasi's activities took place abroad (especially in West Germany), its most insidious work was with its own citizens. By 1989 the Stasi had over 90,000 full-time employees—out of a population of only seventeen million. With one secret agent for every 180 citizens, the GDR was arguably the most watched-over society in the history of the world.

Two aspects of this surveillance inspired particular terror in the population. For one, the Stasi was a law unto itself, so even being suspected of any un-communist beliefs and activities could have catastrophic consequences. Individuals disappeared without trial; torture was a common occurrence in Stasi prisons; and lives and careers could be ruined without warning—and without any possibility for redress. Even worse, the Stasi recruited the infamous Inoffizielle or Informelle Mitarbeiter, the innocuously named unofficial or informal co-workers known simply as IM. These were individuals who voluntarily (or under pressure) agreed to spy on friends and neighbors and report back to the Stasi. The existence of IM was an open secret in the GDR, but only after its demise did it become known how deeply they had permeated society: in the 1970s, at their zenith, there were over 200,000 IM, and even in 1989 there were still over 170,000. These informants eroded the fabric of civil society since you could never know if the person you trusted, even a family member or spouse, was not actually spying on you.

Unsurprisingly, the Stasi was not exactly popular, and "Stasi—Nein danke!" (No thanks!) was one of the slogans in the 1989 protests that led to the fall of the East German regime. After that, Stasi offices became targets for the demonstrators; the Stasi headquarters in Lichtenberg was occupied by protestors on 15 January 1990 in order to stop officials from destroying records. The reunified

German government created a specific department to deal with the Stasi past, which was long known simply as the Gauck-Behörde after Pastor Joachim Gauck, the first head of the agency (and now President of Germany, partly on the reputation he acquired in his previous position). Here, individuals can read their Stasi files, often finding out who was spying on them. Some IM were spectacularly exposed, and many East Germans—and some West Germans—were shocked to find that they were even deemed worthy of surveillance. Not many IM have since been legally prosecuted, but at least knowledge of their activities has both deepened understanding of the GDR's methods and contributed to healing the wounds of the past. The Lichtenberg headquarters has been turned into a museum, and the Stasi has been portrayed (in somewhat romanticized guise) in the Oscar-winning 2006 movie *The Lives of Others* (see pp.128–29).

Sex, Drugs, Guns, and Organized Crime

Where the state does not commit its own crimes, its citizens and institutions—legal and illegal—are happy to jump into the breach. Yet some of the main factors that lead to such crime—guns, prostitution, and drugs—are not much of an issue in Berlin. Guns are heavily regulated (at least compared to the US): owners have to be at least 25 years old (with some exceptions involving psychiatric evaluation), need a license and registration, and must demonstrate that their arms are stored properly. These regulations are probably responsible for the low number of gun-related offenses: in 2010 only 621 crimes were committed in Berlin involving guns of any description (out of a total of over 475,000 crimes), and a firearm was actually discharged in only 365 cases.

Prostitution is decriminalized in Germany (and Berlin). A law of 2002 guarantees sex workers the right to compensation for their services, entitles them to join health insurance schemes, and separates their trade from considerations of morality. In turn, the city and state can more effectively collect taxes from them. Since 1985 Berlin prostitutes' interests had been represented by Hydra, a self-proclaimed "whores' organization," and the 2002 law led to the founding of the Bundesverband Sexuelle Dienstleistung, a national organization for sexual services headquartered in Berlin. These groups have tried to make prostitution, if not reputable, at least accepted and safe for the women involved, and to a large extent they have been successful. Today, there are estimated to be about 8,000 sex workers in Berlin. According to a recent survey, about a third of Berlin students could imagine earning money through prostitution. Of course, the sex trade will always include abuse, and there are persistent allegations of women being kidnapped from Eastern Europe, Asia, and Africa and forced into prostitution, while there are always men and women who turn to prostitution to support their drug habits.

Berlin has never had a central red light district, and streetwalkers have frequented various locations over the years. The Kurfürstenstrasse had a reputation for particularly young prostitutes in the 1980s and 1990s, the Strasse des 17. Juni was known for more expensive sex workers and in Oranienburger Strasse today there seem to be more tourists gawking at scantily clad women than would-be clients trying to pick them up. There are also several hundred officially registered brothels, including ones with long traditions like Bel Ami near the Olympic Stadium, where Helmut Newton took pictures of the women (and which closed in 2011). Today's most famous brothel is probably Artemis, which calls itself a "nude sauna club and wellness brothel" and where forty prostitutes work in an environment that includes a pool, saunas, and two cinemas. There is a standard entrance fee (€80/$110) and a standard price for half an hour of intercourse (€60/$82); everything else can be negotiated with the prostitutes. According to most accounts—like Thomas Brussig's exploration of prostitution, *Berliner Orgie*—the Artemis has a clean and professional atmosphere that makes sex seem like any other business transaction.

Of the three crime factors (guns and vice being the first two), drugs have been the most significant in Berlin. The 1978 autobiography *Wir Kinder vom Bahnhof Zoo* told the story of the drug victim Christiane F., who came from a broken family with divorced parents and an alcoholic father. Christiane started smoking marijuana around Zoo Station at twelve, was addicted to heroin at fourteen, and prostituted herself among the children on Kurfürstenstrasse—without her mother finding out for a full two years. Reporters from the *Stern* magazine became aware of Christiane's situation and told her story in a series of articles and subsequently a book. Turned into a film in 1981, *Wir Kinder* shocked Berlin and led to serious attempts to deal with the city's drug problem. Berlin's drug commissioner now tries a four-pronged approach: prevent drug use; support addicts with consultation and treatment; offer short-term assistance like safe houses and overnight shelters; and protect the population from the effects of the trade and use of drugs by working with the police to fight the illegal drug trade and drug-related crime. This kind of work has helped many addicts, but success with Christiane F. herself was mixed. The young woman managed to stay clean for many years and started a career as an actress and singer, but apparently she relapsed in 2008 and lost custody of her son. She recovered, but was once again questioned during a drug raid in early 2011.

Today there are some 165,000 people in Berlin who consume illegal drugs, mostly marijuana (although marijuana, in small quantities, is widely tolerated, adding to Berlin's allure for young visitors). Approximately 8–10,000 are addicted to opiates such as heroin. In 2009 a total of 155 drug-related deaths were recorded in Berlin. Kottbusser Tor in the poorer part of Kreuzberg was once considered the center of the city's drug scene, though the area is now being gentrified. Addicts used an abandoned car park in the vicinity, but when it was sealed off, many once again took to the streets. Entrances to apartment buildings, underground passages, and any patches of green around Kottbusser Tor are now often occupied by the addicts (who are frequently homeless as well) or covered with excrement and discarded drug paraphernalia. Police and residents remain uncertain about how to respond to the situation. Simply arresting the addicts is no solution since it is usually impossible to prove criminal activity (and their time in the justice system rarely helps them); providing safe spaces to consume drugs is controversial; and there is still some disagreement about whether drug addiction is a medical condition or a lifestyle choice. There does not seem to be much large-scale criminality associated with the drug trade and consumption, so most Berliners, much less tourists, are hardly ever confronted with drugs.

Like any other modern metropolis, Berlin has its share of organized crime. Berliners tend to blame outsiders, and the Italian mafia does indeed seem to be active, as are gangs of Vietnamese, Turks, and Arabs—but Germans hold their own as criminals as well. After the end of the Cold War in the 1990s gangs of Eastern European criminals—especially the alleged *Russenmafia* (see p.184)—established new headquarters in Berlin. The Kantstrasse in Charlottenburg, formerly a street of boutiques and small restaurants, was transformed into a series of import/export stores that seemed to function as little more than fronts for illicit activity. Many of these gangs are involved in prostitution and the drug trade, but they also engage in cigarette smuggling, art fraud, extortion (especially of businesses and restaurants), and money counterfeiting and laundering. Still, Berliners and tourists are rarely in serious danger or victims of anything worse than car theft: cars are stolen by gangs in Berlin and driven over the border to the east, where they are sold for large profits. Berlin is Germany's capital of car theft—every sixth incident in the country occurs in Berlin—and the numbers are rising. Fortunately, not much of this activity involves violence, and even when it does it is mostly within or between the gangs.

Criminal Histories

Again like any big city, Berlin has its history of famous and infamous individual criminals and gangs. Many of their stories are retold in Carl Peter Steinmann's *TatOrt Berlin*, titled as a pun on the longest-running German crime drama. These stories range from the humorous to the gruesome and from the passionate to the professional. In some cases, even characterizing these individuals as criminals is problematic.

For instance, Carl Schurz (1829–1906) could be considered a criminal or a freedom fighter. Following the 1848 revolution (see p.74), the journalist Gottfried Kinkel had been incarcerated at Spandau jail, where Schurz liberated his fellow revolutionary in a daring and adventurous mission on the night of 6 November 1850. Schurz and other supporters of Kinkel had collected money to plan an escape, and they managed to bribe Georg Brune, a sympathetic prison guard, to purloin a key to Kinkel's cell and release the prisoner. Schurz arrived at the appointed meeting place armed with pistols and a rapier and shoes muffled so as not to be detected, but his co-conspirators never appeared. Brune, meanwhile, had not been able to duplicate the key in time, but the guard offered an alternative plan: he would spirit Kinkel to the roof of the jail and lower him to the ground on a sixty-foot rope. Once again, a key went missing, but Brune broke down the last door between Kinkel and freedom with an axe. On the street, Schurz picked Kinkel up and took him to the inn of another supporter, where the prisoner changed his clothes and, strangely, was toasted by a group of policemen who happened to be having a party. Through a series of relays, the two escaped to a port on the Baltic coast, from where they took passage to England on a boat supplied by another sympathizer. The episode made the news internationally—with the true story and many additions and embellishments. Kinkel went on to teach in London and Zurich, while Schurz—his reputation much enhanced—moved to the US, where he became a successful lawyer and politician, the first German-American to join the Senate. From a Prussian perspective, however, Schurz remained a criminal.

Similarly, Friedrich Wilhelm Voigt (1849–1922), better known as the "Hauptmann von Köpenick," was technically a criminal, but he harmed nobody physically and provided both entertainment and food for thought with his crime. Voigt, a cobbler by trade, had a troubled past involving theft, fraud, and robbery. After being released from prison in 1906, he was exiled from the province of Mecklenburg-Schwerin as well as greater Berlin, making it almost impossible for him to earn a living. Instead, he dreamed up and executed an amazing scam. From second-hand clothes stores he put together a fake army uniform, posed as a captain, and commandeered a group of soldiers to execute a non-existing order to arrest the mayor of Köpenick. He marched the soldiers to the town hall, occupied and barricaded the building, detained the mayor and other officials, had the cashier bring the city's petty cash, and "confiscated" it. He accomplished all of this without any questions about his authority, without resistance, and without needing to use any violence.

After commanding his soldiers to secure the building for another half hour, Voigt walked away and boarded a train to Berlin, where he changed back into civilian clothes—and was discovered and arrested ten days later. Even the emperor, it seems, had laughed at his escapade, and he pardoned Voigt after only two years in prison. Voigt was then able to capitalize on his notoriety with appearances at amusement parks and circuses—there was apparently even a tour to the US. He continued to be championed by the lower classes, but was hardly popular among those officials with whom he still had to register as a criminal on parole. In 1910 Voigt emigrated to Luxemburg, where he descended back into poverty and died in 1922. His story was immortalized in Carl Zuckmayer's 1930 drama *Der Hauptmann von Köpenick* and in a subsequent film based on the play starring Heinz Rühmann, one of Germany's most popular actors. Voigt's story still resonates because it raises questions about the supposedly and stereotypically German trait of unquestioning obedience to bureaucracy and authority (see above).

If he had not dreamed up his brilliant plan, Voigt could have joined one of the Ringvereine, union-like clubs that promoted crime in Berlin in the first half of the twentieth century. Officially, the Ringvereine were simply organizations of former prisoners who wanted to support each other—and recognized each other through signet rings that gave the clubs their name. In good German tradition, they officially registered with the authorities, posing as choirs or athletic clubs. The romantic nature of these organizations can be seen in their names such as Immertreu (always faithful) or Apachenblut (Apache's blood), and their members had colorful monikers like Muscle-Adolf or Sailor-Willy. The first Ringverein was founded in Berlin in 1890, and in 1898 various clubs formed an umbrella organization. By the late 1920s there were somewhere between 25 and 50 such clubs in Berlin.

The real purpose of the Ringvereine was in fact for criminals to help each other out with theft, robberies, prostitution, fraud, black-market trade, illegal casinos, and even alibis and witness intimidation. The pursuit of these goals was financed with a cut of the loot that members turned over to the organization. When members in good standing were arrested by the police, the Ringvereine found lawyers; when they became old and sick, the clubs gave them financial aid; and even wives whose husbands were in prison received food and rent. On the other hand, members who committed unacceptable crimes such as sexual violence or murder, or who informed on their comrades to the police, were disciplined—often killed—by the Ringvereine themselves. In at least one instance there was a kind of pitched battle between two Ringvereine at the Schlesischer Bahnhof railway station that left one dead and several severely injured. The Ringvereine were finally eliminated by the Nazis, and attempts to resurrect the organizations after World War II failed.

The Lawless 1920s

In keeping with the decade's reputation, the 1920s witnessed a number of both colorful and nasty criminals. Carl Grossmann (1863–1922), known as "the beast of Schlesischer Bahnhof," was probably Berlin's worst serial killer. A sadist and pedophile, this sociopath perhaps unsurprisingly chose the profession of butcher. After stints in various parts of Germany—and in jail for a variety of crimes including assault and rape—Grossmann moved to Berlin, where he lived in Friedrichshain, which then endured so much crime that it was known as "Berlin's Chicago." Between 1918 and 1921, at the height of the Depression, the dismembered corpses of at least 23 women were found here, but no suspect was identified. The case was solved by accident: on 21 August 1921 neighbors heard screams coming from Grossmann's apartment and called the police, who broke down the door and caught him *in flagrante delicto* (and discovered burned human hands in his stove). It turned out that Grossmann had approached desperate women in the streets, lured them to his apartment by offering them a position as housekeeper, and then killed and dismembered them. According to various rumors, he either ate his victims or turned them into sausage that he sold at his stand at Schlesischer Bahnhof—but neither of those stories was ever confirmed. Grossmann confessed to killing three women, but was probably responsible for anywhere between 25 and 100 murders. He was never sentenced since he committed suicide in his prison cell on 5 July 1922.

In contrast, Friedrich Schumann (1893–1921) met a more dramatic end when he was beheaded at the Plötzensee prison on 27 August 1921 as punishment for at least fifteen attempted and seven successful murders—each of the latter carrying the death penalty. Schumann committed his crimes, which also included rape, at gunpoint in the Falkenhagen forest on the northern edge of Berlin. Apparently, he considered the forest "his" and any visitors or intruders had to be stopped, so he may have been mentally ill in addition to (or instead of) being a sociopath.

Franziska Schanzkowsky (1896–1984), also known as Anna Anderson, was either mentally ill or a fraud. In 1920 she was rescued from a suicide attempt in the Landwehrkanal and admitted into a mental institution. Since she refused to divulge her name, she was registered as Miss Unknown. In 1922 the rumor surfaced that Schanzkowsky was Anastasia, the daughter of the last Russian czar, and for the rest of her life she maintained that this was her true identity. For several decades she moved from supporter to supporter, across Germany and the world, trying to establish her claim to the Romanov fortune. In Germany's longest-running court case, from 1938 to 1970, she attempted to gain official recognition as Anastasia, but ultimately lost. Ten years after her death, DNA analysis proved that she was not related to the czar's family, but it remains unclear whether she made her claim fraudulently or because she actually believed it. Schanzkowsky's case was famous and curious enough that it inspired the 1956 movie *Anastasia*, which won its star Ingrid Bergman an Oscar.

Franz and Erich Sass (1904–40 and 1905–40) were born in the working-class district of Moabit and lived in a tiny tenement apartment with their parents and three brothers, but grew up to be notorious bank robbers. The two brothers actually only ever pulled off one successful heist, but their near-misses and confrontations with the police kept the public entertained and on their side for several years. They were questioned by the police before they even started their career when they were observed buying a cutting torch, but had to be released for lack of evidence. The Sass brothers always prepared meticulously for their robberies, but something always went wrong. In their first attempt in March 1927 they easily found their way into the safe room of the bank in Moabit they had targeted, but failed to realize that their cutting torch needed more oxygen than the room supplied. In the second case several months later, they slowly worked their way through a wall into a bank in Charlottenburg by scratching out each brick individually, but were accidentally discovered. Next, they cut their way through a ceiling into a bank's safe room in Kreuzberg, disguising the opening during the day, and were only foiled because the night guard mistook the sounds of their work for cats and tried to evict the animals with bright lights. Then, a doorman near the zoo noticed a strange smell coming from the bank next door. The bank was surrounded by the police and curious onlookers, but the Sass brothers escaped through a series of tunnels. In May 1928 Franz and Erich returned to Moabit and tried to steal the World War I reparations Germany was about to pay France, but had to flee because of an off-schedule night guard.

Finally, the Sass brothers ran their one successful heist in January 1929 when they cleaned out a safe room with about 180 individual lockboxes. They blocked the room's entrance from the inside, so for several days the bank simply thought the door was broken. Once the bank staff gained entry, they realized that the robbers had made their way into the room through tunnels and air ducts and escaped the same way—leaving two bottles of wine they had emptied to celebrate their success. The police suspected who the perpetrators were and even arrested the brothers, but were unable to prove it and had to release them—which Franz and Erich celebrated with a press conference. Either because they were now worried about police surveillance, or because they had finally actually got some money, the Sass brothers apparently stopped engaging in illegal activity at this time. They led an ostentatious life, and it was said that they randomly and philanthropically inserted banknotes into postboxes all over their native Moabit, earning them the reputation of Robin Hoods. In 1933 they emigrated to Denmark and restarted their criminal careers, but were soon caught and sentenced to jail. After four years in prison, they were deported to Germany in 1938, where they were put on trial under a dubious Nazi law. They were sentenced to eleven and thirteen years in jail respectively, but murdered by the Gestapo only a few days after their sentence had been pronounced on 27 March 1940. The full amount of their booty has never been established, and neither the money nor the valuables have ever been recovered. Most of the buildings the Sass brothers targeted still survive—though not many as banks.

Post-War Criminals

The first notorious criminal of Berlin's post-war period was Werner Gladow (1931–1950). Inspired by fiction and cinema, Gladow tried to emulate criminals like Al Capone, dressing up in custom-made black suits and white ties at the tender age of sixteen. From black market activity he moved on to petty theft, recruited a gang of ten other young criminals, and graduated to armed robbery. Gladow's speciality was committing crimes in one sector of divided Berlin and fleeing to another, where the military police could not follow him. His exploits were first viewed with amusement by the public, so he began to be even more flamboyant, staging robberies for the press to cover. Sympathy evaporated, however, when his activities began to claim human victims, and he was betrayed by one of his own accomplices, surrendering only after an hour-long gun battle in which his mother helped by reloading his weapons. Gladow was sentenced to death and executed by guillotine—which supposedly jammed and became stuck in the midst of decapitating him.

In the late 1960s the boxing promoter and real estate speculator Klaus Speer (b.1944) and his accomplice, the pimp Hans Helmcke (1917–73), dominated the illegal economy in Berlin. In 1970 the two became engaged in an ongoing conflict with Iranian gangs who were trying to take over their turf. When Speer's gang attacked the Restaurant Bukarest in the Bleibtreustrasse, one Iranian was killed and three injured in an infamous gun battle. Subsequently, Berliners nicknamed the street *Bleistreustrasse*, "scattered lead street." Speer was sent to jail for two years. On his release, he claimed he was going straight, but in the early 1990s the "godfather of Berlin" was again put on trial and convicted.

One of Berlin's more celebrated criminals of the late twentieth century was Arno Funke (b.1950), the extortionist better known under his pseudonym Dagobert (the German version of Scrooge McDuck, Donald's miserly uncle). Funke was an artist, but never achieved success and had to make his living varnishing cars. Perhaps because of the fumes he inhaled in his job he became depressed and suicidal. Yet before taking such drastic action as ending his own life, Funke turned to extortion. In 1988 he demanded half a million DM from the KaDeWe department store and threatened to detonate a bomb if his demand was not met. After the money hand-over was unsuccessful and a first explosive device failed, Funke set off a bomb, causing damage estimated at DM 250,000. The second hand-over succeeded, and for several years he lived off his "earnings." Then, out of money and down on his luck, Funke resorted to extortion again in 1992. This time, he targeted the Karstadt corporation and set off several bombs in department stores in Hamburg, Bremen, Hannover, Magdeburg, Bielefeld, and Berlin between 1992 and 1994. He was finally apprehended during one of the attempts to collect the DM 1.4 million in blackmail money.

Dagobert appealed to the Berlin imagination for a variety of reasons. He seemed to target wealthy corporations in a time of economic crisis, so was perceived as simply stealing from the rich. His bombs were designed to cause no harm to humans, and it was clear he was not out to hurt anyone. Dagobert was also technically gifted and his schemes for receiving ransom money were ingenious and entertaining—and frequent, with some thirty attempts. In one instance he put a tiny trolley on decommissioned train tracks and tried to drive it towards himself over half a mile by remote control (the trolley derailed); in another he prepared a sandbox in which the ransom was buried so that he could get to it from the sewer underneath—there was paper rather than money in the bag he recovered. Finally, Dagobert escaped from the police on several dramatic occasions. Once, police spotted him as he was trying to recover a package with money thrown from a train, but the officer slipped on wet leaves (reported in the newspapers as dog feces); on another occasion he had booby-trapped his escape route with tripwires that set off fireworks, which confused the police enough to let him get away.

In the end, though, Funke was captured and sentenced to nine years and significant fines in 1996. He was released for good behavior in 2000, has published an autobiography, and occasionally works as a cartoonist. The effects of the varnish fumes on his health have apparently been addressed, and Funke now lives a quiet life. Sadly, he has been reduced to appearing in the German version of the reality TV show *I'm a Celebrity… Get Me Out of Here!*

In the new century, criminals as charismatic as Dagobert or the Sass brothers are yet to emerge, with crime such as car theft more commonplace and banal. Sex workers, no longer considered criminals, hoped that the 2006 soccer World Cup would increase business, but apparently in vain. At the same time, the rise of ultra-right-wing politics in Germany is leading to new forms of crime against immigrants and foreigners—at least those easily identifiable by their appearance. Much of this crime is concentrated in high-rise suburban districts of Berlin (Wedding, Marzahn, Hellersdorf). In Germany the use of Nazi slogans or the Nazi swastika is punishable by law—problematic in terms of free speech, but not surprising considering Germany's history. For their part, the police have a museum, the Polizeihistorische Sammlung in Tempelhof, which displays exhibits on crimes that have (more or less) been solved.

12 | Escape
Suburbs and Surroundings

erlin is a green and blue city—with many parks, forests, open
skies, lakes, rivers, and waterways—so many Berliners would
argue that there is absolutely no need to escape. Indeed, West
Berliners were literally unable to escape beyond the borders of their
half-city for forty years, which seems to have been cheerfully accepted by most (the same, of course, did not apply to the citizens of
East Berlin). Moreover, since Berlin is really made up of many separate towns and villages (see p.42), there were always many smaller
centers in the city rather than a single big one. Yet after reunification
the situation changed: a *Speckgürtel* (bacon belt) grew around Berlin
in the state of Brandenburg where on the one hand new, gigantic,
and mostly ugly housing developments sprang up to provide cheap
apartments, while, on the other, wealthy Berliners bought or built
large houses and gardens that would have been impossible to find
space for within the city limits—or at least acquired small allotments
or community gardens to which they could escape from the hectic
city. Now, many Berliners commute to and from these villages with
their villas and developments, infusing the city's surroundings with
energy and money.

Yet regardless of these recent historical developments, the villages and cities of Brandenburg have always been there (some even
longer than Berlin), and they have always had their own culture and
atmosphere, seeking to benefit from the proximity to the metropolis without losing their own character. Whatever direction you leave
Berlin—we will leave to the north and pursue a clockwise circuit
around the city—you will find picturesque hamlets, beautiful land-
scapes, ancient castles, and a great deal of water in the region's lakes
and rivers.

Boitzenburg Castle, seat of the von Arnim family since the fifteenth and sixteenth centuries, on an island designed by Peter Joseph Lenné with buildings in the park designed by Carl Gotthard Langhans, in its latest form renovated as a neo-Renaissance castle 1881–84. (Unify/Wikimedia Commons)

North

The Slavic village of Oranienburg straight to the north is documented as far back as 1216—before the official founding of Berlin—when it was called Bötzow. In 1651–52 Luise Henriette, second wife of the Great Elector Friedrich Wilhelm, had a Dutch-style baroque castle built there on the Havel river with a typically squat horizontal front and snaking gables. Johann Gregor Memhardt, who also built Berlin's Fortification (see pp.28–30), was the main architect, and Johann Friedrich Eosander von Göthe and Johann Arnold Nering worked on later additions. A large garden was designed for aesthetic purposes but used for agriculture as well; Luise Henriette supposedly introduced the potato to Brandenburg—though the same claim is made for Frederick the Great. The entrance to the gardens is a cast-iron monogrammed gate hung between two massive portals fronted by Tuscan columns and topped by allegorical figures of summer and autumn. In honor of the electress, who came from the Dutch royal house of Orange or Oranien, the town was renamed Oranienburg.

During World War II the castle was used as barracks for the SS, and unfortunately Oranienburg is associated with the Nazis to this day because of the adjacent concentration camp at Sachsenhausen. Sachsenhausen was built in the summer of 1936 and housed some 200,000 prisoners: first simply political enemies of the Nazis; later Jews, Jehovah's Witnesses, homosexuals, and Sinti and Roma; then citizens of other European countries; and finally Soviet prisoners of war. A gas chamber was built in 1943. Almost all inmates had died, been killed, or sent on a death march before the concentration camp was liberated by Soviet and Polish troops on 22 April 1945.

Many of the atrocities committed at Sachsenhausen were typical of the Nazi regime in their utter disregard for human rights and dignity: infecting prisoners with diseases to test medication, having them walk 25 miles a day to check the durability of shoes, and, of course, forcing them to work in nearby arms factories. Sachsenhausen was, however, unique in that SS guards were trained here before they were sent to other concentration camps, and therefore it was considered a "model camp." Famous inmates included Rudolf

Breitscheid, the SPD politician after whom the square at the center of former West Berlin is named; Hans von Dohnanyi, father of the long-time conductor of the Cleveland Orchestra; and the theologian Martin Niemöller. After World War II the camp was unfortunately used again, this time as a "special camp" by the Soviet army. Of 60,000 inmates in the period between 1945 and 1950, about 12,000 died. In 1961 a memorial opened among the remnants of the camp (only about a twentieth of the original area) and still serves as a reminder of Germany's dark past. There are ideological and personal disagreements over how much the citizens of Oranienburg knew about the concentration camp on the eastern outskirts of their city, but it is difficult to imagine how they could have remained entirely unaware.

Slightly to the west of Oranienburg, Neuruppin is a reminder of happier times in German history. With a castle (thirteenth-century), a Dominican monastery (1246), a school (1365), and a charity hospital (1490), Neuruppin was a fairly substantial town in the late Middle Ages. In 1512 Elector Joachim I held a three-day chivalric tournament here that was beyond anything Berlin had to offer at the same time. In 1787 the entire city burned to the ground, and in the following fifteen years it was rebuilt in the neoclassical style that still dominates the town's architecture. In 1819 the writer Theodor Fontane was born in Neuruppin, and Fontane is now the most highly visible symbol of the town's identity: there is a Fontane (literary) Prize, a Fontane Festival, and the city is official nicknamed "Fontanestadt." The pharmacy of Fontane's father, where the author was trained in his original profession, continues in that trade, but the house is a private residence. Locally, Fontane wrote about Neuruppin, a famous pear tree in the nearby village of Ribbeck (a poem every German child learns in school), and the state of Brandenburg in general.

The beautiful Ruppiner Land north of Neuruppin, covered with lush farming fields and dotted with picturesque villages, is mostly famous for its 170 lakes and 150 miles of waterways. Frederick the Great spent what he considered his happiest years here at Rheinsberg Castle, and Fontane wrote about the Ruppiner Land. In

Rheinsberg: An Album for Lovers (1912), Kurt Tucholsky's first famous work, an engaged Berlin couple spend three days here and discover both pristine nature and the advent of modernity in the countryside. Today Berliners can find the same contrast between their busy city and the quiet Ruppiner Land. In Fontane's last major novel, *Der Stechlin* (1897–98), written and set in the last decade of the nineteenth century, a nobleman of the (imaginary) Stechlin family on Stechlinsee (a real lake) invites a large group of younger friends and relatives, and the usual shenanigans ensue. Not much actually happens in the novel (one person dies, two get engaged), but the novel is famous for its dialogue, social relevance, and, of course, its depiction of the Ruppiner Land.

Continuing around Berlin in clockwise direction from Neuruppin and Oranienburg is Bernau in the Barnim area. Bernau itself is actually less than ten miles from the Berlin border, though still quite a hike from the city center. Legend has it that Bernau was founded in the twelfth century by Albrecht the Bear because he liked the beer he drank at an inn here, yet sadly there is no documentary evidence to support this story. There is, however, an impressive medieval wall surrounding the town with one surviving gate. As usual, there is a fourteenth-century hospital and a sixteenth-century Gothic church, this one with an impressive altar painted in the style of Lucas Cranach the Elder. The Barnim area, a geological formation that extends to the northeastern districts of Berlin, is also known as the "Berlin Balcony" because it boasts a higher elevation than, and is easily reached from, the city. A little north of Bernau is Chorin Abbey, founded in 1258 by Cistercian monks, built of brick in the early Gothic style and left to decay after secularization in the sixteenth century. Happily, Romantic landscape architecture needed atmospheric ruins (see Frederick the Great's artificial ruins at Sanssouci below), so the ruins of Chorin Abbey were perfect, and the grounds were shaped by none less than Peter Joseph Lenné. Today the reconstructed site is used for exhibitions and concerts that many Berliners visit for a night out.

East

With water all around Berlin, it is no surprise that the tourist industry has capitalized on this natural feature; and one of the most gorgeous long-distance hiking trails, the 66-Lake Trail, goes all around Berlin (and through Potsdam) along these lakes. North of Bernau, the trail passes through the hamlet of Melchow, with a population of about 900 in 2012. North again, partly in the German state of Mecklenburg-Vorpommern to the north and on the border with Poland to the east, is the Uckermark region. Named after the same Slavic word ("border") that gave the Ukraine its name, this is the most thinly inhabited part of Germany, with another 400 lakes and marsh areas. In total, some sixty percent of the administrative district of Uckermark (which only covers part of the geographical region) is comprised of nature reserves, and visitors can take canoe tours along the waterways. The area is nicknamed the "Tuscany of the North," apparently because the landscape is hilly—and there is one (organic) vineyard.

The German Chancellor Angela Merkel was born here in the city of Templin—the "Pearl of the Uckermark"—and still owns a home nearby, and her father lived here until he died in 2011. Oddly, an amusement park outside Templin called El Dorado is supposedly a reconstruction of a town from the American West, where visitors can pan for gold, take a post coach, and watch "Indian" dances. Also in the Uckermark, the city of Prenzlau is obviously the source of the name of the Prenzlauer Berg district in the northeast of Berlin. Some sixty miles north of Berlin, Boitzenburg Castle is located on a peninsula (earlier an island) in the Küchenteich (kitchen pond). Built as a baroque castle, it was renovated in the neo-Gothic style in the early nineteenth century and then later reconstructed in neo-Renaissance fashion. Today the fairy-tale castle, picturesque enough to rival any Sleeping Beauty fantasy, is a family-oriented hotel.

To the south of the Uckermark, so east and slight north of Berlin—continuing clockwise around the city—is the Oderbruch or Märkisch-Oderland. Until the eighteenth century the Oder river formed a huge, swampy inland delta here that regularly flooded. In an amazing feat of engineering (executed under orders from

Frederick the Great), a twelve-mile canal was dug to divert the river, and various smaller channels were cut to drain the swamp into the river. The canal was opened in 1753, and the newly-drained area was settled by colonists from other German-speaking regions. To this day, the new settlements can be recognized by the prefix "Neu-". The Oderbruch still floods on occasion (as it did after a deluge of rain in 2010), but mostly it is a quiet area Berliners visit in order to relax and recuperate. Canoe excursions are available on the lakes and rivers, and there are long-distance bike trails such as the 400-mile Oder-Neisse Bike Trail along the German-Polish border and the Oderbruch Railway Bike Trail, a more manageable ninety miles along decommissioned train tracks. At around 150 feet, the Schermützelsee (not to be confused with the more southerly Scharmützelsee) is unusually deep, and famous for its turquoise water. On its eastern shore in the spa town of Buckow, Bertolt Brecht and his second wife, the distinguished actress Helene Weigel, spent their summers after 1952 in what is now known as the Brecht-Weigel-House to work in peace with a view of the lake.

The Oderbruch region is also home to two significant World War II sites. On the Oder, on the Polish side of the border, the town of Küstrin (Polish Kostrzyn) had been a small regional center since the thirteenth century. The Knights Templar ran the city then, and in the sixteenth century a castle and fortress were constructed on a peninsula in the Oder river. Frederick the Great's friend (or boyfriend) Hans Hermann von Katte was executed here in 1730. Küstrin went into decline in the early twentieth century, but towards the end of World War II the Nazis declared it a bulwark against the Soviet advance. In the ensuing battle ninety percent of the city was destroyed and the entire population either killed or removed. After the war, now on the border between Poland and the GDR, any remaining traces of the old city center were razed, and it became a restricted military zone. After the end of the Cold War the peninsula once again became accessible and now makes for an eerie visit. The layout of streets is still recognizable—with the occasional manhole cover going nowhere—and the foundations of the church and castle are visible, with beginnings of stairs indicating where houses once stood. One entrance gate has been reconstructed, but otherwise Küstrin remains a ghost town reminding Germans and Poles of their violent past.

The other World War II site in the Oderbruch is the Seelower Höhen (heights or hills). After Soviet forces had taken Küstrin, they prepared for the final assault on Berlin. In the four-day Battle of the Seelower Höhen one million soldiers of the Red Army pushed back 100,000 troops of the Wehrmacht between 16 and 19 April 1945. At the western edge of the Oderbruch, the hills rise some 165 feet above the river valley with its swampy ground and thus offered an excellent defensive position. Still, the overwhelming Soviet force bombarded the Germans with approximately 500,000 high-explosive shells on the first day alone and ultimately won out. About 12,000 German and 35,000 Soviet soldiers perished in the encounter, and the way to Berlin was free. Today the remains of weapons, artillery, and even long-dead combatants are still found regularly in the area, and there is an excellent memorial site in the shape of a bunker in the town of Seelow.

Directly to the east of Berlin, the city of Frankfurt an der Oder (as opposed to the probably better-known Frankfurt am Main, Germany's banking capital) is less than an hour by train—as a matter of fact, many people who work here (or in Fürstenwalde along the way, with its beautiful St. Mary's Cathedral) commute to and from Berlin. Frankfurt developed in the early thirteenth century at a ford (*Furt*) in the Oder river and was incorporated in 1253. The city became a member of the Hanseatic League, the organization of merchant cities around the Baltic Sea, and was burned down by Hussite rebels in 1432. In 1506 the Viadrina University was founded; in 1811 it was moved to Breslau. (The university was re-founded in Frankfurt in 1991 as the European University Viadrina.) One of the university's most famous students was the poet Heinrich von Kleist, who was also born in Frankfurt in 1777. Like many cities in the path of the Red Army, Frankfurt was destroyed towards the end of World War II, and reconstruction was not quite able to recapture its original charm. Today the city's identity revolves around its position at the interstices between West and East, between Germany and Poland.

Frankfurt has its fair share of tourist sites as well. The Gothic St. Marienkirche was destroyed in the war but reconstructed starting in 1979. Interestingly, the church was recently the recipient of 111 medieval stained glass window panels that had been removed in 1941, captured by the Soviet army, and kept in Russia for sixty years. The panels were returned in 2002, reinstalled, and opened to the public in 2007. An eighteenth-century former garrison school has been turned into a museum dedicated to Heinrich von Kleist, and the Viadrina Museum (not connected to the university) presents local history and art in the Junkerhaus (squire's house), the Frankfurt residence of the Hohenzollern dynasty. This late seventeenth-century baroque palace was one of the few buildings in Frankfurt to escape destruction and is especially famous for its original stucco ceilings. The town hall is an excellent example of thirteenth- and fourteenth-century *Backsteingotik* architecture—an odd mix of red brick and Gothic shapes—typical of the region and emblematic of Frankfurt.

South

South of Frankfurt and about fifty miles southwest of Berlin is the Spreewald, a forested area along the Spree river. Here the river divides into many channels, which are complemented by even more man-made canals. Culturally, this was the homeland of the Sorbs (aka Wends), a western Slavic ethnic group that lived in today's Germany and Poland. Since the Sorbs never comprised a political entity of their own in modern times, their language and identity were constantly threatened; in the nineteenth century their language was banned in various German states, and in the GDR their culture—though officially recognized—was undermined by educating young Sorbs into (German) socialism. Today Sorb folklore traditions such as Easter horseback processions and the "Bird Wedding" (bird-shaped sweets for children) are alive and well again, and the prime minister of the German state of Saxony, Stanislaw Tillich, is a Sorb. A few schools teach Sorb, but still there are probably only about 50,000 people who speak the language.

From Lübbenau, the center of the Spreewald, visitors can take tours around the canals in punts, i.e., flat-bottomed boats propelled by pole. Originally these boats were built of wood, but today they are usually made of metal. Even the post office apparently uses this kind of barge to deliver mail in some places near Lübbenau at certain times of the year. One of the regional delicacies is the Spreewald gherkin, a particularly bitter pickled cucumber. The ingredients in the pickling mixture are still kept as family secrets but include basil, dill, and lemon balm. In the late 1990s there was a brief Gherkin War in which local farmers successfully defended their exclusive right to use the term *Spreewaldgurke*.

Another delicacy from Brandenburg available every spring and early summer is white asparagus from Beelitz, the next stop in our circuit around Berlin. In the season there are stands offering *Beelitzer Spargel* along the roads leading in and out of Berlin to the south and west, and, of course, in the markets. White asparagus—only known since the nineteenth century—is cultivated in rows of raised soil protecting it from the sunlight that would turn the plant green; in good earth an asparagus stalk can grow up to two inches per day. Harvesting this kind of asparagus is labor-intensive since it involves identifying the stalk under the earth, testing it for ripeness, feeling for the precise point where the stalk starts, and cutting it there with a special tool so that the roots can produce more. No attempts to mechanize this process have so far been successful. In Germany white asparagus can legally only be harvested until the Feast Day of St. John the Baptist, 24 June, a vestige of old traditions meant to give the soil plenty of time to recover. Today the harvest is mostly done by seasonal workers from Poland and Eastern Europe, and considering the labor involved it is disconcerting how cheaply asparagus is available in Berlin.

Beelitz is also home to the eerie Beelitz Sanatorium, over fifty buildings (including its own church and power station) built between 1898 and 1930 in successive Wilhelminian, expressionist, and Art Deco architectural styles. Here the Berlin proletariat was supposed to be cured of the tuberculosis rampant in the city's dank tenement houses. In both World Wars the sanatorium was used as a convalescent home for soldiers, who included, after World War I, a young soldier called Adolf Hitler. Between 1945 and 1994 the site was used as a military hospital by the Soviet army, but was then abandoned. Today it is officially closed (though visitors have been known to sneak in) except for guided tours or for use in film sets: scenes from the German movie *Operation Valkyrie* (2004, different from *Valkyrie*, see p.125), Roman Polanski's *The Pianist* (2002), and German cult director Detlev Buck's comedy *Männerpension* (1996) were shot here. Apart from these intrusions, though, nature is quickly reclaiming the site.

Further southeast beyond Beelitz, tucked in before Luther's Wittenberg in the south and Magdeburg to the east, is the Fläming chain of hills. This area was named after the Flemish settler who came here in the twelfth century—though the name did not come about until the nineteenth—because of devastating floods in Flanders. According to some historians, names of towns here are corruptions of Flemish city names, and a strange traditional local costume has survived into the twenty-first century (though now it only appears on rare festive occasions). There are various nature reserves in the Fläming, all with an excellent tourist infrastructure. One corner of the Fläming is known as *Dreiburgenland* (three-castle-country): Eisenhardt Castle (now home to a museum and local library), Rabenstein Castle (a youth hostel), and Wiesenburg Palace (mostly private apartments, with only the tower accessible) were all first built in the twelfth or thirteenth centuries. Today, all three (as well as the fifteenth-century bishop's residence in Ziesar) can be visited along the hundred-mile Castle Trail (or simply by car). On a more contemporary note, the area is home to Fläming Skate, a network of over 125 miles of paths reserved for those using rollerblades or other non-motorized forms of transportation.

West

North of the Fläming and west of Berlin, almost completing the circle around the metropolis, is the city of Brandenburg (not to be confused with the eponymous state). Brandenburg boasts three historical centers: the old town, the new town, and the cathedral island. The indigenous Germanic group known as the Semnones was replaced (probably peacefully) by the Slavic Hevellians, who gave their name to the Havel river that runs from its source in Mecklenburg-Vorpommern through Berlin and Brandenburg before flowing into the Elbe. Slavic culture is recreated in the Slavic Village museum outside Brandenburg. The Hevellians had an island fortress here that was conquered by the German King Heinrich I from the Luidolfinger dynasty in 928 and supplemented later with a cathedral—the earliest of Brandenburg's historical centers.

The old town—the second center—grew around St. Gotthard's Church around the middle of the twelfth century; its citizens apparently looked down on those of the new town, which, founded in the late twelfth century, was a mere upstart. Brandenburg entered a coalition with Berlin, Cölln, and others and belonged to the Hanseatic League in the fifteenth century. There was a significant Jewish community in the late Middle Ages, which was subjected to persecution about once a century. A Jewish cemetery opened in 1747 was destroyed by the Nazis. The old and new towns, the two later historical centers, had their own city walls and did not unite until the early eighteenth century. The Thirty Years' War had reduced the population from 10,000 to 3,000, and Brandenburg did not recover until the nineteenth century. Since reunification the population has once again dipped, from around 95,000 in 1989 to some 72,000 today.

Most of the medieval walls of both old and new towns are still visible, and four of the towers crowning the bulwark still exist. The largest, the crenelated Steintorturm at over one hundred feet, has ten-foot-thick walls made of local bricks. Apart from protecting one entrance to the city, the tower served as a local jail, and uniquely it even had a heating system to keep the soldiers warm, though probably not the prisoners. Brandenburg town hall is another example of *Backsteingotik* and still serves its original function. In front of city hall in the market square of the new town, a fifteen-foot statue of the hero Roland is a symbol of municipal privileges that can be found in many German cities. Cut from sandstone in 1474, the statue was evacuated in 1941; otherwise it almost certainly would not have survived the bombing of the town.

The foundation for the cathedral on the site of the old Slavic fortress in the city's earliest center was laid in the twelfth century; St.

Gotthard's Church was started in the old town around the same time—though not finished until 1475; while St. Catherine's Church, a relative newcomer from 1401, appropriately stands in the new town. The Dominican St. Paul's monastery from the thirteenth century was destroyed during World War II and left as a ruin until reunification. Restored, it now houses the Archeological State Museum. On the site of an old memorial to Bismarck on the Marienberg hill outside Brandenburg the town built a Peace Tower in 1974 for the twenty-fifth anniversary of the GDR. The nickel and chrome tower has five open and five glassed-in viewing platforms that can only be reached by two spiral staircases with 180 steps (one up, the other down). Apparently the platforms are a mathematical clue as to the anniversary for which the tower was constructed. The other memorial to the GDR in Brandenburg is the N-Ostalgie museum, which punningly celebrates nostalgia for the old East German (Ostdeutsch) regime, or at least culture. Rather than offering a narrative or any kind of explanation (beyond the recreation of a GDR-era living room), this museum is simply an *omnium-gatherum* of artefacts from socialist East Germany: everything from food items, dolls, cigarettes, clocks, and pennants to the obligatory Trabant car.

Potsdam

East of Brandenburg and just on the southwest edge of Berlin is the last stop in our circuit around Berlin: Potsdam, capital of the state of Brandenburg and since 1990 a UNESCO world heritage site almost in its entirety. Potsdam is one of the oldest cities in the area, the first document proving its existence dating from the year 993. Then the village was called Poztupimi, probably a Sorb word for outpost. Throughout the Middle Ages Potsdam was a small market town, but with the rise of the Hohenzollern dynasty from the fifteenth century the city became more important. In 1660 the Great Elector Friedrich Wilhelm made Potsdam his second capital (after Berlin) and began an ambitious architectural expansion project. The human capital—both as settlers and as well-educated specialist craftsmen—was provided by the new Huguenot immigrants, who came to Prussia after

Friedrich Wilhelm's Edict of Potsdam declared religious tolerance in 1685 (see pp.170–71).

Several distinct quarters in Potsdam recall various waves of immigration. Between 1733 and 1740 King Friedrich Wilhelm I in Prussia (grandson of the Great Elector) had his urban planners build the Dutch quarter with 134 red brick houses to attract Dutch artisans. To that end, the houses were given typically Dutch eaves and gables. The plan was not entirely successful (few Dutch came), but the quarter still celebrates Dutch-themed events like the Tulip Festival and a Dutch Christmas market. Next to Potsdam, in the part that is now Babelsberg, Fredrick the Great (son of Friedrich Wilhelm I) built the Nowawes (Czech for "new village") colony for Bohemian weavers in the 1750s. In a kind of early mass production, each building looked very much the same: a main entrance leading to separate living quarters for two families, a shared kitchen, and room under the roof for children and servants. There were 210 buildings for 420 families, and the weavers were even provided with their own church, which provided services in Czech. (Many of them were fleeing Bohemia, now the western part of the Czech Republic, and religious persecution.) The Prussian state planted mulberry trees, necessary for silk production, but the industry never really took off. Today there are a fair number of old houses still left in the area (one of which is a museum) but only a few mulberry trees, and only the street name Alt Nowawes—and Nowawes in the names of shops and bars—serves as a reminder of the quarter's origin.

In the northern part of Potsdam the Prussian King Friedrich Wilhelm III (grand-nephew of Frederick the Great) contributed the Russian colony known as Alexandrowka in 1825. In the Napoleonic Wars a group of Russian soldiers had first been held as prisoners of war in Potsdam (when Prussia was forced to side with France) and then fought with the Prussians against the French. Sixty-two of these soldiers formed a choir that survived the wars and they stayed in Prussia with the blessing and support of Czar Alexander (after whom the colony is named). In 1825, when Alexander died, twelve of the choristers were still alive, and Friedrich Wilhelm III decided to build his colony for them. The original layout in the form of a racetrack overlaid with diagonals is still visible, and most of the log houses with their stereotypically Russian storybook look still exist. Of course, one of them has been turned into a museum.

Beyond entire quarters, individual buildings give Potsdam a cosmopolitan feel, or at least convey the impression that its citizens and rulers were playing at being cosmopolitan. The Chinese House (1755–64) on the grounds of Sanssouci (see below) is a perfect example of eighteenth-century European *chinoiserie*; the building is not so much Chinese as a projection of what Europeans imagined or wanted China to look like, complete with a golden mandarin sitting on the domed roof protected by an umbrella. King Friedrich Wilhelm IV took Orientalism one step further and had the pump station supplying water for the great fountain at Sanssouci by Ludwig Persius (1841–43) disguised as a mosque with an ornamental minaret. The Orangery Palace, also on the Sanssouci grounds, was built from 1851 to 1864 in the style of an Italian Renaissance villa with a Palladian touch reminiscent of the Villa Medici in Rome.

Further architectural pastiches followed. From 1863 to 1877 ten houses were built in the Klein Glienicke district of Potsdam in the style of Swiss chalets, four of which still stand. In the 1890s Emperor Wilhelm II had the naval base of Kongsnæs built in a Norwegian style that was just being developed in Norway itself and included such allusions to the Vikings as dragons in the eaves and braided decorative elements. Most of the base burned down during World War II and even more was destroyed because the Wall ran right through the area. There have been recent attempts to resuscitate the development, however, and in 2010 the foundation was laid to reconstruct one building as a restaurant. Finally, in 1914 Wilhelm II decided to build a palace for his son and heir Wilhelm (who never became Wilhelm III) in the style of a Tudor country house. There are 176 rooms in a half-timbered structure with 55 chimneys, none of which is the same as any other. Named after Wilhelm's wife—who actually lived there until 1945—Cecilienhof Palace is today most famous as the site of the Potsdam Conference where Churchill, Roosevelt, and Stalin met to shape the post-war future of Europe.

Cecilienhof is still used for official occasions like the visit of Queen Elizabeth II in 2004.

But Potsdam is certainly best known for Sanssouci, somewhat confusingly the name both of a specific palace and the entire 715-acre grounds with some two dozen structures including the above-mentioned Chinese House and Orangery Palace. At the eastern edge of the grounds, the palace itself is a rococo structure built from 1745 by Georg Wenzeslaus von Knobelsdorff for Frederick the Great—to resemble and rival the palace in Versailles—and was extended in 1841 by Ludwig Persius for King Friedrich Wilhelm IV. Sanssouci was supposed to be a summer palace that Frederick visited for private pursuits such as philosophy and music. Voltaire possibly lived here as a guest of the king, and Menzel's famous apotheosizing painting of Frederick's flute concert is set here. The palace is situated at the top of a six-terraced vineyard with playful rivulets and a large water fountain at the base.

To the north, the Sanssouci palace looks towards a group of ar-tificial ruins, practically obligatory according to eighteenth-century landscape gardening theory, at the top of a hill. Actually, the ruins disguise a reservoir that provides water, and water pressure, for the fountains at Sanssouci. To the west of the palace there once stood an early eighteenth-century windmill that became legendary in its own time. Tradition has it that Frederick was disturbed by the noise of the vanes and tried to buy the windmill from its owner. When the miller refused, Frederick threatened to invoke his royal power, but when the miller in turn appealed to the rule of law, the king relented—so the legend promotes the idea of Frederick as a humble, reasonable, and enlightened ruler. Another version simply relates that the miller was stubborn and devious, and that Fredrick did not like him very much. Either way, the original windmill fell into disrepair and was replaced in 1787, completely destroyed in World War II and not re-constructed until the 1980s. The grave of Frederick lies right next to Sanssouci palace and is often decorated with potatoes, since he sup-posedly introduced that most useful of crops to Prussia (unless it was his great-great-grandmother Luise Henriette). To the east of the palace is the Picture Gallery, the oldest structure in Germany built by royalty specifically to be used as a museum. Frederick kept his personal collection here, and paintings by the likes of Caravaggio, van Dyck, and Rubens remain in place. Still, it is difficult to decide whether to pay more attention to the paintings or to the gorgeous interior, newly restored in the 1990s.

Across the Sanssouci grounds to the west, the New Palace of 1763–69 is mostly baroque rather than rococo. The building looks like it is entirely red brick, but actually much of the façade is simply painted that way. Similarly, there is a large dome but no interior cupola. On top of the dome, the Three Graces carry the Prussian crown on a small cushion. There are over four hundred sandstone sculptures along the cornices and around the building. Inside, the Grotto Hall is decorated with shells, glass, and brilliant stones to an impressive extent—and to somewhat odd effect. The next gallery has red jasper and white Carrara marble walls and three ceiling paintings depicting allegories of night, morning, and midday. The Marble Hall above was completed so quickly that the water needed to polish the marble seeped into the walls, leaving the room in constant danger of collapsing. The entire south wing of the building is a beautiful rococo theater that is still occasionally used for performances. The New Palace was intended as a guest house, and today some faculties of Potsdam University are lucky enough to be accommodated there.

The rest of the Sanssouci grounds is strewn with smaller buildings including several *faux* temples (in Greek style), the Dragon House (another *chinoiserie* folly), an "Egyptian" obelisk (with characters that look like hieroglyphics but actually are simply invented), and supposedly Roman baths. There are furthermore useful facilities such as stables, a dairy, and a pheasant house. All of these can be visited on long walks through the beautiful park just outside the borders of Berlin.

Further Reading
and Useful Websites

In writing the present volume, my sources were almost exclusively books written in German. However, since this section is for readers rather than for myself, it lists only books in English. (Occasionally, I mention particularly important sources in German in the main text. There are several authors who write knowledgeably and almost exclusively about Berlin—Michael Bienert, Horst Bosetzky, Günter de Bruyn, Wolfgang Feyerabend, and Carl-Peter Steinmann—and all of their books are recommended.) There are several excellent local publishers that specialize in books about Berlin: Berlin Story Verlag (see p.193), Jaron Verlag (especially the series Berlin Kompakt), and Vergangenheitsverlag (see websites below). All three have some titles in English; just in case, Vergangenheitsverlag also has a Berlin guide in Latin. Stadtwandel Verlag produces beautifully illustrated and well-researched short pamphlets on individual buildings and sites; over eighty are available in English.

Non-Fiction

Arendt, Hannah. *Rahel Varnhagen: The Life of a Jewess*. Baltimore, MD: Johns Hopkins University Press, 1997.

Borneman, John. *After the Wall: East Meets West in the New Berlin*. New York: Basic Books, 1991.

Buckley, William. *The Fall of the Berlin Wall*. Hoboken, NJ: Wiley, 2004.

Cobbers, Arnt. *Architecture in Berlin: The 100 Most Important Buildings and Urban Settings*. Berlin: Jaron, 1999.

Erlin, Matt. *Berlin's Forgotten Future: City, History, and Enlightenment in Eighteenth-Century Germany*. Chapel Hill, NC: University of North Carolina Press, 2004.

Evans, Jennifer. *Life among the Ruins: Cityscape and Sexuality in*

Cold War Berlin. Basingstoke, UK: Palgrave Macmillan, 2011.

Feiner, Shmuel and Natalie Naimark-Goldberg. *Cultural Revolution in Berlin: Jews in the Age of Enlightenment*. Oxford: Bodleian Library, 2011.

Friedrich, Otto. *Before the Deluge: A Portrait of Berlin in the 1920's*. New York: HarperPerennial, 1995.

Fritzsche, Peter. *Reading Berlin 1900*. Cambridge, MA: Harvard University Press, 1996.

Gerstenberger, Katharina. *Writing the New Berlin: The German Capital in Post-Wall Literature*. Rochester, NY: Camden House, 2008.

Giebel, Wieland. *The History of Berlin*. Berlin: Berlin Story Verlag, 2010.

Gill, Anthony. *A Dance Between Flames: Berlin Between the Wars*. New York: Carroll and Graf, 1993.

Gröschner, Annett and Arwed Messmer (eds.). *The Other View: The Early Berlin Wall*. Ostfildern: Hatje Cantz, 2011.

Hajdu, Joseph. *Berlin Today*. Berlin: Berlin Story Verlag, 2010.

Haubrich, Rainer (et al.). *Berlin: The Architecture Guide*. Berlin: Braun, 2011.

Hertz, Deborah. *How Jews Became Germans: The History of Conversion and Assimilation in Berlin*. New Haven, CT: Yale University Press, 2007.

Hett, Benjamin. *Death in the Tiergarten: Murder and Criminal Justice in the Kaiser's Berlin*. Cambridge, MA: Harvard University Press, 2004.

Hilton, Christopher. *The Wall: The People's Story*. Stroud, UK: Sutton, 2001.

Kempe, Frederick. *Berlin 1961: Kennedy, Khrushchev, and the Most Dangerous Place on Earth*. New York: Putnam's, 2011.

Ladd, Brian. *The Ghosts of Berlin: Confronting German History in the Urban Landscape*. Chicago: University of Chicago Press, 1997.

Large, David Clay. *Berlin*. New York: Basic Books, 2000.

Larson, Erik. *In the Garden of Beasts: Love, Terror, and an*

American Family in Hitler's Berlin. New York: Crown, 2011.

Lifschitz, Avi. *Language and Enlightenment: The Berlin Debates of the Eighteenth Century*. Oxford: Oxford University Press, 2012.

Lowenstein, Steven. *The Berlin Jewish Community: Enlightenment, Family, and Crisis, 1770–1830*. New York: Oxford University Press, 1994.

MacDonogh, Giles. *Berlin: A Portrait of Its History, Politics, Architecture, and Society*. New York: St. Martin's Griffin, 1999.

Moorhouse, Roger. *Berlin at War*. New York: Basic Books, 2010.

Page, Norman. *Auden and Isherwood: The Berlin Years*. New York: St. Martin's Press, 1998.

Read, Anthony. *Berlin Rising: Biography of a City*. New York: Norton, 1994.

Richie, Alexandra. *Faust's Metropolis: A History of Berlin*. New York: Carroll and Graf, 1998.

Roth, Joseph. *What I Saw: Reports from Berlin, 1920-1933*. New York: Norton, 2003.

Schöne, Jens. *The Peaceful Revolution: Berlin 1989/90—The Path to German Unity*. Berlin: Berlin Story Verlag, 2009.

Taylor, Fred. *The Berlin Wall: A World Divided, 1961-1989*. New York: HarperCollins, 2006.

Taylor, Ronald. *Berlin and Its Culture: A Historical Portrait*. New Haven, CT: Yale University Press, 1997.

Tusa, Ann. *The Last Division: A History of Berlin, 1945–1989*. Reading, MA: Addison-Wesley, 1997.

Ward, Janet. *Post-Wall Berlin: Borders, Space and Identity*. Basingstoke, UK: Palgrave Macmillan, 2011.

Webber, Andrew. *Berlin in the Twentieth Century: A Cultural Topography*. Cambridge: Cambridge University Press, 2008.

Fiction (with original publication date)

Brussig, Thomas. *Heroes Like Us* (1996).

Döblin, Alfred. *Berlin Alexanderplatz* (1929).

Fontane, Theodor. *The Poggenpuhl Family* (1895–96).

Fontane, Theodor. *On Tangled Paths* (1887–88).
Fontane, Theodor. *Effi Briest* (1894–95).
Grass, Günter. *Local Anaesthetic* (1969).
Grass, Günter. *Too Far Afield* (1995).
Isherwood, Christopher. *The Berlin Stories* (1945).
Kaminer, Wladimir. *Russian Disco* (2000).
Kästner, Erich. *Emil and the Detectives* (1929).
Kästner, Erich. *Fabian* (1931).
McEwan, Ian. *The Innocent* (1990).
Özdamar, Emine Sevgi. *Life Is a Caravanserai* (1992).
Özdamar, Emine Sevgi. *The Bridge of the Golden Horn* (1998).
Plenzdorf, Ulrich. *The New Sufferings of Young W.* (1972).
Regener, Sven. *Berlin Blues* (2001).
Schneider, Peter. *The Wall Jumper* (1982).
Schneider, Peter. *Eduard's Homecoming* (1999).
Wolf, Christa. *Divided Heaven* (1963).
Wolf, Christa. *In the Flesh* (2002).

Websites

www.berlin.de (official website of the Berlin government, with most pages translated into English—the ultimate site on Berlin)

www.berlin-fever.com (nice lists of quirky experiences, restaurants, clubs, etc. in Berlin, but with no explanation of who is compiling the lists)

www.berlinerunterwelten.de (organization that gives tours of Berlin's subterranean architecture in English)

www.berlinstory-verlag.de (publisher with various books in English, which unfortunately are difficult to find from the front page)

www.exberliner.com (news journal written specifically for English speakers living in Berlin)

www.jaron-buchshop.de (English books from the Jaron Verlag available through the "Fremdsprachige Bücher" tab)

www.ritter-sport.de (could easily be categorized as food porn)

www.smb.museum/ (official website of the Staatliche Museen zu

Berlin, the organization that oversees all major museums in
Berlin)

www.stadtwandel.de (English pamphlets under "Die Neuen
Architekturführer," then "English Versions")

www.tagesspiegel.de (excellent local newspaper with some articles
in English under the "Welt" tab)

www.thelocal.de (short articles of German news written in
English)

Index